THROUGH THE TAX ASSESSOR'S EYES:

ENSLAVED PEOPLE, FREE BLACKS AND SLAVEHOLDERS IN EARLY NINETEENTH CENTURY BALTIMORE

Noreen J. Goodson & Donna Tyler Hollie

CLEARFIELD

Copyright 2017
Noreen J. Goodson & Donna Tyler Hollie
All Rights Reserved

ISBN 978-0-8063-5858-1

Cover art taken from a page of the 1813 Baltimore City
Tax Assessor's Ledger, Baltimore City Archives

TABLE OF CONTENTS

Introduction	Page 4
Foreword	Page 5
Profiles	Page 10
Ward Maps, 1813 and 1818	Page 14
1813 Tax Assessor's Ledger, Ward 1	Page 15
1813 Tax Assessor's Ledger, Ward 2	Page 26
1813 Tax Assessor's Ledger, Ward 3	Page 39
1813 Tax Assessor's Ledger, Ward 4	Page 49
1813 Tax Assessor's Ledger, Ward 5	Page 55
1813 Tax Assessor's Ledger, Ward 6	Page 62
1813 Tax Assessor's Ledger, Ward 7	Page 74
1813 Tax Assessor's Ledger, Ward 8	Page 91
1818 Tax Assessor's Ledger, Ward 1	Page 99
1818 Tax Assessor's Ledger, Ward 2	Page 110
1818 Tax Assessor's Ledger, Ward 3	Page 123
1818 Tax Assessor's Ledger, Ward 4	Page 133
1818 Tax Assessor's Ledger, Ward 5	Page 141
1818 Tax Assessor's Ledger, Ward 6	Page 151
1818 Tax Assessor's Ledger, Ward 7	Page 169
1818 Tax Assessor's Ledger, Ward 8	Page 185
1818 Tax Assessor's Ledger, Ward 9	Page 193
1818 Tax Assessor's Ledger, Ward 10	Page 206
1818 Tax Assessor's Ledger, Ward 11	Page 222
Glossary	Page 238
Streets where Blacks owned property	Page 244
Surnames that became Street Names	Page 246
Further Reading	Page 247
Index	Page 250

INTRODUCTION

On a very basic level this is a book about slavery in Baltimore Maryland in the early nineteenth century. However, it is much, much more than that, as this introduction will reveal. While conducting genealogical research at the Baltimore City Archives, we met Dr. Edward C. Papenfuse, retired State Archivist for Maryland. He enthusiastically shared with us an old volume titled *Baltimore City Tax Assessor's Ledger, 1813*. Later we saw the ledgers for 1818. After turning a few pages we were equally enthused as we watched these nineteenth century documents reveal their treasures: we read about slaveholders and enslaved people, immigrants and the native born, people who worked for their money and those whose money worked for them, many who owned thousands of dollars in property and some whose property was worth less than $50.00. The invisibility of nineteenth century women became apparent as we saw women identified as extensions of their deceased husbands. There were occupations listed that no longer exist and illnesses that are now known by names that did not exist in the nineteenth century. We saw the citizens of Baltimore whose surnames were given to the streets and neighborhoods we frequented as children. Recognizing what a tremendous resource this could be for historians and genealogists, our immediate thought was that it needed to be shared, and thus this publication was born.

While some of these records are available online and at various archives, we have chosen to use only the tax assessor's ledgers for 1813 and 1818 as these could be viewed in their original format. Additionally these ledgers identified citizens by race and in some cases, nationality. Genealogists, in particularly those of African descent, will find this information invaluable for their research.

We have supplemented the information found in the tax ledgers with data from city directories, census records and books and journal articles about nineteenth century Baltimore and Maryland. We examined newspapers, court records and biographies of some of the more prominent residents mentioned in order to illuminate their lives. For our purposes, prominence is defined not just by financial prosperity but also by the impact on enslaved people, the free black population and the city in general.

Readers will note inconsistencies and discrepancies in this book. There are spelling inconsistencies, particularly in names. For example, Benjamin's surname is Annis in one year's ledger and Ennis in another. Many first names, such as Phyllis/Philis/Felis are phonetically spelled. Citizens of African descent were identified as Black, B, Colored, C, Col, Negro, Mulatto, or Yellow. Periodically tax assessors failed to list an enslaved person's name, age and/or taxable value. In some instances the assessor's handwriting was impossible to decipher, nevertheless our intent is to present the data exactly as written.

Our goal is that this volume will benefit those who read it. Genealogists will glean valuable data about their ancestors such as the streets they lived on, the occupations they followed and the property, both real and human, on which they paid taxes. African American genealogists will be able to discover whether their ancestors were free or enslaved, and if enslaved, to whom they "belonged." Historians will be able to ferret out housing patterns, economic conditions, the role and relationships of women, the institution of slavery and the impact of the port/harbor on the economic development of Baltimore.

We are indebted to Dr. Papenfuse for sharing these records and his knowledge of Baltimore and Maryland with us. We are extremely grateful for the cooperation and support shown by Dr. Robert Schoeberlein, acting Baltimore City Archivist, and by Saul Gibusiwa, Search Room Coordinator at the Baltimore City Archives. Thanks also to Gloria Porter for assistance and encouragement and to Gerald A. Roberts, aka Tony, for interrupting our hard work by making us laugh.

Noreen J. Goodson
Donna Tyler Hollie

FOREWORD

In 1812 as the country and the City of Baltimore prepared for war, and again in 1817 when the city's boundaries were enlarged in a time of rapid economic growth and increasing demand for city services, a concerted effort was made to identify all the taxable property in the city including lots with or without improvements, slaves and personal effects such as furniture, horses, and wagons. This transcription and index focuses on the slaves, the slave holders, and the taxable property of Free Blacks between 1813 and 1818, providing a ward by ward analysis of slaveholding in the city with the names of the slaves, and insight into the degree and distribution of the taxable wealth of Free Blacks in each ward. There were 8 wards in 1813 and initially 11 in 1818 when the city boundaries were expanded by legislative fiat to approximately 15 square miles.

Following in the tradition of Ralph Clayton and Jerry M. Hynson, the authors have painstakingly transcribed and indexed the property tax lists of Baltimore City for 1813 and 1818 for free Blacks, slaves, and slave owners. It is works like this that help put a name, if not a face, to the struggle for economic and personal freedom in the largest urban area in a slave state, and a city that vied for third and second place among all cities in the United States in the years before the Civil War. For the period of time covered by this book, 1813-1818, the Free Black population in Baltimore with a total population of 46,555 (1810), grew from about 5,671 to 10,326 within a total population of 62,738 (1820). At the same time the resident slave population declined from 4,672 to 4,357, a pattern that would continue until slavery was abolished in 1864. Slavery did not thrive in the cities as Richard Wade points out, except perhaps as domestic servants, while manumitted slaves and generations of free Blacks increased as a significant element of the workforce and the religious community of Baltimore.

A number of historians have provided overviews of the rise of the free Black population, and the decline of slavery in Baltimore. Among the best are Barbara Jeanne Fields, *Slavery and Freedom on the Middle Ground, Maryland During the Nineteenth Century*, Christopher Phillips' *Freedom's Port*, Seth Rockman's *Scraping By*, T. Stephen Whitman's *The Price of Freedom*, and Richard C. Wade's *Slavery in the Cities*. Particularly helpful are Barbara Fields, Christopher Phillips, Steve Whitman, and Seth Rockman who provide a clear picture of the struggles of the working poor, black and white, to survive and succeed in a world that became increasingly discriminatory and restrictive. In doing so they make use of the broad brush that manumissions, census records, city directories, petitions to city officials, bank ledgers, and tax records provide, most which can be accessed at the Baltimore City Archives where the originals of the 1813 and 1818 property tax lists transcribed and indexed here, reside (see: **BRG4**: Baltimore City Property Tax Records (*see further information about researching Property Tax Records* for an itemized listing of the surviving tax records). Stephen Whitman uncovered records relating to employers, and with Seth Rockman's study it is possible to better understand the struggle of Black and white wage earners to make a living for themselves in an increasingly industrialized world where labor was at a distinct disadvantage in securing a rightful share of the economic largesse. More recently, Andrew K. Diemer in *The Politics of Black Citizenship* has charted the struggle within the pre-civil war black communities of Baltimore and Philadelphia over emigration and acquiring full citizenship, which is helpful in delineating the black leadership in both communities.

But we still do not know the community as individuals and of their individual accomplishments in a city of limited promise for the Free Black and Slave population. Beginning with Bettye Jane Gardner's *Free Blacks in Baltimore, 1800-1860* (1974), Ralph Clayton's *Black Baltimore,1820-1870*, and Jerry M. Hynson's compilations of fugitive slaves, emigrant free blacks, and blacks in the city and county jails, it has been possible to begin to identify who the slaves and free Blacks were in Baltimore, and to gain some insight into the lives of individuals and their families. Because of Ralph Clayton's *Cash for Blood*, we are also able to better understand who was affected by the domestic slave trade out of Baltimore to New Orleans and other points South, which always posed a threat to the slaves and free Blacks of Baltimore. The former, always in fear of being sold South, the latter always in danger of being stolen and being pulled back into slavery for a journey in which their lives and their futures might well be lost altogether to the relentless appetite of slavery.

This work pushes back to 1813 and forward to 1818, the knowledge of who were the Black property owners and holders of slaves in Baltimore City prior to the 1830s. For the period prior to 1813, Richard Cox and Wilbur Hunter indexed the names on the tax lists of Baltimore City from 1798-1808, but not the race. Apart from the overview that Christopher Phillips provides for that period and a few examples elsewhere, who those Black property owners were and the names of slave owners and their owners in those years remain for future identification, although with Benjamin Ennis, who does appear in these tax lists, it is possible to sample how free Blacks purchased ground rent property and acquired houses for themselves prior to 1813.

What can be known from the Cox index is that only 10 of the Black property owners in this volume assessed with property over $100 appear in the tax records prior to 1808. It is in the years covered by this volume that Black property owners in particular surfaced in Baltimore to be taxed in defense of the city, and they appear to have sustained a presence on the subsequent tax rolls, some of whom, as Christopher Phillips points out, became substantial property owners. While he cites only a few examples such as Thomas Green, and makes the overall argument that there were only 58 free Blacks who owned their own houses, with the tax lists, bank records-especially the Savings Bank of Baltimore, and probate records it is not only possible to know who they were and what they accomplished for themselves and their families, but also that the number of Black owners of housing was quite likely considerably higher. For example in 1815, Phillips located only 58 Black owners, but this volume identifies about 250 Black property owners paying taxes on lots and improvement between 1813 and 1818, of whom approximately 64 were assessed with property worth $100 or more. Isaac Whipper who lived on Tyson Street, owned four brick houses. Moreover of the total number of Black property owners, there were 36 women assessed in their own right. Whether or not they all owned their own houses is not easy to ascertain for certain because of the ground rent system and the loss of the Baltimore City chattel records but it is clear that black property ownership increased dramatically between 1813 and 1818. In all 47 individuals were taxed with lots in 1813, of whom 25 reappeared on the 1818 tax list. In 1818 204 individuals were taxed with lots. Where this property was concentrated is also apparent from the tax lists. See the appendix **Streets and Alleys where Blacks were Taxed for lots and Improvements, 1813/1818,** at the end of this volume.

For much of the pre-Civil War period actual black ownership of housing is obscured by a complex ground rent system for which Baltimore is well known and that today remains a title quagmire that the legislature and the courts are still attempting to resolve. In essence the problem is that the original title to land in the city is rooted in land grants called patents. In developing Baltimore City those who held title under a land grant for the most part did not sell their land outright, but leased it out for development on what is known as ground rents. That freed up the capital that otherwise the lessee/renter would have to sink into the acquisition of the land outright if he or she was required to pay full market value of the land. Instead he or she paid about 6% of the value of the land at the time of the rental as an annual fee for the duration of the lease (often 99 years). The renter was then free to build on the land and in turn sell the building with the ground rent requirement to whomever he or she pleased. Over time many ground rents were subleased and sub-subleased (even sub-sub-sub leased) on often long term leases (99 years). While White owners were able to pass their ground rent holdings on to their heirs through probate, it is not clear whether or not Blacks were able to do likewise with any frequency, but as long as they lived and paid the ground rent the houses they acquired were their own.

The clues to Black ownership of housing are the tax records supplemented by land records.. For the period covered by this volume, take for example Honey Alley, later Hughes Street in West Baltimore. All the lots along Honey Alley between South Charles and Light Street were originally part of Luns Lot, a large tract purchased by Colonel John Eager Howard and renamed Howard's Addition to Baltimore. Colonel Howard had the addition surveyed into 937 lots which he in turn leased out on ground rents. As late as 1831 his estate was still collecting the ground rents on a significant portion of the original addition, although some of the ground rents had been sold. In the portion of Honey Alley bounded by Charles and Light, some of the ground rents to the numbered lots had been subleased to developers such as John McDonogh who in turn subleased portions of the lots he leased from Colonel Howard to Black owners of the houses on the lots who in turn he made responsible for all municipal taxes. Such was the case of Benjamin Ennis of Honey Alley who lived in his frame house on the north side of the alley for at least 33 years. Benjamin Ennis, probably a veteran of the American Revolution, appears first on the municipal tax list of 1813 as Benjamin Annis which is corrected to Ennis by 1818. In both lists he is charged with a lot and improvements. In 1808 Benjamin Annis/Ennis (both names are used in the land records relating to his property) leased a portion of Howard lot 874 on Honey Alley which had been subleased by John Eager Howard to John McDonogh in 1794. In that year John McDonogh subleased the adjoining lots 880, 877, and part of lot 874 (on which Benjamin Ennis's house would be built). It is not clear whether Mcdonogh built the two story frame house, or Ennis did, but in 1808 it was Ennis's on a 99 year ground rent lease payable to McDonogh with a provision that all taxes would be paid by Ennis and that failure to pay the ground rent to McDonogh or his assignee within 60 days of the due date could result in the loss of Ennis's lease and improvements on it. In other words, Benjamin Ennis owned his house as long as he paid the ground rent to McDonogh, while McDonogh was responsible for paying the original ground rent to Colonel Howard. Even if McDonogh failed to pay his ground rent to Colonel Howard, Ennis would still own the house he occupied, as long as he paid the ground rent owed specified in the lease from McDonogh, and the taxes owed the city. After Ennis died it would appear that his heirs failed to pay the ground rent and the property reverted to the person to whom Ennis had owed the ground rent. 6It would take a court case and a land patent to resolve who owned the property, but in the end the Ennis family did not.

A further problem is that apparently Free Blacks rarely appear in probate (wills, inventories, and administration accounts of estates) prior to the Civil War and possibly took pains to hide their wealth. The evidence is anecdotal so far, but it may be that Free Blacks generally kept their liquid assets as cash hidden from view. For example one wealthy Free Black who lost his first fortune in a failed bank, lost his second to robbery. The robber was caught and sent to prison, but it is not known if the money was recovered. Some free blacks, particularly women, did avail themselves of bank accounts, particularly with the Savings Bank of Baltimore which asserted that it was color blind. A forthcoming study of blacks and property owners before the Civil War, including the depositors at the bank by Marcus Allen will illuminate who those depositors were and the extent of their banking wealth. It probably will never be known how many of the over 17,000 free blacks in Baltimore City by the time Frederick Douglass left in September 1838 were owners of their own homes, nor will we fully understand the extent of their personal wealth. It can only be assumed that the tax collector's net captured most and that the bulk of the free black population were renters who moved with some frequency about the city, although some, like James Mingo, the host of the East Baltimore Mental Improvement Society to which Frederick Douglass belonged, apparently lived out his adult life with his family on Happy Alley, in the same frame house without ever making it into the tax lists. If he owned his house, it is obscured by the ownership of the groundrents who happened to be the descendants/heirs of the original owners of Fell's Point. Tracing such details has been made nearly impossible by the much regretted destruction of the Baltimore City Chattel records which recorded the sale and transfer of such personal property as slaves and ground rents. In James Mingo's case the 1813/1818 tax records merely suggest that the Fell family heirs owned the land on which his house was situated and that they owed any taxes due.

With the exception of Leroy Graham's *Black Baltimore*, little has been done to tell the life stories of those Free Blacks who remained to live and work in Baltimore in the years prior to that fateful day in November, 1864, when Maryland abolished slavery. Charles Steffen in *The Mechanics of Baltimore* provides insight into the interaction among slaves, Free Blacks and white workers, including an analysis of the free and slave laborers at the Despeaux shipyard in Fells Point, not far from where Frederick Douglass lived and worked as a caulker, but who those Free Blacks were and what can be known about their lives, let alone what they looked like remains a challenge. The profiles in this volume are an excellent beginning. The authors have provided brief notices of the lives of both slave owners and free blacks found in the tax lists. While far from complete, it is intended to demonstrate what can be done to bring substance to the lives of people, especially free blacks and slaves who contributed so much to the economic and cultural growth of Baltimore City. Sadly there are few images of the pre-Civil War black community. The most famous are of those who left, including Reverend Daniel Coker, Frances Ellen Watkins Harper, and Reverend Darius Stokes. The only known Black portrait painter in Maryland in the antebellum years, Joshua Johnson, a resident of Fells Point, painted only two known portraits of Black residents of Baltimore, both probably pastors, and the one identified, emigrated to Liberia. Indeed the most photographed individual in 19th century America was Frederick Douglass who fled the city, rather than face the uncertainty of a promise of future freedom (in six years) offered by his master.

Bethel Congregation
source: http://hdl.loc.gov/loc.pnp/pga.07916

Black Churches were the focal point of Black Culture in the city and were the primary place of religious and secular education. The only known image of the interior of a Baltimore Black church and its congregation (1845) is symbolic of the difficulty of putting faces to the Free Black community. For the most part the women are obscured by their bonnets, while all but a few of the men are hidden in the crowd. The presiding pastor, Darius Stokes, a Baltimore born drayman by trade, who became a Methodist minister, proved to be an aggressive leader of the Black community centered on Bethel Church, the largest Black congregation in Baltimore. Yet he found the tensions within his congregation too great to bear, especially after one community meeting in which he was bloodied by an angry woman. Rather than emigrate to Liberia or Haiti, he chose to follow the American dream to California with the Gold Rush where he served a number of Black Methodist congregations including one in the capital Sacramento. He was described as a "colored preacher who makes a respectable sermon, and is probably as upright as the majority of Americans." As to his congregation in Sacramento, he lamented that "the few of our brethren who were here, were rushing too madly on in pursuit of mammon." Darius's brother, Reverend Eli Worthington Stokes, for whom there is no known image, fled in the other direction to New England where he became a popular preacher in the Episcopal Church, and died in 1867 as a Protestant Episcopal missionary in Liberia.

Old Hagar, 1834 by Samuel Smith, artist, Hamilton row, Hamilton street, Baltimore, courtesy of the Maryland Historical Society, and *Moses Small*, Newsvendor, 1858 by Thomas Waterman Wood, courtesy of the San Francisco Museum of Fine Arts

Until the black men of Baltimore became soldiers in the Union Army there appear to be no family portraits of the Antebellum Free Blacks of Baltimore. A few Blacks including children are featured as individuals in the paintings of white artists of the 1840s and 50s, but most such images are usually slaves and without identification. Apparently the singular exceptions found to date are Moses Small the newspaper vendor, and Hagar, a former slave, who was said to have lived to 104 when her wooden house in Apple Alley was consumed by fire. Neither Moses, who died venerated by the white community in 1861, nor Hagar who died in 1834, appears in these tax lists, although both were adults and working in the city at the time. While Moses was married and they raised a family, he apparently never owned a home of his own, nor did he have sufficient visible personal property to be taxed, even though he was one of the subscribers to John Fortie's efforts to fund private education for Free Black children in 1838. Indeed literacy among the Free Black population deserves re-thinking, especially among the female population. Again the evidence to date is sparse and largely anecdotal. Only one letter is known to have survived from a Baltimore house slave and that is from 1861, but the Sabbath and possibly the day schools were not limited to males. William Watkins provided Frances Ellen Watkins Harper with a well rounded education which enabled her to begin publishing her poetry which she probably began composing when she was a Free Black domestic servant in Baltimore, while Reverend Stokes and Reverend Fortie, among others saw to it that their congregations had Sabbath and day schools that taught reading and writing. Still, with works such as this, it is possible to begin to systematically piece together the stories of the lives of one of, if not the, the largest urban Free Black communities in the United States before the Civil War. Through collaborative genealogy and profilography (an awkward term I coined for collective biography) in an online setting, mining census schedules, tax lists, city directories, newspapers, court records, and http://mdlandrec.net, it will be possible to acquire a better appreciation of those men and women who struggled to maintain their modicum of freedom in a slave state, deciding not to flee, but to stay, making the most of what the City of Promise, no matter how limited to Free Blacks, had to offer.

Edward C. Papenfuse,
Maryland State Archivist, retired

PROFILES

Solomon Birckhead: A prominent physician, Birckhead was born in 1761 to a family that at one time had been Quakers. He served as Commissioner of Health and was a founding member of both the B & O Railroad and the Union Bank of Baltimore. In 1786 he married Jane McCulloh and they lived in downtown Baltimore opposite the Battle Monument. Later they built a summer home, called Mt. Royal, in the neighborhood known today as Reservoir Hill. In an 1813 letter to President James Madison, Birckhead expressed his concerns about the impact of the War of 1812 on the city of Baltimore and its citizens. In that same year he owned three slaves: 22 year old Levin, 40 year old Nelly and Charles who was twenty. Five years later, in addition to the aforementioned slaves, Birckhead owned a fourteen year old also named Nelly. Records of the Savings Bank of Baltimore indicate that in 1824, Charles "Slave to Solomon Birckhead" had an account worth $417.07. Perhaps Birckhead was assisting Charles in his efforts to become a member of Baltimore's large free black community. In 1836 Birckhead died in a fire at Mt. Royal.

Solomon Etting: Etting was born in York Pennsylvania on July 28th 1764. He moved to Baltimore about 1791 where he was an extremely successful merchant and businessman and was active in civic and political affairs. He was affiliated with the Masons and although he supported numerous charitable causes which benefited the Jewish population, there is no evidence that he ever affiliated with a synagogue. As a member of the Baltimore City Council, between 1799 and 1826 he introduced at least three bills to eliminate references to a Christian God in the Oath of Public Office. A founder of the B & O Railroad, he was also President of the Board of Commissioners charged with rebuilding City Hall following the great Baltimore fire. In 1813 Etting had five enslaved people who appeared to be an intact family. There were four slaves and two free women of color in his household in 1820. By 1830 Etting had no slaves. He died Aug 6, 1847 and was survived by his second wife and children. A west Baltimore street is named for him.

Free Women of Color: Restricted by both race and gender, life was difficult for African American women. Countless women, like **Charity Joice** and **Lucinda Dorsey**, worked as laundresses and domestic servants. **Rebecca Brightman** was one of many market women who sold prepared foods, flowers, groceries, seafood etc. at the harbor and from door to door. A minority of women were skilled workers, such as **Candes Mollach**, who was a seamstress. It was customary in city directories to list women as heads of household if there was no man living with them. Some women were listed either because they were widowed or because they were married to men who worked as sailors and spent the majority of their time away from their families. In spite of low wages and limited occupational choices, many women of color were able to acquire property and erect houses. There were several pockets in the city, such as on Honey Alley, Union Street, Brandy Alley and Hill Street where African American women property owners were clustered.

John Gadsby: English born, Gadsby and his wife migrated to America and settled in Alexandria, Virginia, where he was a tavern owner from 1796-1808. He was the founder of Gadsby's Hotel in Washington DC. In 1808 he took charge of Baltimore's Indian Queen Hotel at Hanover and Baltimore Streets which, under his management, was known as Baltimore's largest and fanciest hotel and the first to have running water. There is speculation that it was from the Indian Queen Hotel that Francis Scott Key watched the bombardment of Fort McHenry. By 1818 Gadsby was the city's largest slave holder, with thirty-five people under his control. His human property numbered thirty-nine in 1830 and he also employed four free Black women at the hotel. He is known to have sold at least one enslaved person and manumitted one, Harriet Dickman, a native of Charles County MD who lived to the age of 105. Gadsby died in 1844 in Washington D.C. In his will he names the seventeen enslaved people bequeathed to his wife.

Jacob Gilliard, Sr.: Born enslaved but emancipated by age 45, Gilliard worked as a blacksmith and had at least one enslaved person working with him as an apprentice. He purchased his sons Jacob Jr. and Nicholas and a fourteen year old named Henry Williams from John Merryman. He manumitted his sons in 1808 and Williams in 1812. A trustee of Sharp Street Church, Gilliard was among those, who dissatisfied with the racist practices of the Methodist Church, withdrew and established Baltimore's Bethel African Methodist Episcopal Church. In fact, Gilliard and another free black man named Richard Russell purchased, in 1801, the two plots of land on which Bethel was erected. Through his church associations and the marriages of his granddaughters to Daniel Coker and George Hackett, Gilliard was connected to some of the most influential men in Baltimore's free black community.

Don Carlos Hall: Hall was born enslaved but emancipated in the will of the slave owner. He had been a member of both Lovely Lane and Strawberry Alley Methodist Churches. He was a leader of the free black community and among the members of Sharp Street Church who planned the withdrawal and the subsequent establishment of Bethel African Methodist Church. He worked as a bootblack and varnish manufacturer and in his 1823 will he left property to his wife and sons along with $6000.00 in public stock securities with the interest to be paid to his wife as long as she remained unmarried. Most importantly Hall instructed his friend, Phillip Thomas to use $1000.00 to purchase the freedom of his daughter, Mary Ann, who had been sold to William Lewis of New Orleans, Louisiana. If the purchase could be arranged for less than $1000.00 Hall wanted his daughter to receive the remaining funds.

Christopher Hughes, Sr.: A native of Ireland, Hughes was born in 1744 and migrated to America about 1791. He worked as a brick maker, silversmith and goldsmith. His shop, on Gay and Market Streets, was called Sign of the Cup and Crown. Hughes, a prominent real estate developer in the inner harbor area, was extremely prosperous. In 1790 he held eight enslaved people; that number increased to thirty-three in 1810. He was taxed for fifteen slaves in 1813 and eleven in 1818. In 1810 he offered a reward of $10.00 for the return of Isaac, a runaway slave who was a skilled brickmaker. A member of Old St. Paul's Episcopal Church, Hughes does not appear to have been active in social or political circles. He was the father of fifteen children, only five of whom survived to adulthood. His daughter Louisa married Gen. George Armistead, who served in the defense of Baltimore at Ft. McHenry during the War of 1812. Hughes died in 1824.

Capt. Joseph Leonard: Leonard owned thirty slaves in 1813. They worked in his brewery at the corner of Conway and Hanover which he purchased in 1809 and operated until his death in 1820. In 1818, Leonard offered $500.00 for the return of five enslaved men who had run away. He had been an English sea captain and imported the bricks for the brewery's storage vault from his native land. Leonard used draymen to deliver his products to the citizens of Baltimore and charged for all bottles that were not returned.

George R. McGill: Several free men of color were members of Sharp St. Methodist Church and, in keeping with the church's practices, were in the forefront of civic, educational and anti-slavery efforts. McGill, who operated an oyster cellar and messenger service, was a lay minister and one of Sharp Street's most active members. He had previously belonged to Lovely Lane and Strawberry Alley Methodist Churches. Born enslaved, he purchased his freedom in 1809 and subsequently purchased the freedom of his father and his siblings. By 1819 he was teaching at Sharp Street Church's African Academy. In December of 1819 McGill headed Maryland's first delegation of African American visitors to Haiti. Unfortunately while there he became ill and had to shorten his visit. In 1827 he migrated to Liberia, remaining until 1832. He indicated in letters that he enjoyed the freedom and the fact that "we do not shudder at the sight of a white man." After his return to America, he continued to advocate for migration as a means for African Americans to obtain the freedom and equality which he found so elusive in America.

William Patterson: A native of Ireland born in 1752, Patterson arrived in America in 1788. He was a merchant who made his fortune supplying the Revolutionary War army with weapons. In 1792, he purchased at auction, land belonging to the Rogers family, owners of what became Druid Hill Park. He deeded six acres to Baltimore City in 1827; this property is now known as Patterson Park. When Baltimore seamstresses, concerned about low wages, petitioned the mayor for assistance, Patterson was one of thirty-five men who supported their efforts. Another example of his civic responsibility was his involvement in raising money for the completion of Fort McHenry. Patterson was the first president of the Bank of Baltimore and one of the incorporators of the B &

O Railroad. He owned seven slaves. Patterson married Dorcas Spear, daughter of a wealthy flour merchant and sister-in-law of Revolutionary War Hero, Sam Smith. The Pattersons had thirteen children, the most famous of whom was Elizabeth, better known as Betsy. Noted for her beauty and vivacious personality, in 1803 she married Jerome Bonaparte, brother of the emperor of France.

William Presbury Patterson: Harford County native Patterson was born in 1788 and died in Baltimore in 1865. A prosperous brickmaker, he was taxed for twenty-five enslaved people in 1810. He was a candidate for the Baltimore City Council in 1826 and for Justice of the Peace in Harford County in 1857. According to the Harford County Maryland census of 1850, Patterson owned six slaves ranging in age from five months to one hundred and two years.

William Price: Price was a shipwright in Baltimore from 1794-1833. He lived in Fells Point and his business was located behind his house on Pitt St. (Currently the house is known as 910 Fell St.) The U.S. Navy's major shipwright in Baltimore, it is likely that he assisted in the building of the Constellation. He served as a gunner on the U.S. Constitution during the War of 1812. Some scholars refer to Price as the largest slaveholder in the city. In addition to the twenty-one people he enslaved in 1813, he also employed those who were enslaved by others. Just prior to his escape from Baltimore slavery, one of those employed by Price was Frederick Douglass. Originally from Hampton, Virginia, where he probably acquired his skills, Price died in Baltimore in 1877 at the age of 85.

Sharp Street Methodist Church Members: This African American institution evolved from Strawberry Alley Methodist Church, which a young Frederick Douglass attended. In addition to religious activities, Sharp Street engaged in raising money to purchase enslaved people, operated a school and hosted meetings for the discussion of African American migration. Additionally the church served as a meeting place for fraternal groups such as the Masons. While the Methodist church had more African American members than any other denomination, black members were not allowed to become elders or itinerant ministers and were always subject to the authority of white bishops. In some cases, seating was segregated by race and people of African descent were served communion after white people. For these reasons, a movement arose to separate from the Methodist Church. Among those who gathered to plan the withdrawal from Sharp St. Church were, ***George Douglass***, a drayman and substantial property owner, and ***Don Carlos Hall***, a bootblack and varnish manufacturer. It was ***Stephen Hill***, formerly a member of Lovely Lane and Strawberry Alley Methodist Churches, who suggested the name The African Methodist Bethel Church Society which continues today in Baltimore as Bethel African Methodist Episcopal Church. As one of eighteen Baltimore delegates to the first political convention of African American Marylanders, held in 1852, **Hill** spoke in favor of emigration to Liberia but was adamant that he was not in favor of immediate and mandatory emigration.

The Rev. John-Marie Tessier: Tessier was born in 1758 in France. He was a founding member of the United States Sulpician Community, a religious order of priests, and worked diligently on behalf of the refugees from the Haitian Revolution who settled in Maryland. In 1810 Tessier became director of St. Mary's Seminary and under his leadership the school was elevated to university status. In contrast to religious thought current during that era, Tessier believed that enslaved people had souls and were intellectually capable of being educated. It was under Tessier's leadership and influence that The Rev. James Joubert aided Haitian refugee Mary Elizabeth Lange in establishing the first African American order of nuns, the Oblate Sisters of Providence. The order continues to educate African American children in Baltimore at St. Francis Academy. 1818 Tessier owned a male slave valued at $125.00 and a female slave valued at $80. He died in 1840.

Jeanne Mathusine Droibillan Volunbrun (aka Jeanne Mathusine Droibillan de Volunbrun): One of the few large female slaveholders and business owners in early 19th century Baltimore, Volunbrun emigrated from Haiti following the revolution led by Toussaint L'Ouverture. Initially she settled with her slaves in New York City but found that atmosphere not conducive to her economic stability as the state had enacted legislation requiring gradual emancipation of the enslaved. In addition, abolitionists claimed that the people Volunbrun held in slavery were actually free as a result of the Haitian Revolution. Armed abolitionists, many with Haitian roots, surrounded her home demanding the release of her human property; this effort was thwarted by local police. Volunbrun then attempted to move the slaves to Norfolk, Virginia for sale but was unsuccessful. Seeking an environment friendlier to slave holders, she moved to Baltimore in 1802 and established a cigar manufacturing operation at 35 Harrison Street, with twenty-three enslaved workers. Several of her slaves ran away and/or sued for their freedom. Volunbrun died circa 1832.

Jean Baptiste, John Joseph and John Augustine: These three men were among the enslaved people brought from Haiti and later removed to Baltimore by Jeanne Volunbrun. Had the men remained in New York, they would have been freed under the state's gradual emancipation laws, however, following Volunbrun's move to Baltimore, their future as enslaved individuals was assured. Abolitionist and attorney Daniel Raymond, whose office was near Volunbrun's factory, filed a freedom suit on behalf of the three men arguing that (1) since France abolished slavery in her colonies in 1794 the men were free before coming to the United States and (2) Maryland's 1796 law made it illegal to import slaves for the purpose of residence or sale. The courts upheld Volunbrun's argument that she was a temporary resident of Baltimore and therefore not subject to the 1796 statute. This ruling was issued in spite of the fact that she had lived in Baltimore for sixteen years at that time. Jean Baptiste, who was born in 1788, was one of four people who were kidnapped and taken to New Orleans. Within three months he had been sold a total of three times.

William Watkins: Teacher, minister, abolitionist, lecturer and writer, Watkins was born in Baltimore circa 1803. He was a pupil of Daniel Coker at Bethel Charity School and succeeded him when Coker migrated to Liberia. Among the subjects Watkins taught at the Academy for Negro Youth were history, geography, mathematics, Greek, Latin, English, music and rhetoric. His niece, the renowned abolitionist and poet, Frances Ellen Watkins Harper was one of approximately seventy students at his school. Based on an 1836 speech in Philadelphia in which Watkins argued that education was essential in preparing slaves for freedom, it is possible that, in addition to teaching free blacks, he surreptitiously taught enslaved people. As a member and trustee of Sharp Street Church, he was active in promoting the well-being of the African American community. He was a founder of the National Convention of Free People of Color and a contributor to *The Liberator,* a newspaper published by abolitionist William Lloyd Garrison. In fact, Garrison credited Watkins as one of the three Baltimoreans who convinced him to move from advocating gradual emancipation to becoming a militant proponent of immediate abolition of slavery. In 1820 Watkins purchased two enslaved people, Rebecca and her son Henry, from John Carroll for $150.00. By 1823, the debt was paid and Carroll issued deeds of manumission. Watkins was opposed to colonization and believed that African Americans were entitled to freedom and equality in the United States of America. Several sources indicate that he migrated to Canada and died there in 1858. Given his anti-colonization stance, a move to Canada seems questionable. Further research is needed to determine if the migrant was him or his son.

Nelson Wells: As did many other African American men in Baltimore, Wells worked as a drayman, transporting a variety of materials throughout the harbor area. He was born in 1786 and married in 1814 in the Episcopal Church. In addition to being hard working he must have been extremely frugal as he amassed an estate of about $3500.00, primarily in Baltimore City Stock, bearing 6% annual interest. Wells died in 1843 and named three Quakers as executors of his estate. One of the executors was Isaac Tyson, Jr., whose family had long been active in abolitionist circles. In compliance with Wells' instructions that his estate be used for the education of African American children, the trustees established the Wells Free School at Hanover Street and Cypress Alley. The school was still operating in 1868. The trustees also donated money to the Baltimore Association for the Moral and Educational Improvement of Colored People which, in turn, established the Baltimore Normal School. That institution, which benefited from Wells' bequest, is currently known as Bowie State University and is Maryland's oldest Historically Black College/University.

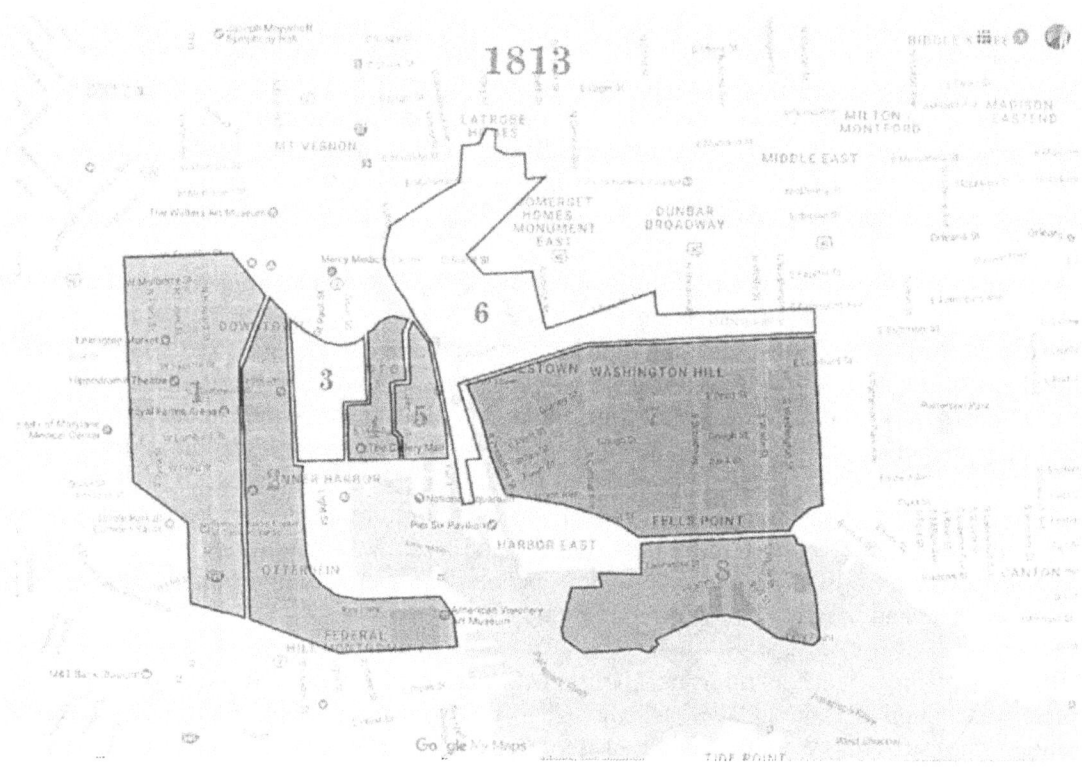

Baltimore City Wards, 1813 and 1818
derived from the maps found on the
Baltimore City Archives Web Site:
https://baltimorecityhistory.net/wards/

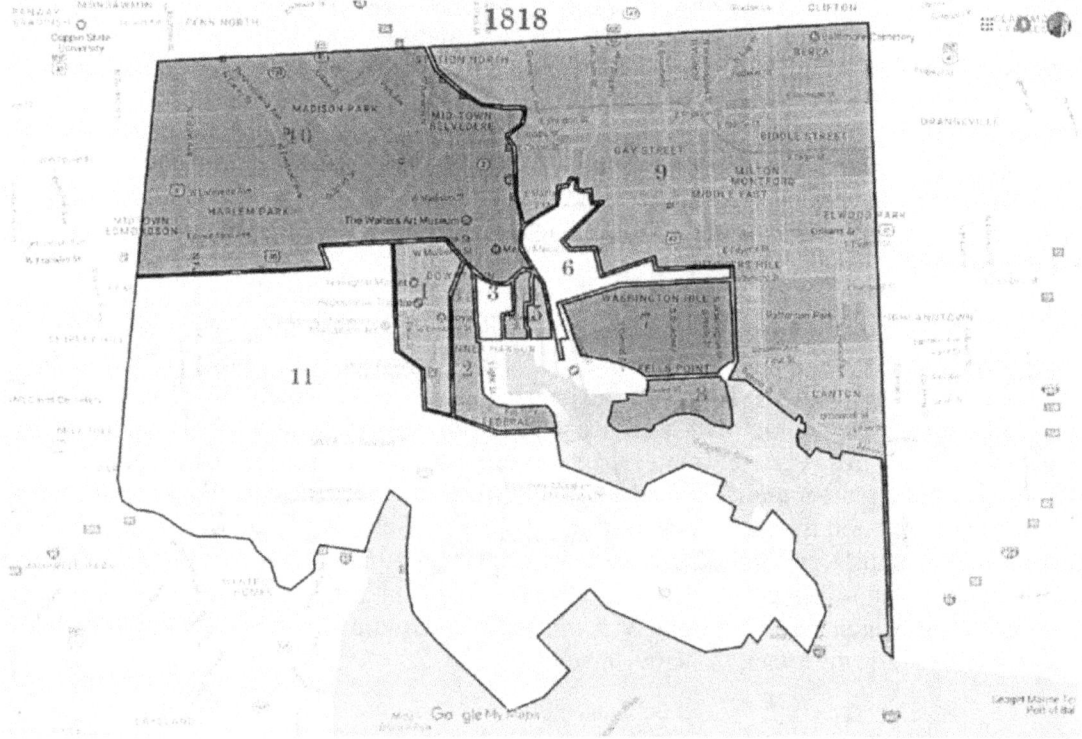

Free Blacks and Slave Owners in Baltimore City Tax Assessor's Ledger, 1813 Ward 1

NAME	RACE/STATUS	RESIDENCE	REAL PROPERTY	OCCUPATION	ENSLAVED PROPERTY Name, Age, Value	COMMENTS
Adams, John		Howard St		Merchant	Henney 20, $80.	
Allen, Owen		Saratoga & Liberty Sts			Hannah 34, $80. Adeline under 8, $20.	
Avisse, Charles		Howard St		Merchant	Jane 17, $80.	
Bailey, Elijah		Ridgeley's addition John St			Betsey 25, $80.	
Bailey, George		Baltimore St		Druggist	George 15, $125.	Property of Nancy Mercer.
Baltzell, Lewis		Liberty St		Merchant	Harriot 17, $80.	
Bare, John		Baltimore St			Sorina 18, $80. Maria 10, $40.	
Barry, Richard		Howard St		Grocer	Paul 30, $125. Isaac 14, $125. Joseph 11, $40. Perrey 9, $40. James under 8, $20. Beck 28, $80. Carline under 8, $20.	
Batturs, Richard		Liberty St		Merchant	Charles 14, $125. Betsey 24, $80.	
Baxley, George		Howard St		Flour Inspector	Isaac under 8, $20.	
Beckley, Henry		Howard St			Sally 20, $80.	
Billard, Martha		Liberty St			John 40, $125. Marani over 36, $40.	
Bixler, David		Howard St		Tobacconist	Ready (f) 18, $80.	
Blair, James		Howard St		Grocer	John 9, $40. Fanney 16, $80.	
Bohn, Charles		Baltimore St		Merchant	Andrew 41, $125. Darkey 23, $80. Daniel 10, $40. Ann 12, $40.	
Bond, Eleanor	Widow	Howard & Pratt Sts			Jessey 18, $125. Sarah 25, $80.	
Bornard, Jambia		Camden & Howard Sts			Omer 30, $80.	Omer is female.
Boyce, Theodore R.S.		German St		Livery Stable keeper	Kitty 20, $80.	
Brice, Henry		Pratt Sr		Merchant	William 10, $40. Bettey over 36, $40. Nance over 36, $40. Peggey 16, $80.	

Free Blacks and Slave Owners in Baltimore City Tax Assessor's Ledger, 1813 Ward 1

NAME	RACE/STATUS	RESIDENCE	REAL PROPERTY	OCCUPATION	ENSLAVED PROPERTY Name, Age, Value	COMMENTS
Brown, Amos		Howard St		Shoe seller	John 11, $40. Arey over 36, $40. Eliza 20, $80. Mary 13, $40. Eliza under 8, $20. Female under 8, $20.	John & Arey owned by Ann Griffith. Eliza & Mary owned by W. Ridgley.
Browning, Peregrine G.		Lombard St		Constable	Julia 14, $80.	
Buchanan, Lloyd		Lexington St		Gentleman	Fanny 18, $80.	
Bull, Jarrett		Howard St		U. S. Gauger for Port of Baltimore	Nelly 15, $80. Hetty 15, $80.	
Byrnes, Samuel		Eutaw St			Male slave 14, $125.	
Campbell, John R.		Eutaw St		Merchant	Perry 14, $125. David 12, $80. Kitty 18, $25.	
Chalmers, James		Howard St		Inspector of butter & lard	Cash 17, $125.	
Chatard, Dr. Peter		Saratoga St		Physician	Bellisarias 20, $125. Charlotta 17, $80.	Bellisarias is male.
Clopper, Edward N.		Howard St			Sam 17, $125.	
Cole, Edward J.		Lexington St			Dilla 25, $80.	
Colhoun, Benjamin		Liberty St			George 21, $125.	
Cook, William Sr.		Baltimore St			Dick, over 45, $60. Ceazer 45, $125. Moses 25, $125. Phoebe over 36, $40. Kittey 27, $80.	
Courage, Anthony		North St			Fanny over 36, $40.	
Croxall, John		German St			William 18, $125. Caleb 15, $125. John 14, $125. Oston 12, $40. Valentine 11, $40.	William owned by T. Ruchels. Caleb, John, Oston & Valentine owned by Philip Fiddeman.
Daley, Daniel		Conway St		Plasterer	Peggy 26, $80. Jinney under 8, $20.	

Free Blacks and Slave Owners in Baltimore City Tax Assessor's Ledger, 1813 Ward 1

NAME	RACE/ STATUS	RESIDENCE	REAL PROPERTY	OCCUPATION	ENSLAVED PROPERTY Name, Age, Value	COMMENTS
Davidson, Sarah		Lombard St			George 17, $125, Sophia 12, $40. Nann 35 infirm, $40. Hanna 26, $80.	
De Butts, Dr. Elisha		German St		Physician	William 12, $40.	
Decker, George		Fayette St		Merchant	Solomon, under 8, $20. Peggy 19, $80.	
Delinotte, Charles		Waggon Alley			Lander 40, $125. Andrew 40, $125. Ordons above 36 $40.	Ordons is female.
Demangin, Charles		Howard St			Joseph 20, $125.	
Denys, Benjamin		North St			Hannah over 36, $40.	
Dinsmore, Henry W.		Liberty St		Merchant	Felis 11, $40.	Felis (f), property of M. Woodland, Eastern Shore.
Donaldson, Joseph		Fayette St		Merchant	Letty 22, $80.	
Donsee, Leypold		Baltimore St		Boot & shoe maker	Julia 22, $80.	
Dorsey, Vachel		Camden St		Inspector of tobacco	Basil 14, $125. Jenney 26, $80. Bell 14, $80. Pheobe under 8, $20.	
Dunbar, George T.		Howard & Baltimore Sts		Cashier of the Commercial & Farmers' Bank	Sukey 26, $80. Beck 17, $80.	
Dunkel, George A.		Liberty St		Physician	Philip 40, $125.	
Earnest, George		German St		Cordwainer	Female 15, $80.	
Eichelberger, George		Camden St		Tobacconist	Bill 12, $40. Charlot 15, $80.	
Elliott, Hartmann		Howard St			Robert 17, $125. Abraham 11, $40. Bill under 8, $20. Nelley 33, $80. Soff 11, $40.	
Elliott, Robert		Lexington St		Paper hanging store	Harriot 13, $40.	
Etting, Solomon		Howard St		Merchant	Daniel 36, $125. Delton 13, $30. Amos 11, $40. Julia 30, $80. Nelly under 8, $20.	Delton is infirm.
Fahnestock, Derick		Howard St		Merchant	Henney 17, $85.	
Fahnestock, Peter		Lexington St		Dry Goods Store	Julia 14, $80.	
Falkonar, Perry		Sharp St		Merchant	Charlot 18, $80. Nancey 15, $80.	

Free Blacks and Slave Owners in Baltimore City Tax Assessor's Ledger, 1813 Ward 1

NAME	RACE/ STATUS	RESIDENCE	REAL PROPERTY	OCCUPATION	ENSLAVED PROPERTY Name, Age, Value	COMMENTS
Fisher, John		Lexington St		Merchant	Mina 18, $80.	
Fisher, John		Liberty St		Currier	Thomas 40, $125. James under 8, $20. Judith over 36, $40. Maria 17, $80. Liza 8, $40.	
Ford, Stephen H.		Sharp St		Merchant	Charlot 10, $40.	
Fox, Mrs. Elizabeth	Widow	Liberty St			Charity 23, $80. Mary 10, $40. Alexander under 8, $20.	
Frailey, Leonard		Pratt St		One of the city gaugers	Henney 16, $80.	
Fry, Samuel		Sharp St			Priscilla 12, $40.	
Fulton, David		Saratoga & Eutaw Sts		Merchant	Michael 40, $125. Lewis under 8, $20. Ned 30, $125. Mint 35, $80. Henry 12, $125. Hannah 30, $80. Jack Lewis 35, $125. Anne 28, $80. Jin 15, $80. Louisa 11, $40.	
Gambrall, John		Liberty & Lexington Sts		Hair dresser	Mary 16, $80.	
George, Archibald		109 Howard St		Merchant	Rachel 13, $40.	
Gibson, John		Pratt St		Gentleman	Jack 36, $125. Tom 28, $125. Anney 17, $80.	
Gilmor, William		Baltimore St		Merchant	Thomas over 45, $60. George 22, $125. Bettey 23, $80.	
Gowan, John		Waggon Alley		Soap, candle, starch & fig blue manu- factoring	Judy 25, $80. Grace 20, $80.	
Griffith, Charles		Howard & Liberty Sts			Nancey over 36, $40. Andrew 13, $40. Charles 12, $40.	
Gwynn, Mrs.	Widow	Eutaw St			Walt 18, $125. Richard 15, $125. Loyd 10, $40. Mary 25, $80. Beck 11, $40. Nancy 10, $40.	

Free Blacks and Slave Owners in Baltimore City Tax Assessor's Ledger, 1813 Ward 1

NAME	RACE/ STATUS	RESIDENCE	REAL PROPERTY	OCCUPATION	ENSLAVED PROPERTY Name, Age, Value	COMMENTS
Hall, Isabella		Sharp St			Jess 20, $125. Maria over 36, $40. Jude 22, $80. Hannah 23, $80. Dinah 9, $40. Susan under 8, $20.	
Harris, Dr. Edward		Dutch Alley		Physician	Sam 33, $125. Joe 28, $125. Alice 34, $80. Anne over 36, $40.	
Hassard, John & Ralph		Howard St		Merchants	Jim 18, $125 rental	Jim is property of Wm. Ringold.
Hawkins, James L.		Liberty & German Sts		Teller @ the Commercial & Farmer's Bank	Mary 22, $80. Nella 20, $80. Polly 13, $40.	
Hennecke, George		Eutaw St		Saddler	Liley 14, $80.	
Hessilius, Mary		Liberty St			Edward 22, $125.	
Hickley, Robert		Howard St		Flour merchant	Louisa 18, $40.	
Hoffman, Daniel		Howard St		Merchant	Limes 19, $125. Lydia 35, $80.	
Hurxthall, Ferdinand		Liberty St		Merchant	Female 16, $80. Washington under 8, $20.	
Hussey, Nathan		Howard St			Sam 35, $125. Preslin 22, $25.	Preslin is infirm.
Irvine, Alexander		Howard St		Merchant	Ann 17, $80.	
Isfett, John		Howard St			Julia over 36, $40.	
Jackson, Henry		Lombard St			Stephen 25, $125.	
Jenkins, Walter		Baltimore St			Frank 8, $40. Charity 10, $40.	
Jessop, Dominic		Liberty St			Polly 30, $80. Charlot under 8, $20.	
Jessop, William		Fayette St		Merchant	Isaacc 17, $125. Henry under 8, $20. John under 8, $20. Lucey 30, $80. Polly 18, $80. Caroline under 8, $20.	
Johnston, Christopher		Fayette St			Hannah over 36, $40. Jane over 36, $40. Harriot under 8, $20. Collins, $60. Thomas 30, $125.	Collins is infirm.
Jones, Talbott		Howard St		Merchant	John 9, $40. Jinney 34, $80.	
Keerl, Dr. Henry		Baltimore St		Druggist	Jack 19, $125. Maria 21, $80. Ann 13, $40.	

Free Blacks and Slave Owners in Baltimore City Tax Assessor's Ledger, 1813 Ward 1

NAME	RACE/ STATUS	RESIDENCE	REAL PROPERTY	OCCUPATION	ENSLAVED PROPERTY Name, Age, Value	COMMENTS
Keyser, Derick		Howard St		China Store	William 16, $125. Charity 25, $80. Harriot 8, $40.	
Keyser, George		Howard St			Linday 15, $80.	
Kimmel, Anthony Sr.		Lexington St			Minley 23, $80	
King, Henry		Howard St		Inn keeper	Febe 15. Rachel 17.	Property of Hoofnagle, $80.
Kipp, John		Liberty St		Merchant	George 30, $125.	
Konig, Frederick		Camden St		Merchant	Anthony 16, $125. Jacob 11, $40.	
Kramer, Frederick		Fayette St		Merchant	Female slave 24, $80. Ellen 12, $40.	
Krebs, John		Conway St		Brickmaker	Henry under 8, $20	
Larantry, Michael P.		Lexington St			Joseph 30, $125. Betsey 25, $80. Gwin 10, $40.	
Laurenson, Philip		Liberty St		Merchant	Simeon 30, $125. Minty 28, $80. Charlot 14, $80.	
Lawson, Elizabeth Mrs.	Widow	Lombard & Eutaw Sts			Sol over 45, $60. Kit 40, $125. Clases (m) 40, $125. Beck above 36, $40. Louisa or Lucy, over 36, $40. Sarah 25, $80. Abbea (f) 30, $80. Maria 17, $80. Louisa 14, $80. Harriot 14, $80. Adeline under 8, $20. Richard under 8, $20. John under 8, $20.	
Lebon, Charles		Howard St		Grocer	Nina (m) 25, $125. John 25, $125. Delile 30, $80. Jorett 30, $80. Lonett 30, $80.	
Lee, Mrs.	Widow	Baltimore & Liberty Sts			Jim 14, $12. Rose over 36, $40. Nelley 35, $80.	

Free Blacks and Slave Owners in Baltimore City Tax Assessor's Ledger, 1813 Ward 1

NAME	RACE/ STATUS	RESIDENCE	REAL PROPERTY	OCCUPATION	ENSLAVED PROPERTY Name, Age, Value	COMMENTS
Leigh, John		Baltimore St		Merchant	Ben 42, $125. Ralph 37, $125. William 25, $125. Thomas 28, $125. Leads 22, $125. George 15, $125. Isaac 12, $40. Andrew 12, $40. Henry under 8, $20. Hannah 36, $80. Jinney 30, $80. Ann 17, $80. Mary under 8, $20.	
Lemmon, Mrs.	Widow	Lombard St			Nat 30, $125. Maria 14, $80. Charlot 13, $40. Margaret 9, $40.	
Levering, Enoch		Lombard St		Grocer	Sam 12, $40.	
Levering, Jesse		Lombard St		Grocer	Charlote 30, $80. Ann 11, $40. Esther 8, $40.	
Levy, Hetty		Pratt & Sharp Sts			Pegg 16, $80.	
Lilley, Elie		Howard & Lombard Sts		Innkeeper	Charles 17, $125. Judith 14, $80.	
Long, Reuben		Camden St North of Hanover St		Merchant	Harriot 8, $40. Ann 19, $80.	
Louerwine, Peter		Howard St			Nelly 18, $20. Milley under 8, $20.	
Lovell, William		Howard St		Baker	Harriot 18, $80.	
Lyeth, John		Dutch Alley			Mary 13, $40.	
Mainard, Foster		Eutaw St		Carpenter	Polly 16, $80.	
Manroe, Jonathan		Baltimore St		Merchant	Jack 20, $125. Isabella 20, $80. Ann 22 infirm $40. Fanny 10, $40. Judith under 8, $20.	
Martin, John		Howard St		Cordwainer	Charity 13, $40 rental	Property of John Hilton, Harford Co.
McCubbin, Moses		North St		Tailor	Jim 18, $125. Dennis 16, $125. Frederick 15, $125. Minty 17, $80. Eliza 8, $40.	
McDowell, Maxwell		Fayette St		Physician	Betsey 21, $80. Peggey under 8, $20.	
Merrica, James		Lexington St			Susan 14, $80.	
Merryman, Job		Fayette St		Accountant	Jin 13, $40.	

Free Blacks and Slave Owners in Baltimore City Tax Assessor's Ledger, 1813 Ward 1

NAME	RACE/ STATUS	RESIDENCE	REAL PROPERTY	OCCUPATION	ENSLAVED PROPERTY Name, Age, Value	COMMENTS
Micry, Augustus		Liberty St			Mary over 36, $40.	
Miltenberger, Anthony		Howard St		Printer & stationer	Nelley 24, $80. Heney 8, $40.	
Moore, George W.		Howard St		Inspector of flour	Bob 40, $125. Jack 10, $40. Tom 18.	Tom property of Wm. Thompson $125.
Mummey, Thomas		Howard St		Merchant	Jane 19, $80. Cecilia 10, $40.	
Negro Ben	B	In W. Biays House	2 horses $15 each 2 drays $10 each Furniture $5			
Neilson, James C.		Lombard St		Fancy & ironmongery store	Clarasa 18, $80.	
Nelson, Rachel		Sharp St			Bob over 45, $60. Will 16, $125. Cornelius 12, $40. Sam under, $20. Elijah under 8, $20. Hannah 36, $80. Rachal 1, $40. Nancy under 8, $20. Nell 8, $40.	
Nicholson, Joseph H.		Baltimore St		President of the Commercial & Farmers' Bank	Charles 42, $125. Perrey 35, $125. Charles 19, $125. Chesterfield 8, $20. Philas 32, $80. Polly 34, $80. Ann 11, $40. Lucey 11, $40. Milley 9, $40.	
Nowland, Dennis		Sharp St			Moses 14, $125.	
O'Rourke, Devizeau Mrs.	Widow	Baltimore St			Viglus 36, $40. Terres 30, $80. Merian under 8, $20. Alfens 23 infirm, $100. Daniel 20, $125.	Only Alfens & Daniel are males.
Peck, Henry		Baltimore St		Show store	Susan 20, $80. Antroge 16, $80.	
Phillips, William		Dutch Alley		Merchant	Rose 19, $80.	

Free Blacks and Slave Owners in Baltimore City Tax Assessor's Ledger, 1813 Ward 1

NAME	RACE/STATUS	RESIDENCE	REAL PROPERTY	OCCUPATION	ENSLAVED PROPERTY Name, Age, Value	COMMENTS
Poughe, Mrs.		German St			Derkey 20 infirm, $40. Grace 12, $40.	Derkey is female.
Puder, Leonard		Howard St	Wagon Alley Pratt St Eutaw & Camden		Sally 18 infirmed, $10.	
Pulett, William		Baltimore St			Heleine 42, $125. Paul under, $20. Laurett 25, $80. Teleilla 25, $80. Agathea 20, $80.	
Purnal, Isaac		Lombard St			Luke 20, $125. Allen 12, $40. Rachal 30, $80.	
Purviance, James		Fayette St		Merchant	Monivia 16, $80.	
Purviance, Robert		Howard St			James 30, $125. Sally 30, $125.	James owned by E. Whitney. Sally owned by Wm. Brewer, Annapolis.
Raborg, William		Eutaw St			Katey 12, $40. Harriottt under 8, $20.	
Reinecker, George		Baltimore St		Merchant	Ceazer 11, $40. Elleck 11, $40.	
Rhees, John		Howard St			Fanny 10, $40.	
Ridgely, Nicholas		Howard St		Tobacco inspector	Charles 22, $125.	
Ringgold, Ann		Baltiimore St		Boarding house	Aaron 18, $125. Perry 12, $40. Isaac 9, $40. Lavinia under 8, $20.	
Robinson, Eve	Widow	Howard St			Sarah 13, $40.	
Sands, Benjamin		Liberty St		Bricklayer	Rachal 11, $40.	
Schultz, Conrad		Baltimore St		Merchant	Joe 12, $40.	
Scott, John		Saratoga St		Stage Proprietor	Clacey over 36, $40. Harriot 9, $40.	
Scott, Joseph		Eutaw St		Flour inspector	Thomas 17, $125. Maria 10, $40.	Thomas, property of Elizabeth Norris.
Scott, Thomas		Conway St			Rachal 23, $80.	

Free Blacks and Slave Owners in Baltimore City Tax Assessor's Ledger, 1813 Ward 1

NAME	RACE/ STATUS	RESIDENCE	REAL PROPERTY	OCCUPATION	ENSLAVED PROPERTY Name, Age, Value	COMMENTS
Simmons, Matthew W.		Sharp St		Brickmaker	Harry 18, $125. Nace 27, $125. Hessey 24, $80. Celia under 8, $20.	Hessey is female.
Simpson, John	Colored Man	Brandy Alley	One lot $30 Improvement $50			12c ground rent to D. Horner.
Slingluff, Jesse		Howard St		Merchant	Elisa 16, $80. Ann 16, $85.	
Snow, Hezekiah or Zedekiah		Liberty St		Merchant	Letty 23, $80. Labia 13, $40	
Starke, George		Saratoga St			Maria 14, $80.	
Stien, George					William 19.	Renting slave owned by Wm. Gamber, AA Co.
Stouffer, Henry		Fayette St			Fanney 13, $40.	
Stouffer, John		Howard St		Merchant	Fanny 13, $40.	
Thomas, Rachal L.		Pratt St			Betsey 22, $80. Charlot 17, $80.	
Walker, Thomas		Howard St			Pat 30, $80.	Pat is female.
Wall, George		Lexington St		Measurer of buildings	Henny 19, $80.	
Wallace, Ruth	Widow	Eutaw St			Nancey 30, $80. Lydia 23, $80.	
Warfield, George F.		Howard St		Merchant	Walter 30, $125. Sam under 8, $20. Esther 30, $80. Palome 16, $80. Poll 18, $80. Rachal 10, $40.	
Warner, Henry		Ridgeley's addition John St			Ben 16, $125.	
Wellmore, William		Baltimore St		Merchant	Mary Ann 9, $40.	
Wells, Benjamin		North & Lexington Sts			Hector above 45, $60. Will 45, $60. Charles under 8, $20. Joe 23, $125. Maria 26, $80.	Dec'd estate, Mary Wells
Wells, Joshua		Liberty St			Tom 16, $125.	
Wetherall, William		Sharp St			Tobias 20, $125. Sam 15, $125. Juno under 8, $20.	Juno is female.

Free Blacks and Slave Owners in Baltimore City Tax Assessor's Ledger, 1813 Ward 1

NAME	RACE/ STATUS	RESIDENCE	REAL PROPERTY	OCCUPATION	ENSLAVED PROPERTY Name, Age, Value	COMMENTS
Wheeler, Leonard		Saratoga St		Carpenter	Priscilla 13, $40. Sidney under 8, $20.	Priscilla Owned by Sarah Green. Sidney is female.
White, George		Dutch Alley			Ann 17, $80. Jerrey 11, $40.	
White, Henry		Howard St		Cordwainer	Bob 18, $125. Rodey 13, $40. Marey 10, $40.	
Wilson, John		Eutaw St		Merchant	Male slave 13, $40. Beck 23, $80.	
Winand, Jacob		Liberty St		Merchant tailer	Leley 17, $80.	
Worley, Joseph		Howard St		Innkeeper	Augustus 22, $125. Harry under 8, $20. Rachel over 36, $40. Clarey 17, $80. Saffer 9, $40. Betsey 15, $80.	
Worthington, Nicholas		Howard St		Grocer	Jane under 8, $20.	

Free Blacks and Slave Owners in Baltimore City Tax Assessor's Ledger, 1813 Ward 2

NAME	RACE/ STATUS	RESIDENCE	REAL PROPERTY	OCCUPATION	ENSLAVED PROPERTY Name, Age, Value	COMMENTS
Allison, Ann		Lombard St. N. side			Henny 18, $80.	
Annis, Benjamin	Colored	Honey Alley	Lot $25 Imp $15			aka Ennis
Baltzell, Thomas		Baltimore St. S. side		Merchant	William 25, $125. Lucy 16, $80. Elisa 8 $40.	
Becker, Simon		Charles St		Merchant	Ann 16, $80.	
Belups, Robert		Charles St			David 33 $125. Jinney 25 $80. Lucey 9 $40.	
Benedict,	Colored	Honey Alley	1 lot $20 Imp $15, Furniture $5			
Berry, Benjamin		Sharp & Lee Sts		Brick maker	George 18, $125. Jacob 16, $125. Isaac 14, $125. William 12, $40. Polly 11, $40.	
Berry, John				Brick maker	Jack $125.	
Black, Vison	Colored	Honey Alley	Lot $20, Imp $15, Furn $5			Paying $23 ground rent to Jacob Young.
Boughan, Augustin					Sarah over 36, $40.	
Brune, Frederick		Hanover St		Merchant	Daniel 25 $125.	
Buchanan, William		Barnett St		Register of Wills	William, 10 $40.	
Burneston, Isaac		King Tammany St			Peter 18, $125.	
Burt, Andrew		Tammany St			Ann 20, $80. Thomas 15, $125.	
Carrol, John		Vulcan Alley & Forrest Lane		Bricklayer	Casse 8, $0.	Casse is female.
Carroll, Charles Jr.		Sharp St E. side			Thomas 22, $125. William 22, $125. John 9, $40. Charity 20, $80. Kesia 18, $80. Beckey 17, $80.	
Carter, Peter	Colored	Bissey Alley	1 lot $40, Imp. $20			

Free Blacks and Slave Owners in Baltimore City Tax Assessor's Ledger, 1813 Ward 2

NAME	RACE/ STATUS	RESIDENCE	REAL PROPERTY	OCCUPATION	ENSLAVED PROPERTY Name, Age, Value	COMMENTS
Casey, Robert		Hanover St			Beck 12, $40. Maria 19, $80.	
Chanehe, Mr.					Gracia over 36, $40. Babe over 36, $40. Justin under 8 $20.	Justin is female.
Chapel, John		Baltimore St		Painter	Ellis 10 $40.	Ellis is female.
Chears, William	Colored	Goodman St	Lot $50 Imp $20			
Cheston, James		Hanover St		Attorney @ Law	Agness 20, $80.	
Clampsel/ Campsall, Michael		Charles St		Livery stable	Beck 20 $80. Louisa 10 $40.	
Coake, James		Lombard St N. side		Physician	John 30, $125. Anthony 12, $40. Peggy 14, $80. Lucy 13, $40.	
Coffield, Martha	Widow	Baltimore St S. side			Joe 35, $125. Nelly 29, $80. Harriot 12, $40. Frances under 8, $20. Catherine under 8, $20.	
Comegys, Cornelius		Baltimore St		Merchant	Francis 34, $125. Maria 15, $80.	
Corrages, James		Conewago St S. side		Baker	John 24, $125. Orlances 32, $80. Rosale 36, $80. Zairac 20, $80.	Orlances, Rasale & Zairac are females.
Count, Stephen		Charles St			Enoch 35, $125. Elie 33, $125. Augustus 32, $125. Bushard 30, $80.	Bushard is female.
Crawford, John		Hanover & German Sts		Physician	Mary 23, $80.	
Crig, Thomas		York St			Charles 13, $40.	
Crosdale, George		Hanover St		Merchant	Patty 25, $80.	
Cummings, John	Colored	Honey Alley	Lot $25 Imp $15 Furn $5			
Dare, Nathaniel E.		Sharp St		Brick maker	Priscilla 14, $80. Jinney over 36, $40. Abigail over 36, $40. Louisa 9, $40.	

Free Blacks and Slave Owners in Baltimore City Tax Assessor's Ledger, 1813 Ward 2

NAME	RACE/ STATUS	RESIDENCE	REAL PROPERTY	OCCUPATION	ENSLAVED PROPERTY Name, Age, Value	COMMENTS
DeBontz/DeBonis, Peter M.		Barre St			Michael, 10, $40. Venus 25, $80. Corlnus 25, $80.	Corlnus is female.
Didier, Henry Jr.		Hanover St		Merchant	Eliza 12, $40.	
Donaldson, James L.		Conewago N. side		Attorney @ Law	Abraham 26, $125. Sophia 20, $80.	
Donaldson, John		Conewago N. side		Lumber merchant	William 20, $125. Rose 12, $40.	
Donaldson, Samuel J.		Hanover			John 14, $125. Fillis 23, $80.	
Dorsey, Allen				Merchant	Bob 40, $125. Hamlet under $20. Charity 23, $80. Henny 14, $80. Jinney 12, $40.	
Dorsey, John E.		Sharp St E. side			Joseph 22, $125. Peter 18, $125. Edward 12, $40. Rachal 25, $80. Louisa 11, $40.	
Dougherty, Theophilus F.		Conway & Sharp Sts		Justice of the Peace, Secretary of the Baltimore Insurance Company	Peggy 30, $40.	Peggy is infirm.
Dounan, Lewis M.		Chatham N. side		Physician	Frances 45, $60.	Frances is a male.
Eaton, William		Sharp St			Amelia 10, $40.	
Edmondson, Thomas & Isaac		Baltimore St		Merchants	Sally 23, $80.	
Eichelberger, Martin		Hanover St		Weigh master	William 20, $125. Lucy 20, 80.	

Free Blacks and Slave Owners in Baltimore City Tax Assessor's Ledger, 1813 Ward 2

NAME	RACE/ STATUS	RESIDENCE	REAL PROPERTY	OCCUPATION	ENSLAVED PROPERTY Name, Age, Value	COMMENTS
Essender, John		Conewago St & Forest Lane		Superintendent of Sweeps	Stephen 16, $125. Jack 15, $125. Stephen 25. $125. William 15, $125. Pollars 11, $40. Perry 12, $40.	Stephen 25 owned by W. Sewell. William & Perry owned by H.I. Mitchell. Pollars owned by W. Crow.
Everett, Thomas		Baltimore St		Umbrella Maker	Amelia 20, $80.	
Ferguson, John Capt		Forrest St			Sukey under 16, $80. Jane under 16, $80. Ann 9, $40.	Ann owned by Benjamin Ferguson.
France, Joseph		Baltimore S		Merchant	Joe 12, $40. Levin 8 $$40. Hannah 35 $80. Margaret under 8, $20.	
Freeberger, John		Forrest St		Baker	Hager 18 $80.	
Freise, Phillip R. J.		Hanover St		Glass manufacturer	Peter 30, $125.	
Gadsbey, John		Baltimore & Hanover Sts		Indian Queen Inn	Thomas 24, $125. Edward 25, $125. Samuel 20, $125. John 24, $125. James 36, $125. Nathan 28, $125. Nace 24, $125. Benjamin 23, $125. James 18, $125. Henry 18, $125. George 8, $40. James 25, $125. James 20, $125. Thomas 30, $125. Robert 38, $125. Gowan over 45, $60. Salsberry 28, $125. Samuel 18, $125. Jerrey 28, $125. William 24, $125. Zachle 28, $125. Runey over 36, $40. Ludey over 36, $40.	Runey is a female.

Free Blacks and Slave Owners in Baltimore City Tax Assessor's Ledger, 1813 Ward 2

NAME	RACE/ STATUS	RESIDENCE	REAL PROPERTY	OCCUPATION	ENSLAVED PROPERTY Name, Age, Value	COMMENTS
					Hannah over 36, $40. Ester over 36, $40. Jane over 36, $40. Amey 18, $80. Prissey 20, $80. Eve 24, $80. Maria 20, $80. Dolly 23, $80. Henny 27, $80. Sarah 24, $80. Rachal 27, $80. Betsy 8, $40. Margaret 18, $80.	
Galloway, William K.		Camden & Sharp Sts		Carpenter	James 17, $125. Bealey 10, $40.	Bealey is male.
Garnett, Henry	Colored	Honey Alley	Lot $30 Imp $10			
Garts, Charles (Deceased Estate)		Hanover St			Michael under 8, $10. Polly 9, $40. Rachal 22, $80.	
Ghequeire, Charles		Charles & Conewago Sts N. side		Broker	Betsey 20, $80.	
Glaveney/ Glavarry, Francis A		Charles St		Grocer	Bett 17, $80.	
Glenn, Elias		Charles St		Attorney @ Law & US Attorney for the district of Md	Isaac 45, $125. Bob 28, $125. Edward under8, $20. Florin 29, $80.	
Goodwin, Caleb D.		Vulcan Alley			Catherine under 8, $20.	
Goodwin, Milcha		Vulcan & Ten Feet Alleys			Juliet 20, $80. Maria 18, $80.	
Gould, Paul		Charles St			George under 8, $20. Adam 18, $125. Charlotte 23, $80.	

Free Blacks and Slave Owners in Baltimore City Tax Assessor's Ledger, 1813 Ward 2

NAME	RACE/ STATUS	RESIDENCE	REAL PROPERTY	OCCUPATION	ENSLAVED PROPERTY Name, Age, Value	COMMENTS
Grahame, William		Conewago, N. side		President of T & U Bank	Fanny 20, $80. Henny 19, $80.	
Grant, Daniel		Baltimore St		Boarding house	Jack 30, $125. Sandey 17, $125. William 14, $125.	
Griffith, Samuel G.		Hanover St		Merchant	James 40, $125. Charles 24, $125. Dinah 28, $80. Ruth 22, $80.	
Grock, John A.		Barre & Hanover Sts			Catherine 25, $80.	
Guthrow, Elizabeth	Widow	Hanover St			William 14, $125.	
Hackeman, Herman Henry		Hanover St		Merchant	Harriot 16, $80.	
Hammond, Harriot		Hanover St			George 30, $125. Peter 19, $125. Henry 12, $40. Thomas 10, $40. Charlot 15, $80.	
Harden, Samuel		Baltimore St		Merchant	Aron 19, $125.	
Harden, William		Conewago St N side			Sarah 20, $80.	
Harmange, Anthony		Baltiimore St			Ann 30, $80.	
Harrison, Hall		Lombard St N. side		Merchant	Dick 12, $40. Fanny 20, $80. Ann 18, $80.	
Hartshorne, William		Hanover St		Merchant	Pegey 30, $80. Chiney under 8, $20.	
Hayward, Harriot		King Tammany St		Young Ladies Academy	Harriot 10, $40.	
Heidelbaugh, John		Pratt St		Merchant	Grace under 8, $20.	
Hewitt, Elie		Forrest Lane		Tobacconist	Dick, 28, $125. Jacob 26, $125. Dick 22, $125. Perry 22, $125. Jacob 18, $125. Dinah over 36, $40. Beckey 18, $80.	
Hall, Stephen	Colored	Bissey Alley	1 vacant lot $40			

Free Blacks and Slave Owners in Baltimore City Tax Assessor's Ledger, 1813 Ward 2

NAME	RACE/ STATUS	RESIDENCE	REAL PROPERTY	OCCUPATION	ENSLAVED PROPERTY Name, Age, Value	COMMENTS
Hoffman, George		Charles St		Merchant	William 40, $125. Fowehill 25, $125. Frank under 8, $20. Nim 11, $40. Charlott 28, $80.	
Hollingsworth, Samuel		Charles St		Merchant	Bendick 28, $125. Dennis 30, $125. Charles 15, $125. Hannah 30, $80. Jane 22, $80. Cara 25, $80. Agness under 8, $20.	
Hoppe, Daniel		Tammany St			Elira 15, $80.	Elira is a female.
Howell, William Sr.		Camden St		Merchant	Kitty over 36, $40. Polly 16, $80.	
Hughes, Christopher Jr.					Bill 20, $125. Cesley 19, $80.	
Hughes, Christopher Sr.		Light & Barre Sts			Julivay 37, $125. Lunden 38, $125. Nero 27, $125. Dinah 24, $80. Charles 35, $125. Carlos 21, $125. Bell 22, $80. Alumsey 15, $125. Harry 18, $125. Leah 31, $80. Gibson 15, $125. Ceazer 35, $125. Crouse 25, $125. Duffer 27, $125. Beck over 3, $40.	Julivay & Alumsey are males.
Johnston, Samuel	Colored	Bissey Alley	1 lot $30, Improve-ment $10			
Johnston, Thomas		Chatham St		Merchant	Nancey 30, $80. Sophia 12, $40.	
Jones, Richard H.		Pratt St		Currier	Dinah 20, $80. Lyle 14, $80.	Lyle is a female.
Kane, John M.		Charles St		Grocer	Sidney (f) 10, $40.	Sidney is female.
Kennedy, John F.		Barnett St			Catherine 34, $80.	
Lanney/Lannay, Lewis J.		Baltimore St		Merchant	Lannany over 36, $40. Patty 25, $80.	Lannany is female. Patty owned by I. Foster.
Larsh, Margaret	Widow	Camden & Sharp			Charlot 11, $40.	

Free Blacks and Slave Owners in Baltimore City Tax Assessor's Ledger, 1813 Ward 2

NAME	RACE/ STATUS	RESIDENCE	REAL PROPERTY	OCCUPATION	ENSLAVED PROPERTY Name, Age, Value	COMMENTS
		Sts				
Leonard, Joseph Capt.		Hanover St		Brewer	George over 45, $60. Samuel 45, $125. James 27, $125. Tom 27, $125. Bill 21, $125. David 25, $125. Daniel 18, $125. Patterson 15, $125. Dick 25, $125. Daniel 14, $125. Washington 14, $125. Michael 14, $125. Colon 14, $125. William 11, $40. Miles 10, $40. Isaac 9, $40. Henry 8, $40. Augustus under 8, $20. Moses under 8, $20. Hannah over 36, $40. Jane over 36, $40. Polly over 36, $40. Fanney 30, $80. Milley 25, $80. Harriot 9, $40. Nancey 14, $80. Kittey 10, $40. Milley 8, $40. Betty 8, $40. Jason 20, $80.	Jason is female.
Levering, Nathan		Hanover St		Merchant	Henry under 8, $20. Harriot under 8, $20. Debby 35, $80.	
Levering, Peter		Hanover St		Merchant	George under 8, $20. Letty under 10, $40.	
Lindenberger, George		Hanover St			George 30, $125. Dick 10, $40. Sarah 16, $80.	
Lister, John		Camden St			Louisa 12, $40.	
Low, Cornelius		Hanover St		Merchant	James 17, $125.	

33

Free Blacks and Slave Owners in Baltimore City Tax Assessor's Ledger, 1813 Ward 2

NAME	RACE/ STATUS	RESIDENCE	REAL PROPERTY	OCCUPATION	ENSLAVED PROPERTY Name, Age, Value	COMMENTS
Magruder, Ellen		Baltimore St			Joe 45, $125. Harry 11, $40. Tom 11, $40. Peter 10, $40. Charles under 8, $20. William under 8, $20. Osborn under 8, $20. Lucey 14, $80. Mary 13, $40. Frances under 8, $20.	
Magruder, William B.		Pratt St		Merchant	Hugh 44, $125. John 2, $125. James 9, $40.	
Martiacq, John					Mary 19, $80. Phillis 25, $80. Susan 16, $80. Suckey 13, $40. Mary 10, $40.	
Martin, William	Colored	Hill St	Lot $40 Imp $25			
McGill, Mary Miss		93 Hanover St			James 18, $125. Betsey 30, $80.	
McKeen, John		McClellans Alley		Merchant	Phoebe 14, $80. Delila over 36, $40.	
McManus, Owen		Charles & Pratt Sts		Grocer	Jacob 20, $125.	
Merfeld, John		Sharp & Barre Sts		Grocer	Benner under 8, $20. Polly 14, $80.	
Miller, Robert		Sharp St. E. side		Merchant	Ephraim 30, $125.	
Moale, Ellen	Widow	Pratt St			Henny 30, $80. Corlus 22, $80. Lydia over 36, $40.	
Molding, John		Camden St			Beck 10, $40.	
Montgomery, John		McClellans Alley		Attorney Gen	Rachal 16, $80.	
Moscrop, Henry		Hanover & German Sts			Fanney 30, $80.	
Mullanphy, John		Charles St			Lidia 22, $80. Beckey 9, $40.	
Mullikin, Benjamin H.		King Tammany St		Merchant	Frank 16, $125. John 20, $125.	
Mushet, Walter		Charles & Conewago Sts north side		Merchant	Joe 21, $125. Milley 25, $80.	

Free Blacks and Slave Owners in Baltimore City Tax Assessor's Ledger, 1813 Ward 2

NAME	RACE/ STATUS	RESIDENCE	REAL PROPERTY	OCCUPATION	ENSLAVED PROPERTY Name, Age, Value	COMMENTS
Myer, Jacob		Conway St		Brick maker	James 35, $125. Dick 30, $125.	
Nance, William		Conewago St south side			Polly over 36, $40.	
Neel, Hannah	Colored	Goodman St	Lot $50 Imp $25			
Nichols, Charlotte		Conewago St north side			Charles 14, $125. Abraham 30, $125. Creadec 33, $125. Fanny 14, $80.	Abraham owned by R.W. Hall.
Norman, Thomas		Hanover St			Rosella 17, $80. Nelly 25, $80. Phillis over 36 $40.	
O'Connor, Hannibal	Colored woman	Montgomery St	Lot $20, Imp $15, Furn $5			
Osborn, William		York St		Lumber merchant	Harry 30, $60. Abigal 30, $80. Charity under 8, $20.	Harry is infirm.
Palmer, Edward					James 2, $125. Maria under 8, $20. Margaret 25, $80. Tunah 13, $40.	Tunah is female.
Payson, Henry		Hanover St		Merchant	David 28, $125. John under 8, $20.	
Perry, Rogius	Colored	Uhler Alley	1 lot $30 Imp $10			
Presstman, William		Hanover St			Aleck 40, $125. Celicea over 36, $40. Kitty 18, $80. Anna 14, $80. Betsy 35, $80.	
Quin, Stephen	Colored	Hill St	Lot $50, Imp $25			
Randall, John		Conewago St N. side		Merchant	Elie 26, $125. Louisa 18.	Louisa owned by W. Hood, $80.
Richards, John C.		King Tammany St		Merchant	William 17, $125.	
Rigden, John E.		Baltimore St		Hardward store	Peggy 14, $80.	
Rollins, James Capt		Forrest St		Sea Capt	Dalphin 20, $80.	Dalphin is female.

Free Blacks and Slave Owners in Baltimore City Tax Assessor's Ledger, 1813 Ward 2

NAME	RACE/STATUS	RESIDENCE	REAL PROPERTY	OCCUPATION	ENSLAVED PROPERTY Name, Age, Value	COMMENTS
Rowe, John K.		Hanover St		Carpenter	Ned 10, $40.	
Ruckle, John		Baltimore St			Rachal 15, $80.	
Schnauber, George		Hanover & Charles Sts		Baker & Grocer	Charles 14, $125. John 11, $80.	
Schultz, John E. C.		Hanover St		Merchant	Male 18, $125. Female 9, $40.	
Schwartz, Frederick		Hanover St		Physician	Tom 20, $125. Arthur 9, $40. Jane 28, $80. Minto 24, $80.	Minto is female.
Shanley, James		Sharp St			Minty under 8, $20.	
Simeon, No 1st name given	Colored Man	Honey Alley	1 lot $20 Imp $15 Furn $5			
Small, Jacob		Conway St		Carpenter	Juliet 12, $40.	
Smith, George		Gilford Alley			Isaac 27, $125. Rose over 36, $40.	
Smith, Robert		Pratt St			Charles 35, $125. Richard 22, $125. Dick 10, $40. Rosella 31, $80. Henney 21, $80.	
Smith, Sally		Pratt St			Peter 10, $40. Eliza under 8, $20.	
Smith, Samuel R.		Pratt St		Merchant	Will 25, $125. Sipphey 30, $80. Beck under 8, $20. Nelly under 8, $20.	Sipphey is female.
Stevens, Mary		Goodman St			Peggy 30, $80.	
Stewart, Richardson		Conewago & Charles Sts			William 40, $125. Ben 25, $125. Polly 20, $80. Vincent 25, $125. Samuel 10, $40. Harry 10, $40. Sally 24, $50.	Sally is infirm.
Strike, Nicholas		Sharp St		Constable	Adam 45, $40. Selvey $40.	Adam is infirm. Selvey, male, is owned by James Gunny.
Stump, Samuel		Hanover St		Merchant	Rezin 35, $125. Charlot 16, $80. Jane under 8, $20. Ann 25, $80.	Resin is male.
Sumwalt, George		Welcome Alley		Measurer of wood	Fanney 12, $40.	

Free Blacks and Slave Owners in Baltimore City Tax Assessor's Ledger, 1813 Ward 2

NAME	RACE/ STATUS	RESIDENCE	REAL PROPERTY	OCCUPATION	ENSLAVED PROPERTY Name, Age, Value	COMMENTS
Sweeton/Sweeting, Thomas		King Tammany St			Milley 20, $80. Lydia 20, $80. Susan under 8, $20. Maria under 8, $20.	
Thompson, Ann	Colored	Honey Alley	Lot $20 Imp $15 Furn $5			Paying $16 ground rent to Jacob Young.
Thornbury, George		Baltimore St, S. side		Merchant	Milly 15, $80.	
Todhunter, Joseph		Forest Lane		Merchant	Samuel 15, $125.	
Travers, Julia	Colored	Hill St	Lot $75, Imp $25			
Trippe, Edward		Hanover St		Capt. of steam boat	Harry 12, $40.	
Tyson, Nathan		Pratt St		Merchant	Nathan 30, $125.	
Uhler, Erasmus		Hanover St		Tanner	John 40, $125. Wark 45, $125. Hark 28, $125. Harry 30 $125. Levin 25, $125. Hannah over 36, $40.	
Uhler, Phillip		Pratt St		Saddler	Beckey 25, $80.	
Walker, Archibald		Hanover St			Nelly 19, $80. Hannah 17, $80.	
Walter, John		Hanover St			Charles 35, $125. Betsy 20, $80. Ann 9, $40.	
Warfield, Charles		Barnett St		Merchant	Catherine 25, $80.	
Watts, Richard K.		Hanover St			Isaac 35, $125. Samuel 13, $40. Henny 18, $80. Maria 13, $40. Harriott 12, $40. Betsy under 8, $20.	
Whelan, Thomas		Charles St			Rachal 8, $40.	
Wilkins, ???? (No 1st name given)	Colored	Bissey Alley	1 lot $30, Improve-ments $10			

Free Blacks and Slave Owners in Baltimore City Tax Assessor's Ledger, 1813 Ward 2

NAME	RACE/ STATUS	RESIDENCE	REAL PROPERTY	OCCUPATION	ENSLAVED PROPERTY Name, Age, Value	COMMENTS
Wilkins, John		Pratt St		Merchant	Iseral 8, $40. Minty 22, $80. Betsey 18, $80.	
Wilkins, Joseph		Hanover St		Merchant	John 12, $40.	
Williams, Benjamin	Colored	Hill St	Lot $50, Imp $20, Furn $5, Horse $15, Dray $15			
Wills, Francis M.		Charles St			Perry under 8, $20. Henny 30, $80.	
Wilmer, John W.		Hanover St		Merchant	James 20, $125. Ann 24, $80.	
Wilmer, Simon					George 20, $125. Emerey 20, $125. Jane over 36, $40. Poll 30, $40. Hagar 15, $80. Sarah under 8, $20.	Poll is infirm.
Wilson, Nixon		Lombard St. north side		Currier	Rachal 14, $80.	
Wilson, William Jr		Hanover St			Jinney 22, $80. Nancey 12, $40.	
Winchester, George				Attorney at Law	Darkes 30, $80. Milly under 8, $20. Henny under 8, $20.	
Winchester, Sarah		Hanover St			Jane over 36, $40. Charity 11, $40. Milkey under 8, $20.	
Woods, William		Pratt St		Grocer	Hester over 36, $40.	
Worrell, Elizabeth	Widow	Camden & Sharp Sts			Perrigoe 12, $20.	Perrigoe is female.
Wyant, Peter		Hanover St		Hackney/ coachman	Alexander under 8, $20. Crowe 32, $80. Jane 10, $40.	Crowe is female.

Free Blacks and Slave Owners in Baltimore City Tax Assessor's Ledger, 1813 Ward 3

NAME	RACE/ STATUS	RESIDENCE	REAL PROPERTY	OCCUPATION	ENSLAVED PROPERTY Name, Age, Value	COMMENTS
Aiken, George		Market St N. side		Jeweler & Goldsmith	Sarah 26, $80	
Aisquith, John (Esq)		Bank St S. side		Justice of the Peace & one of the coroners	Isaac 25, $125. Ralph 16, $125. Sarah 24, $80. Jane 19, $80.	
Aitken, Robert		South St W. side		Apothecary	Bill 16, $125. Milly 22, $80.	
Alexander, Dr. Ashton		St Paul's Lane		Physician	Lewis 20, $25. Charlotte 16, $80. Letty 18, $80. Sarah 8, $40. Milley 15, $80.	
Alexander, Mrs. Isabella		St. Paul's Lane W. side			Stephen 18, $125. Cyrus 8, $40. Mary 40, $40. Hetty 15, $80.	
Armat, Christopher		Market St S. side		Merchant	Louis 13, $40. Jack 8, $40. Rebecca 30, $80. Harriott 15, $80.	
Atkinson, Angelo		Market St		Cordwainer	Hannah 14 $80.	
Baconais, Louis		Charles St E. side		Young Ladies Academy	Nancy 35, $80.	
Baker, George S.		Charles St E. side		Merchant	Zack 9, $42. Jeff 7, $20. Rebecca 28, $80.	
Baker, Thomas		Market St S. side			Mary 25, $80. Sarah 5, $80.	Tenant to Joseph Biays.
Baker, Thomas B.		Market St S. side		Merchant	Edward 12, $40.	
Barney, John H.		Light St. E. side		Merchant	Tom 38, $125. Alia 35, $80. George 30, $63. Rachael 15, $80. Sarah 20, $80. Sall 23, $80. Jane 10, $40.	George sickly, half price.
Bayreau, Monsier		Charles St			Adeline 10, $40.	Tenant to John Bankson.
Benson, Joseph		Market St N. side		Ships Carpenter	James 20, $125. Peter 25, $125. John 14, $125.	

Free Blacks and Slave Owners in Baltimore City Tax Assessor's Ledger, 1813 Ward 3

NAME	RACE/ STATUS	RESIDENCE	REAL PROPERTY	OCCUPATION	ENSLAVED PROPERTY Name, Age, Value	COMMENTS
Betts, Solomon		St. Paul's Lane W. side		Merchant	Abraham 22, $125. Benjamin 16, $125. Samuel 10, $40. Lydia 35, $80. Hester 28, $80. Charlotte 11, $40. Caroline 40, $20.	
Birckhead, Solomon		Chatham St S. side		Doctor	Levin 2, $125. Charles 20, $125. Nelly 45, $40.	
Biscoe, James		Calvert St E. side		Ironmonger & hardware merchant	Winney 26, $80. Clara 22, $80. Maria 18, $80. Young Maria 11, $40. Hopey 7, $20. Walter 15, $125.	
Bonnefin, Nicholas		Market St		Grocer	Francis 25, $125. Edward 10, $40.	
Boyd, James P.		Calvert St E. side		Attorney at Law	Susana 30, $80. Mary 11, $40. Thomas 7, $20.	
Boyd, Miss Elizabeth and Mary		Market St			Lile 30, $80. Henry 12, $40.	Lile is female.
Branson, William		Market St		Hatter	Louis 23, $125. Joseph 21, $125.	Louis prop. of John Neale, soldier. Joseph prop. of Mrs. Mallett of A. A. County.
Brice, Nicholas		New Church St		Attorney at Law	Hannah 35, $80. Maria 18, $80. Charlotte 12, $40. Sam 23, $125. Matthew 20, $125. Johnson 9, $40.	
Brown, Alexander		Market St		Merchant	Ellen 50, $40. Eliza 28, $80. Peggy 19, $80. Harry 35, $125. Gabriel 23, $12. James 13, $40.	

Free Blacks and Slave Owners in Baltimore City Tax Assessor's Ledger, 1813 Ward 3

NAME	RACE/ STATUS	RESIDENCE	REAL PROPERTY	OCCUPATION	ENSLAVED PROPERTY Name, Age, Value	COMMENTS
Brown, Samuel		New Church St S. side		Teacher	Agnes 16, $80. Priscilla 33, $80. Mary 8, $40. Elizabeth 6, $20.	
Buchanan, James A.		Calvert St		Merchant	Prince 45, $125. Robert 45, $125. Abraham 16, $125. Priscilla 45, $40.	
Buchanan, Thomas (Esq)		St. Paul's Lane E. side			Jacob 19, $125. Washington $40. Cass 20, $125. Milley 17, $80. Harriett 14, $80.	Cass is male.
Calhoun, James		Market St N. side			Prince 45, $125. Louis 45, $125. Jane 22, $80.	
Calhoun, Mrs. Lydia	Widow	East St			Henry 20, $125. Charlotte 36, $80. Venus 36, $80. Jane 16, $80. Girl 12 $40.	
Campbell, James		Market St S. side		Merchant	Mary 45, $40. Jacob 54, $60.	
Chavilier, John R.		Roger's Alley			Milley 16, $80.	
Chew, Philemon	Tenant in Dunn's house	Market St			Mary 18 $80.	Tenant in Dunn's house.
Cochran, William		Market St S. side			Sarah 40, $40.	
Cohen, Jacob J. Jr		Market St N. side		Lottery & exchange office	Eliza 18, $80.	
Cole, John		Calvert St W. side		Stationer & book seller	Perry 10, $40.	
Cook, George		Wine Alley			Sophia 20, $80.	Tenant in Cloydsly's House.
Coulter, Alexander		Market St N. side		Saddler	Sophia 12, $40.	
Cox, James		Market St N. side		Cashier	Female 45, $40. Henry 16, $125.	
Cox, Joseph		Public Alley E. side		Hatter	James 45, $125. Tom 10, $40.	
Crocket, Mrs. Jane		St. Paul's Lane			Solomon 25, $125.	

Free Blacks and Slave Owners in Baltimore City Tax Assessor's Ledger, 1813 Ward 3

NAME	RACE/ STATUS	RESIDENCE	REAL PROPERTY	OCCUPATION	ENSLAVED PROPERTY Name, Age, Value	COMMENTS
Cromwell, Dr. John		New Church St N. side		Physician	William 30, $125. Will 6, $20. Elijah 5, $20. Mary 8, $40. Nancy 31, $80.	An intact enslaved family?
Davidge, Dr. John B.		New Church St N. side		Physician	Abraham 25, $125.	
Deagan, Mrs. Mary	Widow	Chatham St			Clarissa 22, $80. Pegg 12, $40.	
Delvecchio, Peter		Calvert St E. side		Print shop, carver & guilder	Harriett 30, $80.	
Dickehut, George		Market St S. side		Confectioner	Appy 25, $80.	Appy is female.
Dorsey, Walter		New Church St		Attorney at Law	Crowley 4, $125. Clemm 32, $125. Prudence 40, $40. Louisa 8, $20. Mary 6, $20.	
Dosh, John M.		Ruxton Lane		Grocer	Patience 16, $80.	
Douglass, George	Black man	Light St W. side	Lot $400, Imp. $500 Furn $10, 3 oz Plate $3, horse $20	Drayman		
Dublin, Thomas	Black man	Primrose Alley	Lot $50, Imp $30			
Farnandis, Samuel		St. Paul Lane E. side			Sarah 15, $80.	
Fissour, John M.		Light St W. side		Merchant	Solime 13, $40. Rosie 8, $40.	
French, William		Calvert St E. side		Merchant	Rachael 25, $80. Caroline 12, $40.	
Gitchell, Increase		Market St		Merchant	Nace 10, $40. Maria 16, $80. Rose 15, $80.	
Gould, Capt. Peter		Charles St E. side			Nancy 25, $80. Julia 18, $80. Joseph 30, $125.	
Griffith, Catherine		Calvert St			Flora 23, $80.	

Free Blacks and Slave Owners in Baltimore City Tax Assessor's Ledger, 1813 Ward 3

NAME	RACE/ STATUS	RESIDENCE	REAL PROPERTY	OCCUPATION	ENSLAVED PROPERTY Name, Age, Value	COMMENTS
Gwynn, William (Esq.)		Chatham St S. side		Attorney at Law, Editor & Proprietor of the *Federal Gazette*	Job 40, $125.	
Hall, Dr. Richard W.	Batchelor (sic)			Physician	Priscilla 30, $80. Hager 20, $80. Jacob 10, $40.	
Harris, John F.		Chatham St N. side		Justice of the Peace	Nancy 14, $80.	
Harvey, Samuel		Calvert St.			Michael 45 $125. York 23, $125. Lydia 19, $80. Eliza 4, $20. Charlotte 16, $80. Patience 12, $40.	
Hayes, Reverdy		Market St		Merchant	Henry 17, $125. Maria 19, $80.	
Heide, George		Pratt St			Samuel 17, $125. Maria 25, $80.	
Henck, Frederick W.		Ruxton Lane			Susan 10, $40.	
Hill, George		Market St N. side		Stationer	Cloe 20, $80.	
Hodges, Benjamin M.		Chatham St		Merchant	Talbot 24, $125. Perry 20, $125. Frederick 10, $40. Eliza 19, $80. Flora 17, $80.	
Hoffman, John		Market St S. side			Lucy 35, $80. Rachael 38, $40. Barnet 30, $125. Harry 14, $125. Harriett 23, $80.	
Hoffman, Peter Jr.		New Church St N. side		Merchant	John 25, $125. Charles 18, $125. William 21, $125. Deborah 24, $80. Grace 18, $80. Charity 15, $80.	
Hollingsworth, Racheal L.		County Wharf			Matilda 24, $80. Eliza 16, $80.	
Hollins, John		Calvert St			Henry 25, $125. Tom 25, $125. David 48, $60. Stepney 30, $125. Edward 18, $125. Suckey 15, $80. Elizabeth 28 $80. Sophia 12 $40.	

Free Blacks and Slave Owners in Baltimore City Tax Assessor's Ledger, 1813 Ward 3

NAME	RACE/ STATUS	RESIDENCE	REAL PROPERTY	OCCUPATION	ENSLAVED PROPERTY Name, Age, Value	COMMENTS
Howard, Dr. Henry		Chatham St S. side		Physician	Hetty 15, $80. Sarah 18, $80.	
Hubble, Josiah	Tenant to Duchemin	New Church St N.side		Merchant	Rose 28, $80. Louisa 11, $40. Enois (m) 100, $40.	Enois is male.
Inglis, Rev. James		East St north side		Pastor of the First Presbyterian Church	Ellen Maria, 6 $20.	
Jarrett, John		Pratt		Merchant	Gassaway 8, $40. Fanny 40, $40. Adeline 7, $20.	
Jenkins, Michael		Chatham St S. side		Cabinet maker	Phobe 7, $20.	
Jenkins, Thomas C.		Charles St			Lucy 16, $125.	
Joshua Brown	Yellow man	Primrose Alley	Lot $400, Imp. $20	Carter		
Kaminsky, Christopher		Bank St		Innkeeper	Richard 27, $63. Charles 12, $40. Maria 27, $40. Lydia 19, $80.	Richard has fits, half price. Maria is lame, half price.
Lansdale, William M.		Charles St E. side			Andrew 28, $125. Henry 25, $125. Milley 10, $40. Ann 5, $20.	
Librou, Anthony		Water St N. side		French barber	Nelly 21, $80.	
Lindenberger, Jacob		New Church St N. side		Merchant	Beda 20, $125. Lydia 20, $80.	Beda is male.
Littig, Philip		Market St		Brush & comb factory	Charles 25, $125. Abraham 14, $125. Mary 22, $80.	
Littlejohn, Miles		Light St W. side		Physician	Male 9, $40. Female 35, $80. Female 14, $80.	
Lock, Nathaniel		Calvert		Cordial distiller	Hinson 18, $62. Peggy 25, $80.	Hinson is crippled, half price.
Love, Elizabeth		East St			Sophia 20, $80.	

Free Blacks and Slave Owners in Baltimore City Tax Assessor's Ledger, 1813 Ward 3

NAME	RACE/ STATUS	RESIDENCE	REAL PROPERTY	OCCUPATION	ENSLAVED PROPERTY Name, Age, Value	COMMENTS
Mactier, Alexander		St. Paul's Lane W. side			Brutus 8, $40. Jane 16, $80. Abby 23, $80. Milly 35, $80.	
Mann, Dr. Anthony		Market St N. side		Apothecary	Sandy 18, $125.	
Martin, Luther (Esq.)		Charles St E. side		Attorney at Law, Chief Judge of the court of Oyer & Terminer	Fanny 45, $40. Rachael 35, $80. Louisa 7, $40. Bill 8, $40. Isaac 35, $125.	
McIlvaine, Alexander		County Wharf		Clothier	Flora, 18, $80.	
McKim, John Jr.		Market St N. side		Merchant	Abraham 52, $60. Richard 48, $60. John 8, $40. Betsy 32, $80. Clarissa 24, $80.	
McMechen, William		New Church St N. side			Jack 22, $125. James 18, $125. Abraham 17, $125. Phyllis 40, $40. Peggy 18, $80. Anna 10, $40.	
Merryman, John		Calvert St W. side			Peter 26, $125. William 20, $125. Mary 40, $40. Susan 38, $40. Anna 22, $80.	
Mitchell, Mrs. Margaret		Calvert St W. side		Boarding house	Rachael 14, $40. Samuel 16, $125.	
Muller, Caspar Otto		East St			Laura 13, $40.	
Mullikin, Richard D.		Charles St. E. side		Merchant	Patience 8, $40. Samuel 12, $40.	
Neal, Abner & Bosley, Daniel		Light St W. side		Bacon Store	Martha 35, $80. Sarah $80.	
Owen, Dr. John		Chatham St		Physician	David 24, $125.	
Partridge, James		Chatham St			Thomas 25 $125.	
Patterson, Robert		South St W. side			Edward 30, $125. Peter 40, $125. Judy 30, $80. Mary 21, $80. Rachael 20, $80.	

Free Blacks and Slave Owners in Baltimore City Tax Assessor's Ledger, 1813 Ward 3

NAME	RACE/ STATUS	RESIDENCE	REAL PROPERTY	OCCUPATION	ENSLAVED PROPERTY Name, Age, Value	COMMENTS
Pew, Peggy		Charles St E. side			Charles 26, $125. Henry 39, $125. Little Henry 10, $40. Mary 27, $80.	
Pew, Rebecca		Charles St E. side			Abraham 17, $125. Adam 19, $125.	
Poor, Moses M.		Calvert St W. side		Merchant	Monacy 13, $40. Anna 25, $80.	Monacy is female.
Pratt, John H.		Market St N. side		Comb manufactory	Jacob 18, $125. Anna 18, $80. Hager 20, $80.	
Quail, Robert		Public Alley		Cooper	Phillis 21, $80.	
Repold, George (Estate of)		Market St			Tom 21, $125. Stephen 17, $125. Frank 6, $20. Ann 37, $40. Maria 15, $80. Silva 4, $20.	
Rescaniere, Monsier		Primrose Alley			Johnpier 22, $125. Colma 20, $125. Joseph 25, $125. John 25, $125. Mars 25, $125. Congo 15, $125. Angel 30, $80. Lora 30, $80. Geo 25, $80. Nancy 12, $40.	Colma is male. Geo is female.
Robinson, Joseph		Market St N. side		Printer, bookseller & circulating library	Sarah 18, $80.	
Sadiler, Philip B.		Market St		Silversmith, Jeweler	Jacob 15, $125.	
Schroeder, Henry		Charles St E. side		Merchant	Tom 14, $125. Daphne 18, $80. Milly 8, $40.	
Schroeder, Henry Jr.		Charles St E. side		Merchant	Lorey 16, $80.	
Scott, John		Chatham St S. side		Judge	Prudence 31, $80. Harriot 28, $80. Hannah 15, $80. Anne 9, $40. Jane 16, $80. Alexander 14, $125. Charles 20, $125. Disaac 25, $125. William 23, $125. Samuel 40, $125. Nat 11, $40.	Disaac is male.
Sellers, Abraham		Calvert St E. side		Merchant Tailor	Patty 26, $80.	

Free Blacks and Slave Owners in Baltimore City Tax Assessor's Ledger, 1813 Ward 3

NAME	RACE/ STATUS	RESIDENCE	REAL PROPERTY	OCCUPATION	ENSLAVED PROPERTY Name, Age, Value	COMMENTS
Shortt, John		South St W. side		Mineral Water Warehouse	Easter 16, $80.	
Simington, James	Tenant of Henry Rogers	Bank St S. side			Lucy 25, $80.	
Sloan, James		Calvert St E. side		Bootmaker	George 50, $60. Moses 45, $125. James 30, $125. Charles 28, $125. Tom 35, $125. Sam 13, $40. Racheal 12, $40.	
Smith, Dennis A.		Calvert St		Cashier	John 16, $125. Henry 19, $125. Lydia 24, $80.	
Smith, Dr. James		Chatham St N. side		Physician	Charles 16, $125. Sarah 40, $40. Dolly 10, $40.	
Smith, Ralph		Charles St E. side		Merchant	Harriett 12, $40.	
Smith, William		County Wharf			Paul 15, $125. James 14, $125. Sarah 40, $40.	
Spiknell, John	Tenant in Dunn's house	Market St			Bedy (m) 12, $40. Elizabeth 20, $80.	
Swan, General John		Market St			Benjamin 47, $60. Edward 17, $125. Nat 10, $40. Caroline 26, $80. Dinah 14, $80. Fanny 13, $40.	
Taylor, Lemuel		East St N. side		Merchant	Charles 30, $125. Isaac 25, $125. Winney 40, $40. Girl 4, $20.	
Taylor, William		Calvert St W. side		Merchant	Male slave 30, $125.	
Tensfield, Zachariah		Primrose Alley		Blacksmith	Peg 16, $80.	
Thomas, John		Chatham St S. side			Male 36, $80. Female 10, $40. Male 15, $15. Male 11, $11.	
Tiernan, Luke		Market St S. side			Tom 15, $125. Sarah 26, $80.	

Free Blacks and Slave Owners in Baltimore City Tax Assessor's Ledger, 1813 Ward 3

NAME	RACE/ STATUS	RESIDENCE	REAL PROPERTY	OCCUPATION	ENSLAVED PROPERTY Name, Age, Value	COMMENTS
Tryall, Joshua	Black man	Public Alley	Large Lot $400, Imp. $50			Paying ground rent to Caleb Hall $200.
Vincent, Samuel		Market St S. side		Clerk to the City Commissioner's Office	Female 25, $80.	
Walker, Samuel P.		Market St N. side		Merchant	Stephen 20, $125. Essex 10, $40. Ann 45, $40. Susan 45 $40. Fanny 6 $20.	
Walraven, John		Market St			Budger Door 21, $125.	Budger Door is male.
Walsh, Robert		New Church St			Isaac 25, $125. Henrietta 19, $80.	
Ward, Elizabeth		Calvert St E. side		Boarding house	Thomas 10, $40. Phyllis 18, $80.	
Weise and Boehm		Market St		Confectioners	Naea 14, $80. Charlotte 25, $80. Mary 14, $80. Emery 18, $125. Lingo 17, $125.	Naea is a female.
Wilkins, Henry		Light St w. side		Physician	James 40, $125.	
Williams, Nathaniel		New Church St N. side		Attorney at Law	Louisa 19, $80.	
Williamson, David		Charles St E. side			Selina 18, $80. Milley 14, $80. Samuel 12, $40.	
Wilson, William		Calvert St. E. side			Priscilla 45, $40.	
Wood, Thomas	Tenant @ Mechanics Hall	Light St W. side			Nat 19, $125. Greenberry 9, $40. Eliza 14, $80.	
Young, Miss Ann		Calvert St			Charles 10, $40.	

Free Blacks and Slave Owners in Baltimore City Tax Assessor's Ledger, 1813 Ward 4

NAME	RACE/ STATUS	RESIDENCE	REAL PROPERTY	OCCUPATION	ENSLAVED PROPERTY Name, Age, Value	COMMENTS
Allison, Mrs.		Gay St			William 19, $125. Sarah 26, $80.	
Ball, William		Market St		Silversmith	Emy 22, $80.	
Bishop, Charles		Lovely Lane			Esther 10, $40.	
Bonner, Hugh		South St		Coppersmith	Maria 20 $80.	
Bosley, James		Water St		Merchants	Zack 20, $125. Sall 17, $80.	
Bosley, William		Water St		Merchant	Phillis 20, $80. Nelly 16, $80.	
Boyd, Ann Mrs.		Holliday St			Nelly 25, $80. Ellen 5, $20.	
Bradenbauch, John		Fish St			Parker 60, $60. Lucy 16, $80.	
Brandt, Jacob		Market St			Jack 14, $80. Richard 9, $40. Tom 5, $20. Mary 22, $80.	
Briscoe, Alexander		Water St		Boot maker	Nancy 20, $80. Kitty 20, $80.	
Brown, Dr. George		Holliday St		Physician	Jim 40, $125. Harry 19, $125. Leah 34, $80. Sophia 27, $80.	
Brown, John		East St		Shakespeare Tavern	Bristo 16, $125.	
Brown, Stewart		Holliday St		Lumber merchant	Susanna 35, $80.	
Brunelot, Francis B.		Water St		Dancing Master	Aglae 20, $80. Nancy 20, $80. Cassy 40, $40. Bill 13, $40. Theodore 9, $40.	Aglae is female.
Buchanan, Miss		Gay St			Matilda 29, $80.	
Campbell, William		Corner of South St		Merchant tailor	Jenny 48, $40. Peggy 18, $80.	
Carrere, John		East St		Merchant	Jeremiah 40, $125. Nicholas 36, $125.	
Cochran, William G.		South St		Secretary to the Baltimore Insurance Co.	Frisby 15, $125. Charlotte 25, $80.	

Free Blacks and Slave Owners in Baltimore City Tax Assessor's Ledger, 1813 Ward 4

NAME	RACE/ STATUS	RESIDENCE	REAL PROPERTY	OCCUPATION	ENSLAVED PROPERTY Name, Age, Value	COMMENTS
Dawes, James		Market St		Cashier at Franklin Bank of Baltimore	Willis 16, $125.	
Donnell, John		Water St		Merchant	Empson 14, $40. Norris 10, $40. Jack 8, $40. Maria 13, $40.	
Dowell, George M.		Market St			Dinah 26, $80.	
Dunwoody, Robert		Pratt St			James 13, $40. Crassa 14, $80.	
Fonerden, Adam		Market St			Ann 14, $80.	
Frelet, Claude Joseph		Second St.		Cordial distilller	Roman 23, $125.	
Fulford, William		Market St			Sarah 28, $80. Venus 20, $80. Harriett 14, $80.	
Gilmor, Robert Jr.		Water St			John 25, $125. Frank 10, $40. Nelly 20, $80. Isabella 12, $40.	
Gilmor, Robert Sr		Water St		Merchant/ Counting House	John 26, $125.	
Giraud, Dr. John J.		South St		Physician	Jack 49, $60. Charlotte 39, $40. Susan 24, $80. Ann 17, $80.	
Haslet, William		Market St		Merchant	James 20, $125.	
Hollingsworth, Thomas		South St		Merchant	Robert 25, $125. Gilbert 25, $125. Polydor 22, $125. Phillis 18, $80. Prudence 16, $80. Hannah 45, $40. Louisa 9, $40.	
Howard, Henry		Holliday St			Theodore 35, $125.	
Hubball, Ebenezer		Gay St		Brass Founder	Maria 17, $80	
Jenkins, Edward		South St		Sadlery store	Ben 14, $125. Jane 30, $80. Sarah 10, $40.	
Jenkins, William		Water St		Currier	George 9, $40. Sarah 30, $80. Amelia 18, $80.	
Jones, Joshua		Market St			Priscilla 20, $80. Lydia 9, $40.	

Free Blacks and Slave Owners in Baltimore City Tax Assessor's Ledger, 1813 Ward 4

NAME	RACE/ STATUS	RESIDENCE	REAL PROPERTY	OCCUPATION	ENSLAVED PROPERTY Name, Age, Value	COMMENTS
Keener, John		Water St		Gunsmith	Kate 35, $80. Two black children under 5 $20 each.	
Kell, Thomas		Gay St		Attorney at Law	Jack 40, $125. Stephen 22, $125. Scipio 50, $60. Abraham 6, $20. Casper 26, 60. Henney 25, $80. Susanna 14, $80.	Casper is sickly.
Key, Abner		Pratt St		Tailor	Priscilla 17, $80. Harriett 10, $40.	
Leypold, Frederick		Gay St		Grocer	Peter 14, $80. Elizabeth 43, $40. Daphne 16, $80.	
Liggett, George		Commerce St			Negro Jack 12, $40.	
Macatee, Francis		Water St			Abraham 18, $125.	
Mackall, Richard		Market St			Betty 10, $40.	
Maggs, Jane		Gay St			Milley 35, $80.	
Martin, James		Lovely Lane		Cabinet Maker	Lucy 7, No value. Ann 12, $40.	Lucy is "a cripple." Ann property of Mr. Lindsey.
McCleary, William		Calvert St		Bootmaker	Rachael 36, $80. Jim 8, $40.	
McConky, James		Holliday St		Innkeeper	Maria 26, $80.	
McFerran, John		Second St		Baker	Loyd 12, $40. Kitty 17, $80.	
McKenzie, George		Corner of Water St			Milly 30, $80. Two children between 4 & 6, $20 each	
Mills, Levin		Gay St			Nancy 30, $80. Betty 29, $80. Charles 12, $40. Isaac 5, $20.	
Moale, Samuel		Gay St		Attorney at Law	Charles 41, $125. Harry 10, $40. Rachael 35, $80. Milley 35, $80. Sarah 22, 80. Jane 7, $20.	
Myers, Jacob		Holliday St		China Merchant	Patty 12, $40. Mary 10, $40.	
Norris, William		Market St		Dry Goods Merchant	Hannah 17, $80.	

Free Blacks and Slave Owners in Baltimore City Tax Assessor's Ledger, 1813 Ward 4

NAME	RACE/ STATUS	RESIDENCE	REAL PROPERTY	OCCUPATION	ENSLAVED PROPERTY Name, Age, Value	COMMENTS
Norris, William Jr.		Market St			George 38, $125. Jeremiah 25, $125. Sabina 40, $40.	
Oldham, John		South St		Chair maker	Ennalls 17, $125. Darky 20, $80. Sidney 18, $80.	Sidney is female.
Owens, Joseph		Market St		Shoe store	Jack 14, $80. Kitty 11, $40.	
Pannell, Edward		South St			Binah 45, $40. Ann 19, $80	Binah is female.
Parker, Elizabeth		South St			Moses 25, $125. Comfort 22, $80. Maria 14, $80.	Comfort is female.
Patterson, William		1. South St and 2. Corner of Pratt St. McClure's Wharf		Merchant	William 40, $125. Abraham 20, $125. David 17, $125. Elias 8, $40. Jane 40, $40. Binah 20, $80. Ann 15, $80.	
Pinkney, William (Esq.)		Gay St		Attorney and counselor at law	Henry 42, $125. Sam 26, $125. Dick 25, $125. Loyd 18, $125. Lucy 11, $40. Grace 8, $40.	
Pontier, Anthony		Market St		Perfume & fancy store	Ritar 35, $80.	Ritar is female.
Porter, William		Market St		Dry goods merchant	Kitty, $80.	
Raborg, Christopher Jr.		South St		Brass founder	Phebe 30, $80.	
Raborg, Christopher Sr.		Water St		Brass founder	Frank 35, $125. Harry 18, $125. Nelly 18, $80.	
Raborg, Samuel		Water St			Sam 10, $40.	
Rawlings, Benjamin		Market St		Merchant	Mary 12, $40. Susan 9, $40.	Mary's owner on Eastern Shore. Susan lives on Fells Point.

Free Blacks and Slave Owners in Baltimore City Tax Assessor's Ledger, 1813 Ward 4

NAME	RACE/ STATUS	RESIDENCE	REAL PROPERTY	OCCUPATION	ENSLAVED PROPERTY Name, Age, Value	COMMENTS
Readel, John		Gay St		Bottler	Flora 30, $80. Charlotte 27, $80. Nelson 7, $20.	
Riggs, George W.		Market St		Jewelry & fancy store	Maria 18, $80. Fanny 5, $20.	
Rogers, Jacob		South St		Hatter	Anthony 22, $125. David 20, $125. Clara 22, $80. Kitty 12, $40.	
Ross, Reuben		Pratt St		Grocer	Eliza 8, $40.	
Sewell, William H.		Market St		Cordwainer	Rachael 15, $8.	
Sherlock, John		Water St			Ben 30, $125. Yorick 12, $40. Maria 19, $80	
Singleton, Mrs.		Gay St			Alice 22, $80.	
Slater, William		Market St			Esther 35, $80.	
Small, John		Market St		Merchant	James 24, $125. Sarah 23, $80.	
Smith, Gen. Samuel		Water St		Merchant	Stetson 16, $125. Rebecca 45, $40. Female 45, $40. 3 black children under 6, $20 each. Dolly 15, $80. Lydia 12, $40.	
Starr, Hezekiah		Calvert St		Tobacconist	Polly 28, $80.	
Steuart, Dr. James		Holliday St			Susan 20, $80. Peggy 18, $80. Daniel 10, $40.	
Stiles, Edward		Lovely Lane			Fanny 30, $80. Eliza 15, $80. Rolet 5, $20.	Rolet is female.
Sweetser, Seth		Calvert St		Boot maker	Isaac 20, $125. Charles 14, $125. Grace 10, $40. Bet 14, $80.	
Taylor, Thomas		Pratt St		Cooper	Nace 4, $125. James 7, $20. Harriett 11, $40.	
Tilden, Marmaduke		South St		Merchant	Minta 20, $80.	
Urie, James		Pratt St		Blockmaker	Kitty 15, $80.	

Free Blacks and Slave Owners in Baltimore City Tax Assessor's Ledger, 1813 Ward 4

NAME	RACE/STATUS	RESIDENCE	REAL PROPERTY	OCCUPATION	ENSLAVED PROPERTY Name, Age, Value	COMMENTS
Urie, Jeremiah		Pratt St		Blacksmith	Sam 24, $125.	
Vallette, Charles		Market St		Wine & Liquor Store	Jemima 22, $80. Eliza 11, $40.	
White, John		Gay St			Phillis 23, $80.	
Williams, Catherine Mrs.		Commerce St			Tabitha 25, $80.	
Wilson, James of William		Holliday St			Pheaton 27 $125. Clara 24 $80.	
Wilson, Robert		South St		Cashier Bank of Maryland	Joseph 17, $125. Nace 8, $40.	
Winchell, James F.		South St			Nace 36, $125.	
Winchester, David		Holliday St			Valentine 22, $125. Nackey 20, $80.	Valentine is male.
Wintkle, Elizabeth		Holliday St			Sam 22, $125. Andrew 13, $40. Jefferson 5, $20. Patty 28, $80. Hetty 16, $80. Ruthy 16, $80.	

Free Blacks and Slave Owners in Baltimore City Tax Assessor's Ledger, 1813 Ward 5

NAME	RACE/ STATUS	RESIDENCE	REAL PROPERTY	OCCUPATION	ENSLAVED PROPERTY Name, Age, Value	COMMENTS
Aldridge, Andrew		Market St			Judy 25, $80. Fanny 7, $20. Bill 12, $40.	
Allen, Richard		Market Space			Dolly 6, $20.	
Arnest, Dr. John		Frederick St			Steuart 4, $20.	
Baque, Margaret		Frederick St			Mary 15, $80	
Barry, Robert		Gay St		Consul	Dafn 35, $80. Ann 10, $40.	
Billington, William		Market Space			Jerry 22 $125.	Property of Benjamin Clark.
Blondell, William		Market Space		Goldsmith & jeweler	Lucy 20, $80.	
Boggs, Harmanus		Market Space		Dry goods merchant	Letty 13, $40.	
Bosley, Daniel		Market Space			Abraham 19, $125. Joseph $40.	
Boyd, Peter		Frederick St			Perry 19, $125. George 13, $40.	Perry property of Mr. Garland.
Brunett, John F.		Cumberland Row			Emily 16, $80.	
Buck, Jacob		Water St		Tailor	Daniel 12, $40.	
Camp, William		Water St		Cabinet maker	Lambert 25, $125. Charlot 27, $80. Mary 11, $40. Little Mary 5, $20.	
Carnigham, James		Frederick St			Juliet 16, $80.	
Carr, Joseph		Market St			Dark 30, $80. Bill 14, $125.	
Cator, John		Duggans Wharf			Philip 11, $40. Phillis 14, $80. Charlott 9, $40.	
Cole, William		Gay St			Henry 30, $125. Joe 10, $40. Thomas 6, $20. Sam 4, $20. Phillis 35, $80.	
Diffenderffer, Peter		Market St		Hardware merchant	Sarah 33, $80.	

Free Blacks and Slave Owners in Baltimore City Tax Assessor's Ledger, 1813 Ward 5

NAME	RACE/ STATUS	RESIDENCE	REAL PROPERTY	OCCUPATION	ENSLAVED PROPERTY Name, Age, Value	COMMENTS
Donaldson, James W.		Market St			Lewey 13, $40. Whiney 42, $40.	
Ducatel, Dr. Edme	Aka Edmond Ducatel	Market St			Anette 30, $80. Agnes 30, $80.	
Ducatel, Germain		Tripolets Alley			Mary 28, $80. Sally 18, $80. Jacob 26, $125.	
Dugan, Cumberland		Duggans Wharf			Ned, Jacob & Dick all over 60. Cassia 30, $80. Milley 30, $80. Allen 12, $40.	No value given for Ned, Jacob & Dick.
Dukehart, Elizabeth	Widow	Market St			Rachel 16, $80.	
Duon, Honore	Widow	Pratt St			Sally 40, $40. Virginia 20, $80.	
Edwards, Jonathan		Gay St		Merchant	Flora 26, $80.	
Faure, Blanc	French woman	Water St			Venus 45, $40. Nancy 18, $80.	
Finley, John & Hugh		Gay St			Betty 12, $40.	
Foreman, Elijah		Duggans Wharf			James 15, $125. Claire 9, $40.	
Frick, Peter		Frederick St. and Gay St			Harriet 20, $80. Leah 16, $80. William 8, $40.	
Galland, John B.		Gay St			John 15, $125. Sydney 18, $80.	
Gants, Adam		Duggans Wharf			Polly 9, $40.	
Garetson, Mary		Gay St			Flora 26, $80.	
Gill, John				Notary	Sally 37, $40.	
Glassgow, Dr. John & Hannah		Frederick St			Ann 12, $40.	
Godfraid/Godfroid, William		Water St		Cigar maker	Jane 16, $80. Bet 13, $40. Carlile 14, $80. Alben 13, $40. Dick 9, $40.	
Gooding, John		Harrison St			Sophia 15, $80. William 5, $40.	

Free Blacks and Slave Owners in Baltimore City Tax Assessor's Ledger, 1813 Ward 5

NAME	RACE/ STATUS	RESIDENCE	REAL PROPERTY	OCCUPATION	ENSLAVED PROPERTY Name, Age, Value	COMMENTS
Griffith, Susanna		Gay St			Zachariah, 45 $125. John 30, $125. Betty 25, $80. Joshua 9, $40. William 6, $20.	
Hamilton, Pliny		Dugans Wharf			James 15, $125.	
Hanson, Charles W.		Frederick St			David 15, $125. Samuel 9, $40. Nancy 30, $80. Peggy 30, $80. Susan 15, $80. Ellen 5, $20.	
Harper, Robert G.		Gay St			Jerry 32, $125. John 16, $125. William 10, $40. Joseph 4, $20. Nancy 34, $80. Harriet 34, $80. Polley 22, $80. Julia 16, $80. Little Julia 8, $40.	
Haskins, Govert		2nd St		Merchant	James 25, $125. Alley 25, $80. Robert 4, $20.	
Hindman, James		Gay St			William 32, $125. Mary 38, $40. Maria 26, $80. Peggy 12, $40.	
Hollins, John S.		Water St			Peyton 28, $125.	
Hutchins, John		Frederick St			Charity 12, $40.	
Hutton, James		Market St			Marchall 19, $125.	
Ireland, Edward		2nd St			Suck 26, $80. Nelly 18, $80. Anna 24, $80. Jenny 7, $20.	
Ives, James		Water St		Cordwainer	Betey 15, $80.	
Jamison, Joseph		Frederick St			Hester 14, $80.	
Jones, Awbreay		Cumberland Row			Hannah 29, $80.	
Kaylor, George		Cumberland Row			Paris 15, $125. Kitty 10, $40.	
Keys, John		Duggans Wharf			Charles 13, $40.	
Lacy, Hannah		Cumberland Row			Jacob 10, $40.	
Larsh, Abraham Jr.		Gay St			Henry 20, $125	

Free Blacks and Slave Owners in Baltimore City Tax Assessor's Ledger, 1813 Ward 5

NAME	RACE/ STATUS	RESIDENCE	REAL PROPERTY	OCCUPATION	ENSLAVED PROPERTY Name, Age, Value	COMMENTS
Lauden, Michael		Water St		Boarding house	Fortune 20, $125. August 21, $125. Mary 20, $80. Ann 30, $80.	
Legrand, Samuel D.		Market Space			Hannah 10, $40. Harriet 9, $40.	
Love, Dr. John		Market Space			Hannah 5, $20.	
Lovering, Francis		Frederick St			David 13 $40.	
Maerst, James M.		Gay St			Rose 38, $40. Hannah 8, $40.	
Marche, John		Gay St			Puntine 17, $80. Harry 20, $125.	
McKim, Samuel		Frederick St			Beck 5, $20.	Beck property of George Chancey.
McKinze, John		Frederick St			Frederick, 36 $125.	
Middleton, Richard		Market St			Clem 16, $125.	
Milhau, Michael		Water St		Merchant	William 50, $62. Nancy 38, $40. Rachel 30, $80. Mary 22, $80.	
Miller, John Jr.		Market Space			Maria 20, $80.	
Mitchell, Alexander		Frederick St			Lydia 23, $80. Harriet 20, $80.	
Mohler, Henry		2nd St			Mary 20, $80. Janet 20, $80. Caroline 11, $40.	
Newburn, Mary		Market St			Margaret 7, $20.	
Nicholas, Bathesard		Market St			Louisa 20, $80.	
Norris, Harriet		Frederick St			Caroline 22, $80.	
Norris, John		Harrison St.			Bill 17, $125.	
Oliver, Robert		Gay St		Merchant	George 34, $125. Jerry 40, $125. Moore 30, $125. Kitty 30, $80. Nelly 28, $80.	
Owens, William		Duggans Wharf			Jack 35, $125. James 32, $125. Nancy 13, $40. Grace 11, $40. Aaron 33, $125.	Aaron property of Thomas Owens.
Perkins, John		Frederick St			Hetty 12, $40. Grace 20, $80.	

Free Blacks and Slave Owners in Baltimore City Tax Assessor's Ledger, 1813 Ward 5

NAME	RACE/ STATUS	RESIDENCE	REAL PROPERTY	OCCUPATION	ENSLAVED PROPERTY Name, Age, Value	COMMENTS
Poncet, Lewis		Market St		Gold & silver smith	Amint 25, $80. Candis 25, $80. Dick 6, $20.	
Presbury, George G. 1st		Gay St			Shade 42, $125. Moses 45, $125. Charlott 28, $80. Moll 9, $40.	
Ridgley, Lot		Market St		Merchant	Priscilla 20, $80. Milley 16, $80.	
Ringold, Catherine		Market St		Fancy store	Moses 28, $125. Perry 24, $125. Curtis 20, $125. James 16, $125.	All slaves belong to the estate of James Ringold.
Roney, William		Frederick St			Jack 24, $125.	
Shedden, John		Gay St			Sam 8, $40. Mary, $40.	
Smith, Arnold		Gay St		Blacksmith	Peter 28, $125. Jack 11, $40. Prud 15, $80.	
Smith, Job		Frederick St		Baker	Becky 35, $80. Caroline 7, $20.	
Smith, George C.		Gay St		China Store	Reman 14, $125. Susan 16, $80.	
Sollers, Basil		Market St		Hatter	Carry 46, $80. Lucy 35, $80. Sally 23, $80.	
Sprigg, Thomas		Dugan's Wharf		Merchant	Will $125.	Has 8 years to serve.
Sprole, William		Market Space			Charity 33, $80. Bet 13, $40.	
Stallings, Benjamin		Market St			Harriet 12, $40. Henry 9, $40.	
Sterett, Col. Joseph					Sophey 11, $40.	
Sterett, Samuel					Frank 25, $125. Peter 10, $40. Juliet 27, $80.	
Sterrett, James		Gay St at City Bank			Charles 12, $40. Maria 18, $80. Charlot 18, $80.	
Stewart, David		Gay St			Maria 45 $40. Charlott 16 $80. Maria 14 $80. Hetty 16 $80. Emily 12 $40. Fanny 15, $80. James 14, $125.	

Free Blacks and Slave Owners in Baltimore City Tax Assessor's Ledger, 1813 Ward 5

NAME	RACE/STATUS	RESIDENCE	REAL PROPERTY	OCCUPATION	ENSLAVED PROPERTY Name, Age, Value	COMMENTS
Tapiau, Vital		Gay St			John 25, $125. Tousant 20, $125. Finetee 20, $80. Soline 22, $80. Rosetta 23, $80.	
Thompson, Hugh		Gay St			Sampson 45, $125. Charles 35, $125. James 30, $125. Abraham 17, $125 Priss 22, $80. Julia 40, $40. Hager 13, $40.	
Tolbert, John		Gay St			Duchess 13, $20.	
Torrance, Charles		Harrison St			Mary 38, $40. Fanny 23, $80. Levin 22, $125.	
Vanwyck, William		Pratt St			Bristol 34, $125. George 10, $40. Sally 36, $80. Milley 20.	Milley has fits, no value.
Volunbrun, Jean M.		Harrison St			Nelson 30, $125. Gentas 26, $125. Jean Joseph, 24 $125. Leveque 27, $125. I.Nago 36, $125. Tranquilla 37, $125. Bishop 27, $125. Nicate 20, $80. Francais 36, $80. Prudence 30, $80. Adele 16, $80. Athelie 32, $80. Sanite 30, $80. Popote 30, $80. Soline 26, $80. Trevoline 6, $20. Aguste 7, $20. Charles 30 $125 Roel 25 $125. Barite 32 $125. Jane Baptiste 36, $80. Maria 31 $80. Nataline 9 $40.	Charles, Roe, Barite, Jane Baptiste, Maria & Nataline property of Jacques N, Bourget.
Waters, Richard		Water St			Hannah 40, $40. Robert 13, $40.	

Free Blacks and Slave Owners in Baltimore City Tax Assessor's Ledger, 1813 Ward 5

NAME	RACE/ STATUS	RESIDENCE	REAL PROPERTY	OCCUPATION	ENSLAVED PROPERTY Name, Age, Value	COMMENTS
Weise, Felix		Frederick St			Nelly 21, $80.	
West, John		Cumberland Row		Tailor	Peggy 30, $80. Joe 5, $20. Kitty 13, $40.	Kitty property of Polly Smallwood.
Wilson, Gerard		Gay St			James 22, $125.	
Winkler, John		Dugans Wharf			Charlot 20, $80.	
Wirgman, Charles		S. Gay St			William 26, $125. Larkin 10, $40. Lydia 19, $80. Julia 16, $80.	
Wright, James I.		Gay St			Levy 10, $40.	
Zollers, Dr. Charles		Frederick St			Harriet 19, $80.	

Free Blacks and Slave Owners in Baltimore City Tax Assessor's Ledger, 1813 Ward 6

NAME	RACE/ STATUS	RESIDENCE	REAL PROPERTY	OCCUPATION	ENSLAVED PROPERTY Name, Age, Value	COMMENTS
Albers, Solomon G.		McElderrys Wharf			Daniel between 8 & 14, $40.	
Amos, John		High St		Hatter	Mill between 14 & 36, $80.	
Amos, William H.		Front St.		Potter	Susan between 14 & 36, $80.	
Armstrong, James		McElderrys Wharf		Grocer	Jack between 14 & 45, $125. Bob between 14 & 45, $125. Sarah between 14 & 36, $80. Jack between 14 & 45, $50. John under 8, $20. Caroline under 8, $20. James between 14 & 45, $10.	James is infirm. Jack, worth $50, is infirm.
Baker, James		Jones St		Surveyor	Henry between 14 & 45, $125. James between 14 & 45, $125. Trylus between 8 & 14, $40. Flora between 14 & 36, $80. Betsy between 14 & 36, $80. Lucy between 14 & 36, $80.	
Barrickman, Hannah		Bridge St		Hardware Store	Fan between 8 & 14, $40.	
Barry, Lavallin		Bridge St		Clerk	Peggy between 14 & 36, $80. Cass under 8, $20.	
Basset, Ann	Widow	Milk Lane			Sarah between 14 & 36, $50.	Sarah is infirm.
Berteau, Peter		Pitt St		Tailor	Susan between 14 & 36, $80.	
Black, James	Tenant			Teacher of languages	Rose between 8 & 14, $40.	
Bond, Peter		High St		Merchant	Rachel between 14 & 36, $80. George under 8, $20.	
Bond, Thomas W.		Bridge St			Edward under 8, $20. Frank under 8, $20. Phoebe between 14 & 36, $80.	

Free Blacks and Slave Owners in Baltimore City Tax Assessor's Ledger, 1813 Ward 6

NAME	RACE/ STATUS	RESIDENCE	REAL PROPERTY	OCCUPATION	ENSLAVED PROPERTY Name, Age, Value	COMMENTS
Bonnett, Joseph	Tenant			Merchant	Philipon between 14 & 45, $125. Noel between 14 & 45, $125. Zemere above 36, $40. Ilet above 36, $40. Jane above 36, $40. Louisa between 14 & 36, $80. Mary between 14 & 36, $80.	
Bray, Joseph (Estate of)		Fish Market			Betty between 14 & 36, $8. Isaac between 8 & 14, $40.	
Briscoe, Samuel	Tenant	Front St		Merchant	John between 14 & 45, $125. Jack between 14 & 45, $125. Jonas between 8 & 14, $40.	
Brown, Jehu		Sleys Lane			Julia under 8 $20.	Property of William Beatty of Baltimore Co.
Bryson, Nathaniel G.		Bridge St		Grocer	Charles between 14 & 45, $125. Dick between 14 & 45, $125. Tom between 24 & 45, $125. Polladore between 14 & 36, $40. Till $40. Henrietta between 8 & 14, $40.	
Butler, James		Potter St		Carpenter	Jacob, between 8 & 14, $40.	
Cappeau, Ann	Widow Tenant	Great York St North side			Zamore 45, $10. Addal under 8, $20.	Zamore is infirm.
Carson, Andrew		Great York St North side		Blacksmith	George between 8 & 14, $40. Esther between 14 & 36, $80.	
Chenoweth, Richard		Front St		Blacksmith	Simon between 14 & 45, $125. Violet between 14 & 36, $80.	Simon property of Miss Younger of Kent Co.
Cole, Matthew		Eden St East side			Lydia between 14 & 36, $80	Property of John Vansant.

Free Blacks and Slave Owners in Baltimore City Tax Assessor's Ledger, 1813 Ward 6

NAME	RACE/ STATUS	RESIDENCE	REAL PROPERTY	OCCUPATION	ENSLAVED PROPERTY Name, Age, Value	COMMENTS
Coleman, John		Pitt St		Slater	Minty between 14 & 36, $80. Susan under 8, $10.	
Collins, George C.		Addison St		Carpenter	Nelly between 14 & 36, $80. Sam between 8 & 14, $40. Jane between 8 & 14, $40.	
Constable, Charles		Addison St		Lumber merchant	Charles between 8 & 14, $40.	
Conway, William		Market Space		Iron merchant	Harriet between 8 & 14, $40.	
Cook, John L.		Liberty St		Printer	Lucy between 8 & 14, $40.	
Crook, Walter		Market Space		Cabinet maker	James between 14 & 45, $125.	
Cross, Andrew & John		High St		Lumber merchants	William between 14 & 45, $125. Bob between 14 & 45, $125.	
Cross, Andrew		High St		Lumber Merchant	Harriet under 8, $20.	
Cross, William S.		High St		Carpenter	Mary between 8 & 14, $40. Nick under 8, $20.	
Crow, Ann		Pitt St			Leonard between 14 & 45, $125. Barbara above 36, $40.	
Curran, John		Mechanical St			Sarah between 8 & 14, $40.	Sarah is property of Arch Gittings of Baltimore Co.
Davidson, Margaret	Widow	Baltimore St			Rebecca under 8, $20. Kitty under 8, $20.	
Dawson, Capt. Henry		Pitt St			Eleanor between 14 & 36, $80	
Deffenderffer, John D.		NW corner of York & High Sts		Merchant	Tom between 14 & 45, $125. Milkey between 14 & 36, $80. Harriet between 14-36, $80.	
Derkheim, Capt. Meyer		Mechanical St			Daniel between 8 & 14, $40.	
Dew, Ann		High St			2 female slaves between 14 & 36, $160	

Free Blacks and Slave Owners in Baltimore City Tax Assessor's Ledger, 1813 Ward 6

NAME	RACE/ STATUS	RESIDENCE	REAL PROPERTY	OCCUPATION	ENSLAVED PROPERTY Name, Age, Value	COMMENTS
Diffenderffer, Michael (Estate of)		McElderrys Wharf		Physician	Paul between 14 & 45, $125. Rose between 14 & 36, $80. Jude between 14 & 36, $80. Bill between 8 & 14, $40.	
Dobbin, George (Estate of)		Harrison St		Printer	Nelly between 14 & 36, $80.	
Doddral, James		Front St		Currier	Mary between 14 & 36, $80.	
Egerton, Charles C.		Aisquith St			Priscilla between 8 & 24, $40.	Priscilla property of Mordecai Jones, St. Mary's Co.
Elliott, John		Straight Lane		Plasterer	Charles between 14 & 45, $125.	
Esmanard, John B.		Great York St North side			George between 14 & 45, $125. Sarah above 36, $40.	Tenant
Evans, Griffith		Water St		Cooper	Caroline between 14 & 36, $80.	
Evans, Joseph		Addison St		Cordwainer	Rachel between 8 & 14, $40.	Rachel property of John Wooden of Balto. Co.
Fitzhugh, John		Aisquith St			Ralph above 45, $40. Bill above 45, $40. Henry above 36, $40. Letty between 8 & 14, $40. Harriot between 8 & 14, $40. Scilla under 8, $20.	
Flanagan, William		Concord St			Ben between 14 & 45, $125. Caleb between 14 & 45, $125. John between 14 & 45, $125. Ally between 14 & 36, $40. Sally between 14 & 36, $40. Harriet between 8 & 14, $40.	
Franciscus, William		Milk Lane			Ann between 14 & 36, $80	

Free Blacks and Slave Owners in Baltimore City Tax Assessor's Ledger, 1813 Ward 6

NAME	RACE/ STATUS	RESIDENCE	REAL PROPERTY	OCCUPATION	ENSLAVED PROPERTY Name, Age, Value	COMMENTS
Fusselbaugh, John		East St			Richard between 14 & 45, $125. Jack above 45, $20.	
Geuiran, Isadore		Baltimore St			Jenny between 14 & 36, $80. August between 8 & 14, $40.	
Giles, Rebecca	Tenant	Dulany St.			Fanny above 36, $40.	
Glenn, John W.		Front St		Paint & oil store	James between 14 & 45, $125. Phillis between 14 & 36, $80. Nelly between 14 & 36, $80. Cornelia under 8, $20.	
Goldsmith, Sarah	Widow	Pitt St			Rachel above 36, $40. Aquila between 14 & 45, $125. Lucy between 8 & 14, $40. Matilda between 8 & 14, $40. Nancy between 8 & 14, $40. Isaac between 8 & 14, $40. Abraham under 8, $20. Zachariah under 8, $20.	
Gorsuch, Joshua		Bridge St		Merchant	Henrietta between 14 & 36, $80. Susan between 14 & 36, $80.	
Gorsuch, Nicholas		N.E. corner of High & Low		Innkeeper	Richard between 14 & 45, $125. Jacob, between 14 & 45, $125. Rebecca between 8 & 14, $40.	
Govins, Daniel	Black man	Bridge St	Lot $40, Imp $20			
Gracy, Redmond		Baltimore St			Nanny between 8 & 14, $40.	Nanny owned by N. Sewell of St Mary's Co.
Graham, Robert		High St		Carter	Harry between 14 & 45, $125. Tracy between 14 & 45, $125.	

Free Blacks and Slave Owners in Baltimore City Tax Assessor's Ledger, 1813 Ward 6

NAME	RACE/ STATUS	RESIDENCE	REAL PROPERTY	OCCUPATION	ENSLAVED PROPERTY Name, Age, Value	COMMENTS
Hanna, Ann		Great York St North side			Sarah between 14 & 36, $80. Sukey between 14 & 36, $80. Charlott between 14 & 36, $80.	
Hays, John		Union St			Hannah between 14 & 36, $80.	
Hays, William		Fish Market		Grocer	Minty between 14 & 36, $80.	
Hicks, John		S.E. corner of High & Low			Jane between 14 & 36, $80. James between 8 & 14, $40.	
Hillen, John		Pitt St			Joe between 14 & 45, $125. Esther, between 14 & 36, $80.	
Hoffman, Frederick G.		S W corner of High & Pitt Sts		Grocer	Hetty between 14 & 36, $80. Rose under 8, $20.	
Honeycomb, John		Bridge St		Baker	Kitty between 14 & 36, $80.	
Hurst, Shadrach		Bridge St		Butcher	Charles between 14 & 45, $125.	
Hutchings, Daniel	Yellow Man	Mechanical St	Lot worth $33 Imp $20, Plate 1 oz. & furniture $2			
Karthause, Peter A.		Great York St North side		Merchant	Frank between 14 & 45, $125.	
Kempton, Samuel A.	Tenant	Great York St North side		Merchant	2 female slaves between 14 & 36, $160.	
Kittinger, Michael (Say Heddinger)		Sleys Lane			Isaac between 14 & 45 $125. Betsy between 14 & 36 $80.	
Lawder, Benjamin		North St		Feed store	Archy, between 14 &45, $125.	
Letta, Thomas		High St			Rachel between 14 & 36, $80.	Rachel owned by Richard Daugherty of Balto. Co.
Long, Henry		Jones St		Soap factory	Charles between 14 & 45, $125. Fannie between 14 & 36, $80. Dick between 8 & 14, $40.	

Free Blacks and Slave Owners in Baltimore City Tax Assessor's Ledger, 1813 Ward 6

NAME	RACE/STATUS	RESIDENCE	REAL PROPERTY	OCCUPATION	ENSLAVED PROPERTY Name, Age, Value	COMMENTS
Lupeerre, Clelie		Union St			Alexandrie between 14 & 36, $80. Terris between 14 & 36, $80.	
Magauran, James		Dulany St			Lucy between 14 & 36, $80.	
Maidwell, John		Harrison St			Charity between 14 & 36, $80.	
McAllister, Robert		Fish Market		Innkeeper	Ann between 14 & 36, $80. Dinah between 14 & 36, $80. Rhoda under 8, $20.	
McGinnis, John		Fish Market		Innkeeper	Rachel between 14 & 36, $80. Jacob between 14 & 45, $125. Ann under 8, $20.	Jacob owned by A. Gambrall of Anne Arundel Co.
McLaughlin, Peggy		High St			Jenny between 14 & 36, $80. Henny between 14 & 36, $80.	
Meeteer, Samuel & William		Baltimore St		Paper manufacturers	Tobias between 14 & 45, $125. Mary between 14 & 36, $80.	Tobias belonging to Isaac Quinton of Eastern Shore.
Meyer, Andrew		Pratt St			Tom between 14 & 45, $125. Scott between 14 & 45, $125. Rachel between 14 & 36, $80.	
Miles, John		High St		Merchant	Case between 14 & 36, $80.	
Miller, George		Hawk St		Blacksmith	Sam between 14 & 45, $125. Zack between 8 & 14, $40. Matilda above 36, $20.	
Miller, George W.		Fish Market		Innkeeper	Ben between 14 & 45, $125. Cloe between 14 & 36, $80. Jenny between 14 & 36, $80. Esther between 8 & 14, $40. Milly under 8, $20.	
Miller, Jacob		Bridge St		Tanner	Jack between 14 & 45, $125. Tom between 14 & 45, $125. Tobias between 14 & 45, $125.	

Free Blacks and Slave Owners in Baltimore City Tax Assessor's Ledger, 1813 Ward 6

NAME	RACE/STATUS	RESIDENCE	REAL PROPERTY	OCCUPATION	ENSLAVED PROPERTY Name, Age, Value	COMMENTS
Miller, John		Great York St North side			Betty between 8 & 14, $40.	
Morgan, Edward	Tenant	Pitt St			Charlotte between 14 & 36, $80 Austin between 8 & 14, $40. Minty between 8 & 14, $40.	
Morin, Francis		On the Falls			Edward between 14 & 45, $125. Virgin between 14 & 36, $80.	
Morrin, James		High St			Siloa between 14 & 36, $80.	
Myers, Elizabeth	Widow	S W Bridge & High Sts			Mill between 8 & 14, $40.	
Myers, Jane		Great York St North side			Susan between 8 & 14, $40. Jacob under 8, $20.	
Myers, William		Pitt St			Mary between 8 & 14, $40.	Property of Mrs. Jacobs of Anne Arundel Co.
Nicholson, John		Front St			Sina between 8 & 14, $40.	
Okely, John		Pitt St		Merchant	Thomas between 14 & 45, $50. Dolly between 14 & 36, $80.	Thomas is infirm.
Onion, Elizabeth	Widow	Union St			Basil between 14 & 45, $125. Edward between 14 & 45, $125. Philip between 14 & 45, $125. Jane between 14 & 36, $80. Lucy between 8 & 14, $40. Julia 20, $20.	Julia is infirm.
Page, Daniel		McElderrys Wharf		Grocer	Venus between 14 & 36, $80.	
Parks, Maybury		High St		Inspector of fish	Sophia between 14 & 36, $80.	
Partridge, Rosanna		Youngs Alley			Hagar above 36, $40.	
Person, Jesse		Pitt St			Charles under 8, $20.	

Free Blacks and Slave Owners in Baltimore City Tax Assessor's Ledger, 1813 Ward 6

NAME	RACE/ STATUS	RESIDENCE	REAL PROPERTY	OCCUPATION	ENSLAVED PROPERTY Name, Age, Value	COMMENTS
Phenix, Elizabeth	Tenant				Hannah between 14 & 36, $80. Basil between 14 & 36, $80. Betsy between 14 & 36, $80. Basil between 14 & 45, $125. Thomas between 14 & 45, $125. George between 14 & 45, $125. Henry under 8, $20. Fanny under 8, $20. John under 8, $20.	
Presbury, George G. III		Pitt St		Justice of the peace	James between 14 & 45, $125. Charlotte between 14 & 36, $80. Henry under 8, $20.	
Priestly, Edward		Liberty St		Cabinet & chair maker	Brooks between 14 & 45, $125. Fanny between 14 & 36, $80.	
Renshaw, James		High St		Innkeeper	Violet between 14 & 36, $80. Luce between 8 & 14, $40. Jeff between 8 & 14, $40. Sam under 8, $20. Dinah under 8, $20.	
Richards, Rev. Lewis		Pitt St		Pastor of the 1st Baptist Church,	Lucy between 14 & 36, $80.	
Ridgely, Greenbury		Pitt St		Merchant	Rebecca between 14 & 36, $80. George between 8 & 14, $40. Mary between 8 & 14, $40.	
Ridgely, Noah		Pitt St		Proprietor of Lee's family medicines	Kitty between 14 & 36, $80.	
Rogers, Richard Jr.		High St		Carpenter	Leonard between 8 & 14, $40.	

Free Blacks and Slave Owners in Baltimore City Tax Assessor's Ledger, 1813 Ward 6

NAME	RACE/ STATUS	RESIDENCE	REAL PROPERTY	OCCUPATION	ENSLAVED PROPERTY Name, Age, Value	COMMENTS
Rogers, Thomas		Pitt St		Notary public & city collector	Hannah between 14 & 36, $80. Caroline between 8 & 14, $40. Hany between 8 & 14, $40. Brister under 8, $20. Nanny above 36, $40.	
Ruso, Peter		McElderrys Wharf			Rose between 14 & 36, $80.	
Schmidt, William L.		High St		Merchant	Polly between 14 & 36, $80.	Property of Jacob Franklin of Anne Arundel Co.
Sellman, Jonathan		Market Space			George between 14 & 45, $125.	
Sewell, James H.		High St			Joe under 8, $20.	
Shutt, Bartholemew		Green St			Sarah between 8 & 14, $40.	
Simpson, John		Pitt St			Hetty between 14 & 36, $80.	Property of James Hamilton of Balto. Co.
Smith, Capt. Joseph		Pitt St			Nelly between 14 & 36, $80. Jenny between 14 & 36, $80. Eliza between 8 & 14, $40. Bell between 8 & 14, $40.	
Smith, Capt. Robert		Pitt St		Sea captain	William between 14 & 45, $125. Peter between 14 & 45, $125. Winne between 14 & 36, $80.	
Smith, James		East St			Nace between 8 & 14, $40.	
Sprague, Charles		High St			Minty between 14 & 36, $80.	Property of John Hardesty, Kent Co.
Stall, Edward H.		Bridge St			Sophia between 14 & 36, $80.	Since removed to Cincinnati.
Stansbury, William of Abraham		Mechanical St			Charlotte between 8 & 14, $40.	

Free Blacks and Slave Owners in Baltimore City Tax Assessor's Ledger, 1813 Ward 6

NAME	RACE/ STATUS	RESIDENCE	REAL PROPERTY	OCCUPATION	ENSLAVED PROPERTY Name, Age, Value	COMMENTS
Stansbury, William of Elijah		Union St		Carpenter	Phoebe between 8 & 14, $40.	
Stevenson, Dr. Cosmo		Harrison St		Physician	Jacob between 14 & 45, $125. Mill between 14 & 36, $80. Fanny under 8 $20.	
Stevenson, Josias		Front St		Tobacco inspector	Caleb about 45, $60. Potee about 45, $60. Sirah between 14 & 45, $125. Sarah between 14 & 36, $80. Henry under 8, $20.	
Stewart, John		Mechanical St			Slave above 36, $40.	
Stickney, Henry		Pitt St		Ship chandler	Lavina under 8, $20.	
Sykes, John		High St		Innkeeper	Ned between 14 & 45, $125.	
Tanner, P. & L.		North St			Maria between 14 & 36. $80. Mill between 8 & 14, $40.	
Thompson, John		McElderrys Wharf			Nice between 14 & 36, $80.	
Travis, Susan		High St			Draper between 14 & 46, $125.	
Tupper, Nathan		Pitt St			Lucy between 14 & 36, $80. Lydia between 8 & 14, $40.	
Wall, John E,		Baltimore St			Peter between 14 &45, $125.	
Whitaker, Thomas		Green St		Carpenter	Hetty between 8 & 14, $40.	
Willhelm, John		North St		Innkeeper	John between 14 & 45, $125.	

Free Blacks and Slave Owners in Baltimore City Tax Assessor's Ledger, 1813 Ward 6

NAME	RACE/STATUS	RESIDENCE	REAL PROPERTY	OCCUPATION	ENSLAVED PROPERTY Name, Age, Value	COMMENTS
Williams, William N.		McElderrys Wharf			Preston between 14 & 45, $125. Nathan between 14 & 45, $125. Solomon between 14 & 45, $125. Charlott between 14 & 36, $80. Maria between 14 & 36, $80. Harriet between 8 & 14, $40. Michael under 8 $20.	
Wilson, James		Bridge St		Justice of the Peace	Abram between 14 & 45, $125. Mary between 14 & 36, $80.	
Wilson, John		Baltimore St		Grocer	Ann between 14 & 36, $80. Henny between 14 & 36, $80.	
Winder, Rider H.		Aisquith St			George between 14 & 45, $125.	
Winder, William		Great York St North side		U. S. brigadier general commanding 10th military district	Louisa above 36, $20. Henny between 14 & 36 $80. Delilah between 14 & 36 $80. Jane between 8 & 14 $40. Jamaica between 14 & 45 $125. Sam between 14 & 45 $125.	Louisa is infirm.
Winstanley, William H.		High St		Merchant	Sophia between 14 & 36, $80. Jerry between 8 & 14, $40.	Jerry owned by Margaret Wilson of Harford Co.
Woods, Corfel		Bridge St		Grocer	Ann between 14 & 36, $80.	
Woodyear, Edward G.		Front St		Attorney	Maria between 14 & 36, $80.	
Worthington, Henry		Pitt St		Harness maker	Bob between 8 & 14, $40.	
Yates, John		Great York St North side		Tenant	Negro Patty between 14 & 45 $80. Hannah under 8 $20.	
Young, John		Brittons Alley			Hagar above 36, $40. Mary between 8 & 14, $40.	

Free Blacks and Slave Owners in Baltimore City Tax Assessor's Ledger, 1813 Ward 7

NAME	RACE/ STATUS	RESIDENCE	REAL PROPERTY	OCCUPATION	ENSLAVED PROPERTY Name, Age, Value	COMMENTS
Abraham, Capt. Wolbert		Market St E. side		Sea captain	Charlott 25, $80. Julia 4, $10.	
Adams, Capt. Alexander		Fleet St N. side		Sea captain	Pamela 40, $50. Grace 8, $40.	
Addison, Elizabeth		Wolfe St W. side			Jacob 12, $40.	
Adkinson, William		Albemarle St E. side		Painter agent	Vialet 13, $40.	At William P. Cloppers
Allen, Elizabeth		Albemarle St E. side			Binder 22, $125. Joseph 27, $125. Ishmael 22, $125. Mary 15, $80. Affey 12, $40. Lydia 8, $40.	Allen is tenant to John Cunningham.
Almeda, Capt. Joseph		Duke St N. side		Sea captain	Jem 12, $40. York 10, $40. Sam 6, $20.	
Anthony, Daniel		Aliceanna St N. side		Ships carpenter	Charles 25, $125.	Anthony is tenant to Dyer.
Arcambal, Madame		King George St N. side			Maria 16, $80.	Arcambal is tenant to W. guestier
Armour, Mrs. Mary		Great York St S. side			Henny 30, $80. Phillis 16, $80.	
Atkinson, Joshua		Aliceanna St		Carpenter	Ann 17, $80.	
Baartsheer, William		Bond St W. side			Rachel 42, $60. Also crippled boys of no value.	Baartsheer is tenant to Capt. Low.
Bailey, Rachel R.	Widow	Albemarle St W. side			Sarah 12, $40.	
Bandel, George		Pete Alley E. side		Supt. of Sweeps	Tom 13, $40. Perry 10, $40. Elijah 10, $40. Sophy 2, $80.	
Barker, William		Aliceanna St N. side		Ship carpenter	Jane 45, $40. Jane the younger 7, $40.	

Free Blacks and Slave Owners in Baltimore City Tax Assessor's Ledger, 1813 Ward 7

NAME	RACE/ STATUS	RESIDENCE	REAL PROPERTY	OCCUPATION	ENSLAVED PROPERTY Name, Age, Value	COMMENTS
Barns, Whitly		Gramby St E. side			Rebecca 25, $80.	
Beneland/ Benillant, Stephen		Fleet St N. side		Ship carpenter	Ceaser very old $40. Joe $125.	
Bier, Jacob		Aliceanna St N. side		Cashier of the Marine Bank	Nelly 40, $50.	
Bosley, James		Gramby St E. side		Merchant	Male slave Cyrus, {Say Stephen} 6, $20	Bosley is tenant to Carroll.
Boss, Hays		Woolf St W. side		Pilot	Peter 12, $40. Shadrach 22, $125.	
Bowen, Richard		King George St S. side		Cordwainer	Lemmon 28, $125. John 6, $20. Darcus 50, $25. Eliza 10, $40.	
Bowser, Rebecca	Black	Hammonds Alley	Lot $50, Imp. $25			
Boyce, Prettyman		Fleet St		Ship carpenter	Clarissa Harlow 18, $80.	
Brannon/Brannan, John Francis		Albemarle St W. side		Distiller	John Miller 22, $125. Sally 26, $80. Josephine 15, $80.	
Brister, Moses	Black	Caroline St W. side	Lot $75, Imp. $15			
Brown, Valentine		Albemarle St E. side		Tailor	Sherry 22, $125. Exter 11, $40. William 8, $40. Jess 7, $30.	Brown is tenant to Ennis.
Buck, Benjamin		Queen St S. side			Rebecca 22, $80. 2 small children, $0.	
Bunbury, Capt. M. S.		Aliceanna St N. side			Jack 13, $40. Tom 7, $30.	
Cane, Anthony		Fleet St N. side			Cassey 23, $80.	
Carroll, Acquilla		Gramby St E. side		Constable @ Hart's Tavern	Nanny 24, $80. Eliza 7, $25. Levin 5, $15.	
Cathel, Capt. Clement		Aliceanna St		Sea captain	Hester 18, $80.	Cathel is tenant to Thompson.

Free Blacks and Slave Owners in Baltimore City Tax Assessor's Ledger, 1813 Ward 7

NAME	RACE/STATUS	RESIDENCE	REAL PROPERTY	OCCUPATION	ENSLAVED PROPERTY Name, Age, Value	COMMENTS
Caton, Richard		Duke St S. side			3 males $125 each. 1 male $40. 3 females $80 each. 1 female $40. 1 female $20.	
Chapman, Christopher		Market St W. side			Harry 14, $125. Ann 25, $80.	
Chater, Capt. James		Market St E. side			Bet 15, $80.	
Clark, John L.		Gramby St E. side		Sea captain	Celia 50, $40. Tom 6, $20.	Clark is tenant to McConkey.
Clery, Madame		Albemarle St E. side			Jean Baptiste 28, $125. Misirie 22, $125. Chire 8, August 2 & Henrie 2. Felix 19, $80. Kezi 26, $80. Emitie 19, $80. Acinthe 20, $80. Virginie 6 & Eliza 5.	Clery is tenant to Hanan. Chire, August & Henrie together worth $40. Virginie & Eliza together worth $25.
Coates, William	Black	Pet Alley W. side	Lot $45, Imp. $25			
Collins, Benjamin		Little York St S. side		Sail maker	Dolly 14, $80	
Colvin, Miss Rachel		Great York St S. side			Jefferson 6, $25. Eliza 15, $80. Ann 13, $40.	
Comegys, Jesse		Gramby St W. side		Baker	Richard 22, $125. Jude 14, $80.	Comegys is tenant to I.T. Ford
Connoway, Darcus		Bond St			Lucy 13, $40.	
Conway, Robert		Bond St. E. side			Maria $15. Tom $5.	
Cook, Robert		Little York St S. side		Captain	Ruth 14, $80. Nance 10, $50.	

Free Blacks and Slave Owners in Baltimore City Tax Assessor's Ledger, 1813 Ward 7

NAME	RACE/ STATUS	RESIDENCE	REAL PROPERTY	OCCUPATION	ENSLAVED PROPERTY Name, Age, Value	COMMENTS
Corner, James		Market St W. side		Sail maker	Moses 20, $125. Risden 15, $125. Ennalls 10, $40. Rebecca 32, $80. Louisa 4, $10.	
Coulter, Dr. John		King George St N. side		Physician	Cyrus 46, $100. Rache 50, $30.	Coulter is tenant to Van Bibber.
Coward, Capt. Thomas, Jr.		Aliceanna St N. side		Sea captain	Hetty 23, $80.	
Craig, Capt. James		Great York St S. side			Anna 25, $80. 2 children of no value	
Craig, Henry		Queen St S. side			Leah 15, $80.	
Dalrymple, John		Albemarle St W. side			Mary 33, $80.	
Dalrymple, William		Harris Creek			Ned 31, $125. Somerset 30, $125. David 25, $125. Delphid 24, $125. Ben 24, $125. Anna 15, $80.	
Davis, Henry		Bond E. side			Cato 17, $125.	Davis is son-in-law to William Smith.
Davis, Peter		Wilks & Wolfe St			George 7, $30. Fan 26, $80.	
Deshon, Christopher		Gramby St E. side		Merchant	Priscilla 12, $33.	
Dewees, Andrew		Queen St S. side		Merchant	Molly 30, $80.	Dewees is tenant to Herron.
Doda, Julian		King George St S. side			Moffee 40, $60. Sophi 40, $60.	
Dorry, Dr. Henry		Market St W. side		Druggist	Rachel 18, $80.	Dorry is tenant to Mrs. Wheeler.
Dunkin, Peregrine		Aliceanna St N. side		Sea captain	Rhoda 16, $80. Rose 15, $80.	
Dyer, William B.		Aliceanna St N. side			Ebbin 25, $125.	
Ennis, Joshua		Market St W. side			Cato 20, $125. Phill 18, $125.	

Free Blacks and Slave Owners in Baltimore City Tax Assessor's Ledger, 1813 Ward 7

NAME	RACE/ STATUS	RESIDENCE	REAL PROPERTY	OCCUPATION	ENSLAVED PROPERTY Name, Age, Value	COMMENTS
Ensor, Luke & William		Exeter St		Brickmaker	Nat 20, $125. Brister 15, $125. Sam 18, $125. Sarah 17, $80.	
Fennell, Caleb		Strawberry Alley		Grocer	Grace 10, $40.	
Fitch, William of H.		Philpot St S. side			Lucy 7, $30.	Fitch is tenant to Bouldin.
Ford, Joseph T.		Queen St		Wheelwright	Bill 6, $20. William 10, $40. Rosina 14, $80.	William property of William A. Shaw
Fowler, Col. Benjamin		Dulany St S. side			Unnamed female slave 13, $40.	
Franciscus, John		Albemarle St W. side		Sugar refiner	Kitty 14, $80.	
Frazier Capt. James		Fleet St N. side		Sea captain	Mary 40, $50.	
Fry, Elizabeth	Widow	Ann St E. side			Milley 30, $80. Rachel 35, $80. Mary 12, $40. Beck 12, $40.	
Galloway, James		Albemarle St E. side			Delia 18, $80.	Galloway is tenant to Hanan.
Gavot/Gavet, Capt. John		Wolfe St E. side		Sea captain	Peggy 18, $80.	Gavot is tenant to Capt. Thomson.
Gemmell, Capt. David Heirs of		Fleet St N. side			Jane 25, $80.	
Gibson, Capt. James		Ann St E. side		Sea captain	Sam 15, $125. John 5, $15. Grace 45, $40. Ann 22, $80.	
Giles, James	Black	Gough St N. side	Lot $100, Imp. $25, Furniture $5			
Gist, Job		Bond St W. side		Methodist local preacher	Maria 9, $40.	

Free Blacks and Slave Owners in Baltimore City Tax Assessor's Ledger, 1813 Ward 7

NAME	RACE/ STATUS	RESIDENCE	REAL PROPERTY	OCCUPATION	ENSLAVED PROPERTY Name, Age, Value	COMMENTS
Glendy, Rev. John		Great York St S. side		Pastor of 2nd Presbyterian Church	Hester 20, $80.	
Glenn, James		Gramby St E. side		Saddler	Minta no age, $80.	Glenn is tenant to McConkey.
Goldthwait, Mrs.		Albemarle St E. side			Darcus 23, $80. Child $20.	Goldthwait is tenant to Reell.
Graham, Dr. William T.		Dulany St S. side			Montania, 16 $125.	
Graham, Hamilton		Albemarle St W. side		1st Clerk @ the Bank of Maryland	Ann 18, $80. Nathan 4, $15.	Graham is tenant to Stirling.
Graves, Robert		Bond St E. side		Carpenter	Maria 9, $40.	
Gray, Lynch		Bond St E. side			Lydia 33, $80. Lyd 15, $80. Betty 10, $40.	
Gregg, John		King George St N. side		Grocer	Jane 36, $60. Hetty 14, $80.	Gregg is tenant to heirs of McElderry.
Griggs, James		Exeter St W. side		Pilot	Abraham 14, $125. Joe 12, $40. Isaac 9, $40. Ellen 18, $80. Eliza 16, $80.	
Guestier, Peter A.		King George St S. side		Merchant	George 25, $125. Ursell 30, $80. Reine 30, $80. Thisbe $80.	
Haley, Mrs. Mary		Albemarle St W. side			Bridget 18, $80. Tom 8, $0.	Tom is blind.
Hall, Capt. John		Market St E. side		Sea captain	Violet 35, $80.	Hall is tenant to Roche.
Hall, George		Market St E. side		Measurer of lumber	Daniel 50, $78. Bet 15, $80.	
Hanan, John		Gramby St W. side		Carpenter	Bett 15, $80. Louisa 6, $20.	
Hanna, Alexander B.		Great York St S. side		Cordwainer	Milcah 25, $80. Caroline 12, $40. George 4, $10.	

Free Blacks and Slave Owners in Baltimore City Tax Assessor's Ledger, 1813 Ward 7

NAME	RACE/ STATUS	RESIDENCE	REAL PROPERTY	OCCUPATION	ENSLAVED PROPERTY Name, Age, Value	COMMENTS
Hardester, Benjamin		Queen St N. side			Berry Brooks 7, $30. Lloyd 4, $10. Unnamed female 40, $50.	
Hargrove, Rev. John		Great York St S. side		Pastor, of the New Jerusalem Church & Register, of the City of Baltimore	Unnamed slave 12, $40.	
Harris, Samuel		Duke St N. side		Merchant	Dolly 30, $80.	Harris is tenant to P. Durkee. Dolly property of Mrs. Rogers.
Hart, Capt. Robert		Gough St		Sea captain	Alexander Timothy 20, $125. Alice 30, no value.	Hart is tenant to F. Shaffer. Alice is decrepit.
Hart, Joseph		Still House St		Innkeeper	Maria 35, $80. Moses 25, $125.	Hart is tenant to Philpot. Moses owned by Joseph Hart, Sr. of Balto. Co.
Hays, Martha		Little York St S. side			Eliza 12, $40. Bill $15.	Hays is tenant to Owen Allen.
Hays, Walter C.		Gramby St E. side			Martin 12, $40.	
Heddricks/Hedrick, Thomas		Queen St S. side		Sail maker	Kitty 12, $40	
Herring, Ludwig		Queen St S. side		Lumber merchant	Minta 15, $80.	
Hill, George, Jr.		Smith St N. side		Clerk	Rachel 20, $80.	
Hodgkin, Mrs. Susanna	Widow	Granby St E. side			Elijah 16 yrs. old or upwards, $125. Old Lavinia 65, $0. Young Lavinia 15, $50.	Young Lavinia is defective in sight.
Holbrook, Capt. Joseph		Great York St S. side		Sea captain	Peggy 30, $60.	Peggy unsound.

Free Blacks and Slave Owners in Baltimore City Tax Assessor's Ledger, 1813 Ward 7

NAME	RACE/ STATUS	RESIDENCE	REAL PROPERTY	OCCUPATION	ENSLAVED PROPERTY Name, Age, Value	COMMENTS
Hooper, William	Black	Bond St W. side	Lot $50, Imp. $10			
Huberts, Dr.		Albemarle St W. side			Augou 30, $125. Aslep 30, $125. Augustine 30, $80. Zelia 3, $5. Montoueh $25.	Hubert is tenant to #18 Albemarle St.
Hughes, Jonas	Black	Woolf St W. side	Lot $35, Imp. $15, Furn $5, Horse $10, Cart $10			
Ingles, Silas		Caroline St W. side		Boat builder	Dennard 12, $40.	
Isaacke, Elizabeth		Wolfe St E. side			Allen 40, $125. Ben 18, $125. Dick 18, $125. Little Dick 18, $125. Maria 9, $40. Jane 20, $80.	Jane hired with Mrs. Norris.
Jacobs, Capt. Wm.		Granby St E. side			Hagar 18, $80.	
James, James W.		King George St N. side		Baker	Bill 9, $40.	
Jamison, Caecilius		Albemarle St E. side			Carlton 27, $125.	Jamison is son of Mrs. G.
Jenkins, Mrs. Sarah	Widow	Wilks St			Lewis 22, $125. Anthony 18, $125. Basil 12, $40. Jack 12, $40. Bill 10, $40. Alexander 5, $15. Margaret 50, $30. Milley 45, $40. Caroline 14, $80. Harriet 14, $80. Catherine 11, $40. Airy 10, $40. Matilda 8, $40.	Jenkins is tenant to White.
Johnson, David	Black	Salsbury St	Lot $100, Imp. $25, Old horse $7.50, old dray $7.50	Carter		

Free Blacks and Slave Owners in Baltimore City Tax Assessor's Ledger, 1813 Ward 7

NAME	RACE/ STATUS	RESIDENCE	REAL PROPERTY	OCCUPATION	ENSLAVED PROPERTY Name, Age, Value	COMMENTS
Johnson, Edward (Esq.)		King George St. S. side		Mayor of the city	Ben 35, $125. Tom 35, $125. David 18, $125. Harry 16, $125. Beck 45, $40. Sarah 50, $30. Teresa 20, $80. Priscilla 20, $80.	
Kemp, Thomas		Fountain St		Ship carpenter	Robert 25, $125. Jim 1, $125. Tom 10, $40. Dick 5, $15. Mary 35, $80. Poll 35, $80. Molly 17, $80.	
Killburn, Capt. Russell		Ann St W. side			Tilley 10, $40.	
King, James	Black	Fleet St. S. side	Lot $100, Imp. $50, Furniture $5			
Leeke, Nicholas		Ann St S. side		Scrivener	Eliza 11, $40.	
LeLoup, Monsier Louis F.		King Geoge St N. side		Vice counsel pro temp from France	Douzie 30, $125. Lornette 25, $80.	
Leone, Jasper/Gasper		Fleet St N. side		Grocer	Betty 23, $80.	Leone is tenant to Delaporte.
Loncy, Phoebe	Black	Hammonds Alley	Lot $60, Imp. $25			
Lovell, William Jr.		King George St S. side		Baker	Eliza 10, $40. Charlotte 7, $30.	Lovell is tenant to Smith heirs.
Lytle, Mr.		Dulany St S. side			George 11, $40.	Lytle is tenant to King.
Manning, Capt. Thomas		Ann St W. side			John 6, $20. Martha 12, $40.	Manning died before 1814. Widow is Sarah.
Marshall, Thomas		Gough St			Hanna 22, $80. Darcas 5, $10.	Marshall is tenant to Machan.

Free Blacks and Slave Owners in Baltimore City Tax Assessor's Ledger, 1813 Ward 7

NAME	RACE/ STATUS	RESIDENCE	REAL PROPERTY	OCCUPATION	ENSLAVED PROPERTY Name, Age, Value	COMMENTS
Maxwell, Elizabeth	Widow.	King George St S. side			Peter, $85. Nathan 7, $40. Cassandra 7, $25. Jane $80. John 6, $20.	Peter hired @ farm of E. Johnson. Maxwell is tenant to Dalrymple.
McCombs, Solomon		Aliceanna St N. side		Sea captain	Sall 14, $80.	
McConkey, William		Gramby St E. side			Fanny 30, $80.	
McConnell, Thomas		Market St E. side			Letitia 20, $80. Betty 13, $40.	
McDonald, Col. William		Queen St		Merchant	George 30, $125. Milley 30, $80. Ruth 5, $15.	
McFadon, John		King George St N. side			Lamas $60. Fanny $80.	McFadon is tenant to H. Wilson.
McGill, William		Albemarle St W. side			Rachel 14, $80.	McGill is tenant to Rosk heirs.
McGwinn, William		President St			Lucy 13, $40. Issaler 9, $40. Maria 6, $15.	
McKinzie, Dr. Colin		Albemarle St W. side			Charles 13, $40.	
Merriott, Mary D.		Duke St N. side			John 25, $125. John 10, $40. Eliza 7, $25.	
Messick/Mezick, Capt. Joshua		Aliceanna St N. side		Sea captain	Jem 8, $40. John 6, $20.	
Mince, Joseph		Fleet St			Lucy 23, $80.	
Mitchell, Richard		Duke St S. side			Eliza 12, $40. Ann 6, $20.	
Moore, Philip (Esq.)		Market St W. side		Pres. of the Franklin Bank & Clerk of the U.S. District Court	Phil 12, $40. Fanny 45, $40.	

Free Blacks and Slave Owners in Baltimore City Tax Assessor's Ledger, 1813 Ward 7

NAME	RACE/STATUS	RESIDENCE	REAL PROPERTY	OCCUPATION	ENSLAVED PROPERTY Name, Age, Value	COMMENTS
Mousinier, Madame		Albemarle St E. side			Pauline 14, $80. Gertrude 45, $20.	Gertrude of little value. Mousinier is tenant to Cunningham.
Muller, John C.		Plowman St S. side			Unnamed female 14, $80.	
Muskett, John		Caroline St W. side			Fanny 15, $80.	
Ockerman, George	Black	Bank St S. side	Lot $40, Imp. An old frame, no value			
Page, Fanny	Black	Caroline St W. side	Lot $40, Imp. $20, Furn. $5			
Parks, William		Gough St			Kezia 12, $40.	
Patterson, William and Robert		Rogers' Addition			Ned 50, $60. Peter 46, $75. Jerry 35, $125. Little Peter 28, $125. Scott 27, $125. Anthony 27, $125. Charles 30, $125. Big Bob 25, $125. Levin 25, $125. David 24, $125. Arthur 24, $125. Josias 23, $125. Big Tom 22, $125. Little Tom 22, $125. Jacob 20, $125. Mat 20, $125. Dick 20 $125. Little Bob 20, $125. Essex 18, $125. Cato 18, $125. Charles 18, $125. Christopher 18, $125. Prince 4 & George 2, $15. Cate 24, $80. Hannah 25, $80.	

Free Blacks and Slave Owners in Baltimore City Tax Assessor's Ledger, 1813 Ward 7

NAME	RACE/ STATUS	RESIDENCE	REAL PROPERTY	OCCUPATION	ENSLAVED PROPERTY Name, Age, Value	COMMENTS
Pechin, William		Great York St S. side			Sam 5, $15. Jess 18, $125. Grace 25, $80. Henny 20. $80. Grace 4, $10.	
Peck, Francis	Black	Caroline St E. side	Lot $120, Imp. $40, Furn. $15, 2 horses $30, 2 carts $20			
Penrise/Penrice, Capt. Thomas		Wolfe St E. side		Sea captain	Lucey 30, $80.	
Peterbottom, John		Great York St S. side			Sophia 10, $40.	Sophia property of William Hosier of Eastern Shore. Peterbottom is tenant to M. McFadon.
Peterkin, Capt. William		Market St W. side		Sea captain	Rose 12, $40.	
Philips, Perry	Black	Caroline St W. side	Lot $40, Imp. $20, Furn. $5			
Phillips, Capt. James		Granby St E. side			Ester 44, $45.	Phillips is tenant to Swann.
Pitt, William		Aliceanna St N. side		Grocer	Jem 33, $125. Nancy 33, $80. Lucrutie 7, $25.	
Prout, James	Black	Bond St W. side	Lot $50, Imp. $30			
Ramsey, Joseph		Aliceanna St N. side		Blacksmith	Sam 25, $125. Lydia 30, $80.	

Free Blacks and Slave Owners in Baltimore City Tax Assessor's Ledger, 1813 Ward 7

NAME	RACE/ STATUS	RESIDENCE	REAL PROPERTY	OCCUPATION	ENSLAVED PROPERTY Name, Age, Value	COMMENTS
Raven, Thomas		Fleet St N. side		Ship joiner	Joshua 38, $125. Toney 30, $125. Dan 25, $125. Esther 40, $50. Diana 24, $80. Hetty 15, $80. Till 4, $15.	Raven is tenant to Burgoine.
Reddy, Samuel		Queen St S. side			Fanny 11, $40.	Fanny hired to B.Buck. Reddy is son of John of Patapsco lower.
Ringgold, Dr. Jacob	.	King George St north side			Jem 12, $40. Charles 10, $40. Henry 5, $15. Araminta 41, $50. Sue 29, $80. Fransess 26, $80. Ruth 22, $80. Maria 12, $40. Sarah 12, $40. Araminta 5, $15.	Ringgold is tenant to J. Stevenson on Granby St. Charles at Benjamin Edd's. Fransess at Wm. Ford's. Ruth at W. Davidson on Sharp St. Maria at W. Herbert's.
Robinson, Charles		King George St S. side			Austin 40, $125. Peter 30, $125. Gideon 10, $40. Robin 6, $20. Lydia 17, $80. Nancy 16, $80.	
Robinson, Joseph		Strawberry Alley			Male slave 10, $40.	
Robinson, Mrs. Deborah	Relict of Capt. William Robinson	Albemarle St W. side			Maria 22, $80.	
Robinson, William		Granby St W. side		Merchant @ Market Space	Tamer 45, $40.	

Free Blacks and Slave Owners in Baltimore City Tax Assessor's Ledger, 1813 Ward 7

NAME	RACE/ STATUS	RESIDENCE	REAL PROPERTY	OCCUPATION	ENSLAVED PROPERTY Name, Age, Value	COMMENTS
Rodrigues, Lewis		Bond & Wilks St			Catherine 35, $80.	Rodrigues is tenant to Joseph Biays.
Rowles, Rezin		King George St S. side		Custom house officer	Matilda 7, $25.	Rowles is tenant to C. Robinson.
Sexton, Charles		Wilks St S. side			George 4, $15. Ann $5.	
Sharp, James	Black	Bond St W. side	Lot $50, Imp. $50, Furn $10			
Shaw, John		Gough St		Brick layer	Tom 40, $125. Jack 10, $40.	
Shears, Joseph		Ann St E. side			Vachel 10, $40.	
Smith, George		Great York St		Carver & Gilder	Maria 30, $80. Mary 14, $80. Airy 7, $30.	
Smith, John	Black	Strawberry Alley E. side	Lot $25, Imp. $25			
Smith, Mrs. Mary	Relict of Thorowgood	Granby St E. side			Neilson 30, $80. Keziah 6, $5. Flora 45, $30. Milley 26, $80	
Smith, Richard		Fountain St		Copper refiner	John 40, $125	
Smith, William		Bond St E. side		Rope maker	Eve 60. Patty 22, $80.	
Sorenson, Catherine		Fleet St N. side			Male slave 5, $15. Nice 24, $80.	
Spear, Capt. William		Market St E. side			William $40. Mary $80.	
Stansbury, Charles		Exeter St W. side			Letty 20, $80.	
Stephens/Stevens, Capt. Richard		Bond St W. side		Sea captain	Rebecca 24, $80. Ann 3, no value.	
Sterling, Achsah		Bond St W. side			Bill 7, $30. Nell 60, $10. Grace 12, $40.	Sterling is next to Bevard's.

Free Blacks and Slave Owners in Baltimore City Tax Assessor's Ledger, 1813 Ward 7

NAME	RACE/ STATUS	RESIDENCE	REAL PROPERTY	OCCUPATION	ENSLAVED PROPERTY Name, Age, Value	COMMENTS
Steuart, Major William		Granby St E. side		Stone cutter	Jack 30, $125. Joseph 17, $125. Diana 25, $80. Hannah 20, $80. Priscilla 15, $80. Cassandra 6, $20.	
Steuart, Robert (Esq.)		Duke St N. side			Penny 46, $40.	
Stevenson, Capt. William (Heirs of)		Ann St W. side			Milley 30, $80.	
Stiles, Capt. George		King George St S. side		Merchant	Edward 33, $125. John 20, $125. Jane 40, $50. Ann 25, $80. Bet 8, $40.	
Stoddard, Capt. Seth		Gramby St W. side		Sea captain	Roxbury 13, $40.	
Sumwalt, Philip		Dulany St S. side			Jim 19, $125. Noah 21, $125.	
Taylor, Robert		Granby St E. side		Cooper	Samuel Chase 30, $125. John Chase 28, $125.	Taylor is tenant to Boehme.
Thomas, Barton		Ann St E. side		Pilot	Tab 15, $80.	
Thomas, Richard	Black	Eden St E. side	Lot $50, Imp. $20			
Thompson, Edward	Black	Caroline St W. side	Lot $50, Imp. $10, horse $8, cart $7			
Tinges, Charles		Great York St		Watch maker	Sall 18, $80.	
Towson, Madame Amie		King George St S. side			Harriott $80.	Towson is tenant to Smith's heirs.
Vickers, Capt. Joel		Granby St W. side		Merchant	Beck 12, $40. Jude 20, $80.	Vickers is tenant to Swann.
Walsh, Jacob Jr.		Albemarle St W. side			Isaac 46, $80. Martha 45, $30. Margaret 40, $20.	Walsh is tenant to Dalrymple. Martha crippled in hand. Margaret sickly, little use.

Free Blacks and Slave Owners in Baltimore City Tax Assessor's Ledger, 1813 Ward 7

NAME	RACE/ STATUS	RESIDENCE	REAL PROPERTY	OCCUPATION	ENSLAVED PROPERTY Name, Age, Value	COMMENTS
Waltham, Thomas		Wilkes St S. side		Waterman	Peter 45, $125. Ben 39, $125. Pollidore 21, $100. Leander 10, $40. Richard 8, $40. Blanche 40, $80. 2 children $15.	Waltham is tenant to Jimmet. Pollidore is crippled.
Ward, William		Apple Alley E. side		Sail maker	Elenor 50, $25. Betsy 38, $55.	
Warrell, Thomas		Aliceanna St N. side			Richard 37, $125. Simon 26, $125. Nero 24, $125. Mike 21, $125. Ceaser 19, $125. Hannah 28, $80. Patty 26, $80. Charity 8, $40. Basil 6, $20.	
Waters, Darcus	Black	Hammonds Alley	Lot $60, Imp. $25			
Waters, Sarah		Albemarle St W. side			Moses 33, $125. Emory 22, $125. Priscilla 10, $40. Charlott 16, $80.	Waters is tenant to Dalrymple.
Weeks, Capt. Benjamin		King George St N. side		Sea captain	Fanny 35, $80. Nancy 20, $80. Louisa 4, $15.	
Weems, Capt. Charles		Wilks St S. side		Sea captain	Fanny $80.	
Weems, Dr. William		Gramby St W. side			Hester no age, $40.	Weems is tenant to Ennis.
West, Capt. William		Queen St S. side			Rachel Mills 15, $80.	
West, William		Little York St S. side		Blockmaker	Susan $80.	
White, Capt. Thomas		Fleet St N. side		Sea captain	Frank 25, $125. George 8, $40. Hester $80. Littleton 7, $28.	
White, William		King George St S. side		Wheelwright	James 14, $125.	White is tenant to Bryden.

Free Blacks and Slave Owners in Baltimore City Tax Assessor's Ledger, 1813 Ward 7

NAME	RACE/ STATUS	RESIDENCE	REAL PROPERTY	OCCUPATION	ENSLAVED PROPERTY Name, Age, Value	COMMENTS
Wickham, Capt. Peter		Great York St S. side			Sarah 35, $80.	
Williams, Ezekiel	Black	Caroline St E. side	Lot $100, Imp, $30, Furn. $10			
Williams, Martha		Bond St E. side			Jack 14, $125. Nancy 30, $80.	Williams is tenant to Capt. Dye.
Willis, Joshua		Market St E. side		Ship carpenter	Job 25, $125. Joe 25, $125. Aaron 24, $125. London 18, $125. Tom 14, $125. Jane 18, $80. Minta 13, $40.	
Winchester, Jacob		Albemarle St E. side		Carpenter	Harriot 13, $40.	
Yates, Major Thomas		Albemarle St E. side		Merchant	Neilson 12, $40. Hetty 30, $80.	Neilson property of Mrs. Fisher.
Young, Capt. William		Bond St W. side		Mariner	Sall 13, $40.	
Zane, Peter		Prince St		Cooper	Ells 13, $40.	Zane is tenant to Graham.

Free Blacks and Slave Owners in Baltimore City Tax Assessor's Ledger, 1813 Ward 8

NAME	RACE/ STATUS	RESIDENCE	REAL PROPERTY	OCCUPATION	ENSLAVED PROPERTY Name, Age, Value	COMMENTS
Allender, Dr. Joseph		Fells St S. side		Physician	Isaac 30, $125. Phil 6, $20. Frank 14, $125. Charlotte 40, $50. Sarah 16, $80. Louisa 3, $5.	
Atkinson, Isaac		Aliceanna St S. side		Carpenter	Amie 14, $80.	
Barnes, Capt. James		Ann St W. side		Sea captain	Perry 16, $125.	Barnes is tenant to Kierstead.
Barnes, William T.		Fells St S. side		Sea captain	Lemmon 40, $40. Harry. Joe 4, $15.	Barnes is tenant to Osborne. Lemmon is female. Harry has lost an arm.
Belt, James		Pitt St SW side		Ship chandler	Bob 26, $125. Judy 40, $50.	
Bennett, Fielding/Fielder		Ann St W. side		Pilot	Barsheba 17, $80.	Bennet is tenant to Mrs. Challie.
Biays, Col. Joseph		Fells St S. side		Merchant	Edmond 9, $40. Jack 30, $125. Fanny 35, $80. Caroline 15, $80. Eliza 9, $40. Henny 12, $40.	
Biays, James Col.		Thames St S. side		Merchant	Elisha 60, $5. Simon 50, $40. Richard 50, $40. Harry Smith 48, $50. Charles 35, $125. Stephen 25, $125. Bill 25, $125. John Lubey 30, $125. Frank 30, $125. Ned 30, $125. Jacob 35, $125. Nathan 10, $40. Jane 38, $60. Ellen 25, $80. Alice 16, $80. Keziah 16, $80. Kate 12, $40.	

Free Blacks and Slave Owners in Baltimore City Tax Assessor's Ledger, 1813 Ward 8

NAME	RACE/ STATUS	RESIDENCE	REAL PROPERTY	OCCUPATION	ENSLAVED PROPERTY Name, Age, Value	COMMENTS
Bond, Margaret		Fleet St N. side			Jane 16, $80.	
Bouthier, Peter Francis		Lancaster St			Abelard 12, $40. Virginia 18, $80.	Bouthier is tenant to Feinour.
Burke, David		Corner of Philpot & Thames St		Boat builder	Caleb 35, $120. Mary 26, $80. Maria 10, $40. Harry 7, $30.	
Caduc, Raymond		Fells St N. side			Tom 7, $30. Rosie 39, $60.	Caduc is tenant to Mrs. O'Conner.
Carr, John		Aliceanna St S. side		Ship carpenter	Milley 25, $80.	
Challie, Susanna		Ann St W. side			Ann, $80 & infant	
Chalmers, Capt. Timothy		Queen St N. side			Fanny 30, $80.	
Chase, Thorndick		Thames St S. side		Merchant	John Gill 23, $125. Hannah 35, $80.	
Clendennin, Dr. William H.		Ann St E. side		Physician	Charity 20, $80.	
Cloney, James		Bond St W. side		Grocer	Priscilla 16, $80. Louisa 9, $40.	
Cock, Matthew T.		Ann St E. side			James 21, $125. Rachel 23, $80.	
Cockrill, Thomas		Philpot St S. side		Ships-smith	Robert 30, $125.	
Cordery, James		Philpot St S. side		Ships captain	Female slave 18, $80.	
Cowchois, John		George St S. side			Frank 18, $125. Ante 18, $80.	Cowchois is tenant to Major T.
Crow, Sarah	Widow	Bond St W. side			Polydore 10, $40. Ruth 30, $80. Patty 7, $25.	
Cunningham, Capt. John		Queen St N. side		Sea captain	Ned 12, $40. Letty 30, $80.	
Curtain, Mrs. Mary	Widow	Market St E. side			Charles 60, $20. Davey 20, $125.	
Curtis, Capt. James		Happy Alley		Sea captain	Hannah 35, $80. Ann 9, $40.	

Free Blacks and Slave Owners in Baltimore City Tax Assessor's Ledger, 1813 Ward 8

NAME	RACE/ STATUS	RESIDENCE	REAL PROPERTY	OCCUPATION	ENSLAVED PROPERTY Name, Age, Value	COMMENTS
Dashiell, Capt. Henry		Market St W. side			Robert 25, $125. Julia 18, $80.	
Davey, Capt. Hugh		Pitt St NE side		Sea captain	Sophia 19, $80.	
Davidson, Capt. William		Fleet St. S. side			Horace 12, $40. Henney 36, $80.	Horace @ Capt. T. Gardner's. Henney @ Mrs. Crockett's.
Davis, Joseph		Queen St. N. side			Phoebe 40, $50.	
Deal, Hannah		Market Space E. side		Innkeeper	James 12, $40. Jenny 50, $25.	
Despeaux, Joseph		Philpot St S. side		Ship carpenter	Assour 40, $125. Jerry 23, $125. John Louis 18, $125. Joe 23, $125. Chuffee 7, $25. Lafleur 6, $20. Reddia 30, $80. Maria 25, $80. Malloere 8, $40.	
Dickinson, Mrs. Catherine	Widow	Philpot St N. side			Charles 25, $125. Esther 44, $50. Violet 20, $80. George 7, $30.	
Doxey, Joseph		Corner of Philpot & Thames St		Boarding house	Female slave 19, $80.	Doxey is tenant to D. Burke.
Galt, Peter (Esq.)		Fells St S. side		Justice of the peace	Celia 30, $80. Polly 13, $60.	
Grosh, Capt. John		Pitt St SW side		Sea captain	Delia 20, $80.	Grosh is tenant to Price. Delia property of Mr. Willis, Eastern Shore.
Gunby, Stephen		Philpot St S. side		Ship carpenter	Phil 60, $5. Jem 25, $125. Sarah 22, $80.	Gunby is tenant to Weston.
Hagthrope, Edward		Bond St W. side		Cordwainer	Leah 15, $80.	
Harrison, Thomas (Heirs of)		Bond St W. side			John 12, $40.	

Free Blacks and Slave Owners in Baltimore City Tax Assessor's Ledger, 1813 Ward 8

NAME	RACE/ STATUS	RESIDENCE	REAL PROPERTY	OCCUPATION	ENSLAVED PROPERTY Name, Age, Value	COMMENTS
Henderson, Robert		Pitt St SW side			Female 8, $40.	Henderson is tenant to Price.
Howe, Mrs. Margaret		Queen St N side			Female slave 27, $80.	
Inloes, Joshua (Heirs of)		Bond St W side			Nicholas 6, $20. Rachel 25, $80.	
Jackson, William		Thames St S. side		Block & pump maker	Stepney 50, $60. Dennis 20, $125. Abraham, 12 $40. Two small children, ages 2 & 1, no value. Chloe 45, $40. Susan 22, $80.	
Jacobs, Mrs. Jane		Bond St W. side			London 46, $100.	
James, William		Bond St E. side			David 16, $125.	
Jenney, Rebecca	Widow	Aliceanna St S side			Matilda $80.	
Jones, Capt. Levin		Aliceanna St S side		Sea captain	Bet 14, $80. Phebe 16, $80.	
Kerr, Capt. Archibald		Fells St S side			Robert 50, $40. Lydia 25, $80. Ellen 4, $10. Angelina 12, $40. Grace 12, $40.	Angelina belongs to the estate of Capt. Gemmell.
Kierstead, Luke		Ann St W side		Sail maker	Male slave 40, $125. Molly 30, $80. Three children ages 7, 4 & 2, $30.	
Lawrence, Richard		Aliceanna St S. side		Blacksmith	Elisha 40, $125. Esther 20, $80.	
Lewis, Mrs.		Pitt St NE side			Sam 12, $40.	Lewis is tenant to McKubbin.
Louderman, Frederick (Heirs of)		Bond St W side			Jonas 14, $125. Old Rachel 55, $20. Young Rachel 15, $80.	

Free Blacks and Slave Owners in Baltimore City Tax Assessor's Ledger, 1813 Ward 8

NAME	RACE/ STATUS	RESIDENCE	REAL PROPERTY	OCCUPATION	ENSLAVED PROPERTY Name, Age, Value	COMMENTS
Lourens, Robert		Happy Alley			Hannah 20, $80.	
McGaughan, David		George St N side			Esther 25, $80.	
McNeal, Capt. Daniel		George St N side			Henry Howard 30, $125. Mat 12, $40. Fanny 28, $80. Matilda 3, $80.	
Messick, Baptist		George St W side		Sea captain	Peter 21, $125. Muscal 21, $80.	Muscal is female.
Millard, Joseph Lee		Argyle Alley			George 28, $125. Diana 20, $80.	
Morris, Thomas		Pitt St NE side		Ship joiner	Henny 12, $40.	
Morton, Capt. Robert		Philpot St N side			Anna 25, $80.	
Paduzi/Peduzi, Peter		Market St W side		Grocer	Betsy 33, $80. Alice 17, $80.	
Pamphillion, Thomas		Fells St S side		Marine coffee house	Jack 20, $125. Ben 10, $40. Sall 30, $80. Syka 35, $80. Diana 6 & Lid 2, $25.	
Peirce, John		Market St W side		Innkeeper & Formerly constable	Perry 14, $125.	
Prendiville, Ann	Widow	Fleet St N side			Harry 21, $125. Sophia 18, $80.	
Price, John		Ann St E side			Ned 34, $125. Jesse 34, $125. Joe 24, $125. Clayton 30, $125. Lloyd 16, $125. Ben 25, $125. Levi 14, $125. Isaac 12, $40. Polly 36, $60. Milly 20, $80. Peggy 8, $40. 3 small children $15.	

Free Blacks and Slave Owners in Baltimore City Tax Assessor's Ledger, 1813 Ward 8

NAME	RACE/ STATUS	RESIDENCE	REAL PROPERTY	OCCUPATION	ENSLAVED PROPERTY Name, Age, Value	COMMENTS
Price, William		Pitt St SW side		Ship carpenter. Builder of clipper ships.	Fisher 65, $10. Bill 50, $40. Charles 49, $50. B. Watkins 35, $35. Tom Martin 45, $120. Lloyd 28, $125. Prince 25, $125. Minzo 55, $25. Harry 15, $125. Dan 8, $40. Andrew 2, $5. Betty 50, $20. Bett 40, $40. Harriett 30, $80. Charlotte 25, $80. Henny 11, $40.	
Printz/Prints, Casper		George St N side		Hatter	George 8, $40.	
Ramsey, James		Fleet St S side			Solomon 15, $125. John 7, $30. Rachel 28, $80. Sarah 28, $80.	
Ring, Capt. Thomas		Queen St N side		Sea captain	Female slave, $40.	
Sheppard, Thomas		Fells St S side		Tailor	Jesse 42, $125. Hamilton 17, $125. Hannah 35, $80. Bett 11, $40.	
Smith, John		Fells St S side		Blacksmith	Isaac 25, $125. Emory 27, $125. Silvia 20, $80.	Isaac to serve one year. Emory to serve ten months.
Snyder, Capt. John		Fells St S side		Ship chandler	Lucretia 46, $40.	
Stafford, Capt. Patrick		Pitt St NE side			Harriett 12, $40.	
Stansbury, Nicholas		Bond St W side			Isaac 20, $125. Harry 16, $125. Charles 15 months, no value. Lydia 25, $80 & her 9 month old child, no value. Sophia 18, $80.	

Free Blacks and Slave Owners in Baltimore City Tax Assessor's Ledger, 1813 Ward 8

NAME	RACE/ STATUS	RESIDENCE	REAL PROPERTY	OCCUPATION	ENSLAVED PROPERTY Name, Age, Value	COMMENTS
Steel, Capt. John, (Heirs of)		Pitt St NE side			Davey 40, $125. Jack 60, $20. London 30, $125. Richard 30, $125. Cesar 29, $125. Perry 26, $125. Isaac 26, $125. Jacob 9, $40. Susanna 16, $80.	Jacob property of Mrs. Sterett.
Steward, Mrs. Ann		Fells St S. side			Nelly $50.	Nelly is infirm.
Stockett, Barbara	Widow	Bond St W side			Harriett 8, $40.	
Sunderland, Elizabeth		Philpot St N side			John 19, $125.	
Tenant, Thomas		George St W side		Merchant	Vincent 5, $60. Cesar 30, $125. Henry 22, $125. George 12, $40. Hester 18, $80. Sylvia 50, $40.	
Thompson, Capt. Alexander		Aliceanna St S side		Sea captain	Matilda $50.	Matilda is infirm.
Thompson, Capt. Nathaniel		Fleet St S side		Ship chandler	Bob 28, $125. Grace 18, $80.	
Wagner, George		Philpot St		Blockmaker	Jemima 13, $80.	Wagner is tenant to Thompson.
Waters, Hezekiah		N. E. corner of Pitt & Wolfe Sts		Merchant	Frank 46, $80. Frank 10, $40. Jane 25, $80.	Frank property of Mr. Worrell of Eastern Shore.
Weary, Peter		Pitt St NE side		Measurer of wood	Preston 23, $125. Sippy 30, $80.	
Weems, George		Philpot St N side		Sea captain	George 52, $60. Jem 30, $125. Gabriel 20, $125. Beck 28, $80.	
Wilkinson, Capt. Shubael/Shubal		Wolfe St W side		Sea captain	Charlotte 7, $25.	
Williams, John S.		Fells St S side			Henny 25, $80. Henny 5, $15. Maria 2, $5.	Williams tenant to Farrell.

Free Blacks and Slave Owners in Baltimore City Tax Assessor's Ledger, 1813 Ward 8

NAME	RACE/ STATUS	RESIDENCE	REAL PROPERTY	OCCUPATION	ENSLAVED PROPERTY Name, Age, Value	COMMENTS
Wingate, Capt. Peter		Shakespeare St S side			Ned $125. Female $80.	
Zane, Joseph		Pitt St SW side		Cooper	Phil 20, $125. Sidney 18, $80. Hannah 17, $80.	Phil property of Dr. Davis.

Free Blacks and Slave Owners in Baltimore City Tax Assessor's Ledger, 1818, Ward 1

NAME	RACE/STATUS	RESIDENCE	REAL PROPERTY	OCCUPATION	ENSLAVED PROPERTY Name, Age, Value	COMMENTS
Adams, William		Conway St			Hetty 15, $80.	
Albert, Jacob		Fayette St		Hardware merchant	Jane 15, $80.	
Allnutt, James		Sharp St		Lumber measurer	Harriot 14, $80. Sarah 7, $20.	
Armitage, Benjamin		Howard St			Sarah 24, $80. Mary 3, $10.	
Avise, Charles		Howard St		Fancy store	Jane 22, $80.	
Bailey, James		Fayette St			Rachel 19, $80.	
Bailey, Margaret		Baltimore St			Sarah 25, $80.	
Baker, George S.		Pratt St			Unnamed male 18, $125. Eliza 8, $40.	
Bareman, Joshua		Saratoga St			Nathan 3, $10. Poll 36, $80. Milly 13, $40.	
Barney, John		Baltimore St		Biscuit maker	Phil 40, $125.	
Bassett, Mrs.	Widow	Sharp St			Sall 18, $80.	
Bausman, John		Liberty St			Rosanna 12, $40.	
Beckly, Mrs.	Widow	Pratt St			Sally 25, $80.	
Beho, Moses	Colored	Howard St	Lot $100, Imp $100 on Conway St. Lot $150, Imp $300, Lot $40, Imp $75 on Homespun Alley	Drayman		Behoo per City Directory.
Benson, Peter		Wagon Alley			Susan 15, $80.	

Free Blacks and Slave Owners in Baltimore City Tax Assessor's Ledger, 1818, Ward 1

NAME	RACE/ STATUS	RESIDENCE	REAL PROPERTY	OCCUPATION	ENSLAVED PROPERTY Name, Age, Value	COMMENTS
Berry, John		Sharp St			John 37, $125. Ned 28, $125. Perry 28, $125. Ben 5, $10. Peter 38, $125. Philip 40, $125. Kitty 14, $80.	
Berry, John and Tho. L.		Sharp St			Henry 22, $125. Joe 28, $125.	
Berry, Mrs.	Widow of Benjamin	Sharp St			Jacob 21, $125. Isaac 19, $125. William 17, $125. Patty 16, $80.	
Berry, Thomas L.		Sharp St			Nelly 35, $80. Elsey 10, $40. Nance 7, $20.	
Black, Arthur	Colored	Howard St	Lot $20, Imp $20, 2 horses $40, 2 drays $20			
Blair, Mrs.	Widow	Liberty St			Kitty 10, $40.	
Bond, Ellenor	Widow	Pratt St			Jesse 23, $125.	
Bond, Thomas		Sharp St			Basil 19, $125. Dolly 19, $80. Ann 6, $20.	
Boyce, Theodore R.C		German St			Peter 25, $125. John 3, $10. Henny 25, $80. Moch(?) 18, $80. Juliana 7, $20.	
Brice, Henry		Pratt St		Flour merchant	Ned 10, $40. Milly 37, $80. Milly 18, $80.	
Brown, Amos		Howard St			John 16, $125. Mary 18, $80. Eliza 12, $40. Philia 13, $40.	
Bruff, Mrs.	Widow	Baltimore St			Keziah 12, $40.	
Burrell, Charles		Baltimore St			Frederick 20, $125.	
Campsall, Michael		Liberty St		Proprietor of livery stable	Peggy 35, $80.	

Free Blacks and Slave Owners in Baltimore City Tax Assessor's Ledger, 1818, Ward 1

NAME	RACE/ STATUS	RESIDENCE	REAL PROPERTY	OCCUPATION	ENSLAVED PROPERTY Name, Age, Value	COMMENTS
Carey, Richard	C	Brandy Alley	Lot $30, Imp $50 Lot $20, Imp $50			
Carson, Nehemiah		Sharp St			Jacob 21, $125. Charlotte 28, $80. Caroline 8, $40.	
Child, Richard	C	Conway St	Lot $50, Imp $50			
Clagett, Hezekiah		Eutaw St		Flour merchant	Perry 30, $125. Serena 26, $80. Julia 40, $40. Sally 20, $80. Mitena 8, $40.	
Claggett, Eli		Liberty St		Brewery	Milly 14, $40. Eliza 20, $80. Harriot 16, $80.	
Cohen, Jab. J.		Baltimore St			Sam 14, $125.	
Cook, William (Estate of)		Baltimore St			Harry 16, $125. Cimon 50, $60. Moses 30, $125. Philly 45, $40. Kitty 32, $80.	
Cooper, Wells		North St		Merchant Tailor	Milly 9, $40.	
Creery, John		Pratt St		Teacher	Kitty 9, $40.	
Decker, George		Fayette St		Gentleman	Saul 14, $125. Wgly (??) 2, $5. Peg 25, $80. Harriot 7, $20.	
Delinat, Charles		Wagon Alley		Gentleman	Sandey 45, $125. Andrew 45, $125.	Delinott per City Directory.
Desan, Nicholas		Ridgeley Addition			Peter 20, $125. Polly 24, $80.	
Deweese, Andrew		Pratt St		Wine Merchant	Suckey 15, $80.	
Donaldson, Marriot V.		Lombard St			Sophia 25, $80. Lydia 40, $60.	
Donaldson, Richard		Lombard St			Sam 15, $125.	
Donsee, Leopold		Liberty St		Boot & shoe factory	Julian 27, $80.	

Free Blacks and Slave Owners in Baltimore City Tax Assessor's Ledger, 1818, Ward 1

NAME	RACE/ STATUS	RESIDENCE	REAL PROPERTY	OCCUPATION	ENSLAVED PROPERTY Name, Age, Value	COMMENTS
Dorsey, Allen		Sharp St		Iron & commission merchant	Beth 45, $40. Charity 28, $80. Jenny 18, $80. Sophia 8, $40.	
Dorsey, Bachel (Estate of)		Sharp St			Belle 19, $80.	
Douglas, George	C	Howard St	Lot $50, Imp $75			
Duke, Basil		Eutaw St			Bill 25, $125. Ben 25, $125. Abraham 25, $125. John 20, $125. Jim 16, $60. Harry 10, $40. George 6, $20.	Jim is infirm.
Dunbar, George T.		Howard St		Cashier @ Commercial & Farmer's Bank	Peg 22, $80.	
Dunington, William		Howard St			Richard 13, $40. Hagar 23, $80. Wilson 2, $5.	
Dunkel, George A.		Liberty St		M.D.	David 13, $40. Sarah 35, $80. Nance 5, $20.	
Dushane, John		Sharp St		House Carpenter	Sam 25, $125. Isaac 10, $40. Basel 15, $125.	
Eichelberger, George		Sharp St			Charlotte 20, $80.	
Elliott, Hartman		Eutaw St			Watt 50, $60. Ned 30, $125. Nelly $40. Sophia 14, $80.	
Elliott, Robert		Lexington St			Nathan 10, $40. Harriet 18, $80.	
Ernest, George		German St			Samuel 8, $40. Margaret 3, $10.	
Etting, Solomon		Baltimore St		Merchant	Daniel 41, $125. Amoy 16, $125. July 30, $80. Nell 9, $40.	
Fahnestock, Dederick		Howard St		Merchant	Dick 5, $20. Henry 22, $80. Ann 14, $80.	
Fahnestock, Peter		Howard St		Dry goods merchant	Perry 3, $10. Ann 22, $80.	

Free Blacks and Slave Owners in Baltimore City Tax Assessor's Ledger, 1818, Ward 1

NAME	RACE/STATUS	RESIDENCE	REAL PROPERTY	OCCUPATION	ENSLAVED PROPERTY Name, Age, Value	COMMENTS
Faulks, John	C	Saratoga St	Lot $50, Imp $25	Carter		
Fonderay, William	C	Brandy Alley	Lot $30, Imp $20			
Forney, Peter		Baltimore St		Gentleman	Calvert 14, $125.	
Fox, Mrs.	Widow	Lexington St			Alex 10, $40. Charity 28, $80. Mary 15, $80.	
Frailey, Leonard		Fayette St		City gauger & inspector of domestic liquors	Female slave, 4, $10.	
Gallon, Absalom	C	Howard St	Lot $20, Imp $30	Laborer		
Goetz, Mrs.	Widow	Howard St			Floro 8, $40.	
Goodwin, Thomas	C	North St	Lot $30, Imp $40			
Gowan, John		Lexington St		Soap & candle manufactury	Allen 30, $125. Adam 21, $125. Julia 30, $80. Nell 14, $80.	
Graff, Frederick C.		Camden St		Merchant	Francis 35, $125.	
Grimes, Nero	C	North St	Lot $75, Imp $65			
Gwynn, Mrs.	Widow	Eutaw St			Laid (?) 40, $125. James 2, $5. Henry 4, $10. Peck 15, $80. Nance 12, $40.	
Hall, H. W.		Liberty St			Hannah 28, $80.	
Hane, James	C	Brandy Alley	Lot $25, Imp $25			
Harden, William		Conway St		Merchant	Amey 20, $80.	
Harris, Dr. Edward		Baltimore St			Sam 40, $125. Edward 8, $40. Nelly 50, $30. Kitty 9, $40.	
Hennick, George		Eutaw St		Saddler	Lida 19, $80.	

Free Blacks and Slave Owners in Baltimore City Tax Assessor's Ledger, 1818, Ward 1

NAME	RACE/ STATUS	RESIDENCE	REAL PROPERTY	OCCUPATION	ENSLAVED PROPERTY Name, Age, Value	COMMENTS
Hines, John		Sharp St			Henry 35, $80.	
Hogg, John		Saratoga St		Grocer	Charity 19, $80.	
Holland, Littleton		Baltimore St		Goldsmith & jeweler	Maria 16, $80.	
Hooks, Joseph Jr.		Howard St			Nance 23, $80. Violet 4, $10.	
Hooper, James		Sharp St			Thomas 9, $40. Ann 12, $40. Easter 7, $20. Bett 50, $30.	
Hudson, Jonathan		Liberty St			Edward 20, $125. Harriott 14, $80.	
Hurxthal, Frederick		Liberty St		Accountant	Wash 12, $40. Charlotte 20, $80. Kitty 15, $80.	
Hurxthal, Lewis		Liberty St		Merchant	Jim 14, $125.	
Irvine, Alexander		Howard St			Dench 30, $80.	
Isett, John		Howard St		Proprietor of the Columbian Hotel	Phebe 30, $80. Sally 10, $40. Violet 10, $40. Judy 7, $20. Nancy 3, $10.	
Jackson, Anthony	C	Forest Lane	Lot $50, Imp $150			
Jackson, Bolton		Howard St			Patty 45, $40. Mary 15, $80.	
Jackson, J.E.		Liberty St			Sarah 18, $80. Grace 10, $40. Joshua 35, $125.	
James, Tudor		Liberty St			Philis 40, $40. Emily 5, $20.	
Jennings, Dr. Samuel K.		Lexington St		M.D.	David 10, $40. Rose 15, $80. Nance 12, $40.	
Jennings, Thomas, (Esq.)		Conway St		Attorney & counselor at law	Maria 10, $40.	
Jessop, William		Fayette St			Isaac 22, $125. Henry 12, $40. John 11, $40. Susan 35, $80. Caroline 13, $40.	
Johnson, Christopher		Fayette St			Collin 25, $125. Hannah 50, $30. Jane 50, $30. Harriot 12, $40.	

Free Blacks and Slave Owners in Baltimore City Tax Assessor's Ledger, 1818, Ward 1

NAME	RACE/ STATUS	RESIDENCE	REAL PROPERTY	OCCUPATION	ENSLAVED PROPERTY Name, Age, Value	COMMENTS
Jones, Talbot		Howard St		Merchant	John 15, $125. Matilda 23, $80.	
Karrick, Joseph		Sharp St		Gentleman	James 28, $125. Mary 28, $80. Philis 5, $20. Matilda 2, $5.	
Keenen, Charles		Saratoga St		Collector	Mary 12, $40.	
Keerl, Dr. Henry		Baltimore St		M.D.	Maria 26, $80. Anna 18, $80. Wiley 7, $20.	
Keyser, Diderick		Howard St		China merchant	Harriot 13, $40.	Derick per City Directory.
Keyser, Samuel		Fayette St		China merchant	Kitty 20, $80.	
Kimmel, Michael		Howard St		Hardware merchant	John 15, $125. Ben 7, $20. Israel 4, $10. Phily 40, $40.	
Kipp, John		Camden St		Glass, oil & paint store	Minty 45, $40.	
Kramer, Frederick		Fayette St			Tempy 20, $80. Ellen 17, $80. Harriot 8, $40.	
Krous, George (Estate of)		Howard St			Hannah 28, $80.	
Landsdale, Richard	C	Conway St	Lot $50, Imp $50			
Laurenson, Phillip		Liberty St			Charlotte, 19, $80. Louisa 8, $40.	
Lee, Mrs.	Widow	Baltimore St			Jesse 26, $125. Rose 50, $30.	
Lemonier, Alexander L.		Howard St		Gentleman	Nan 40, $40. Juliet 8, $40.	
Levering, Jesse		Lombard St		Grocer	Ann 16, $80. Easter 13, $40.	
Makeff, Richard		Lombard St			James 14, $125. Patty 17, $80.	
Manro, Jonathan		Baltimore St		Merchant	Jack 25, $125. Isabella 25, $80. Ann 27, $80. Fan 15, $80. Jude 10, $40.	
Mason, Peter		Pratt St		House carpenter	Milly 12, $40. Charlotte 30, $80.	
McCubbin, Moses		Dutch Alley		Tailor	Maria 21, $80. Mary 3, $10.	

Free Blacks and Slave Owners in Baltimore City Tax Assessor's Ledger, 1818, Ward 1

NAME	RACE/STATUS	RESIDENCE	REAL PROPERTY	OCCUPATION	ENSLAVED PROPERTY Name, Age, Value	COMMENTS
McDonald, John		Dutch Alley		Carpenter	Sophia 10, $40.	
McDowell, Dr. Maxwell		Lexington St		M.D.	Betsy 26, $80. Peg 12, $40.	
Meridith, Thomas		Eutaw St			Eliza 19, $80.	
Mingo, John	C	Howard St	Lot $20, Imp $20	Blacksmith		
Mingo, Kitty	C	Camden St	Lot $75, Imp $50			
Mitchell, Francis J.		Liberty St			Ned 25, $125. Peter 25, $125. Tom 21, $125. William 10, $40. Rebecca 46, $30. Rachel 36, $80. Dick 25, $125. Jack 36, $125. Dick 14, $125. Bill 17, $125. Tom 10, $40. John 9, $40. Saul 6, $20. David 14, $125.	
Moore, Molly	C	Brandy Alley	Lot $30, Imp $20			
Mulliken, Rignald		King Tamany St		Tobacco merchant	Hanna 30, $80. Sarah 16, $80. Henny 6, $20.	
Mummy, Thomas		Howard St		Dry goods merchant	Hannah 8, $40.	
Nichol, Samuel		Sharp St			Susan 15, $80.	
Noland, Mrs.	Widow	Howard St			Dick 47, $60. David 14, $125. Bill 11, $40. Charles 8, $40. Suckey 37, $80.	
Philips, William		Dutch Alley			Rose 24, $80.	
Pitts, Spencer	C	Howard St	Lot $50, Imp $25			
Pogue, Elizabeth		German St			Darky 25, $80.	
Porter, Michael		Pratt St		Bricklayer	Richard, 16, $125.	

Free Blacks and Slave Owners in Baltimore City Tax Assessor's Ledger, 1818, Ward 1

NAME	RACE/STATUS	RESIDENCE	REAL PROPERTY	OCCUPATION	ENSLAVED PROPERTY Name, Age, Value	COMMENTS
Proebstino, Theodore C.		Baltimore St.			Dan 14, $125. Cassy 20, $80.	
Prout, Robert	C	Camden St	Lot $75, Imp $125	Cordwainer		
Reese, John		Howard St			Peter 21, $125. Fann 15, $80.	
Reinecker, George		Howard St		Gentleman	Susan 17, $125. Mary 15, $80.	
Reinecker, Mrs. Maria	Widow	Liberty St			Jerry 16, $125.	
Richardson, Robert R		Eutaw St			James 33, $80. Milly 46, $30. Ellen 4, $10. George 8, $40.	
Ridgely, Miss		Howard St			Richard 20, $125. Dick 14, $125. William 12, $40. Lydia 36, $80. Eliza 25, $80. Eliza 8, $40.	
Robertson, George		Sharp St			Nicholas 22, $125. Joe 22, $125. Watson 21, $125. Dennis 10, $40. Alfred 74 20. Susan 50, $30. Leah 17, $80. Sally 10, $40.	
Robinson, Eve	Widow	Howard St			Beck 17, $80.	
Rodgers, Caesar	C	Howard St	Lot $15, Imp $25			
Sands, Benjamin N.		Liberty St			Rachel 16, $80.	
Sauervine, Peter		Howard St		Flour merchant	Jack 18, $125.	Sauerwein per City Directory.
Schultze, Lucy C.	Widow of John	Liberty St			Myers 30, $125. Sally 13, $40.	
Scott, John		Saratoga St		Gentleman	Arthur, 50, $60. Michael 21, $125. Samuel 19, $125. Jim 21, $125. Lewis 9, $40. Harriet 14, $80.	
Scott, Joseph		Eutaw St			Tom 22, $125. Maria 15, $80. Harriet 14, $80.	

Free Blacks and Slave Owners in Baltimore City Tax Assessor's Ledger, 1818, Ward 1

NAME	RACE/STATUS	RESIDENCE	REAL PROPERTY	OCCUPATION	ENSLAVED PROPERTY Name, Age, Value	COMMENTS
Shane, Joseph		Pratt St		Glass, oil & paint store	Cecilia 20, $80.	
Shipley, Richard A.		Conway St			John 28, $125. Charles 28, $125. Philis 22, $80. Charlotte 13, $40. Miranda 11, $40.	
Simpson, John	C	Eutaw St	Lot $30, Imp $100			
Sollars, Joseph	C	North St	Lot $60, Imp $20			
Spalding, Richard B.		Liberty St		Proprietor of the Baltimore Type Foundery	Calvert 18, $125.	
Spies, John P.		Brandy Alley		Comb factory	John 30, $125. Ellen 25, $80.	
Stansbury, Daniel		Howard St		Merchant Tailor	Ellen 13, $40.	
Steinbeck, Christian		Lexington St			Perry 15, $125.	
Sterritt, Benjamin		Fayette St			Maria 20, $80. Susan 30, $80.	
Stokes, William		Sharp St			Milly 12, $40.	
Stonebraker, George		Pratt St		Flour merchant	Sam 13, $40. Dolly 36, $80.	
Stouffer, Henry		Fayette St		Gentleman	Fan 19, $80.	
Swan, John		Lombard St			Unnamed slave 10, $40.	
Taylor, Joseph		Howard St			Betsy 35, $80. Dan 2, $5.	
Taylor, Samuel		Howard St			Susan 9, $40.	
Thompson, William	C	Brandy Alley	Lot $25, Imp $45			
Ward, William	C	Brandy Alley	Lot $25, Imp $75			
Warfield, George T.		Baltimore St		Merchant	Rachel 16, $80. Clara 7, $80.	
Waters, Joseph G.		Sharp St		Accountant	Henry 18, $125. Priscilla 15, $80.	
Watkins, William	C	Camden St	Lot $125, Imp $75			

Free Blacks and Slave Owners in Baltimore City Tax Assessor's Ledger, 1818, Ward 1

NAME	RACE/ STATUS	RESIDENCE	REAL PROPERTY	OCCUPATION	ENSLAVED PROPERTY Name, Age, Value	COMMENTS
Weeks, Samuel	C	Wagon Alley	Lot $75, Imp $50, Furn $10			
Wells, Benjamin (Estate of)		Dutch Alley			Charles 10, $40. Joe 28, $125. Joe 4, $10. Maria 30, $80. Harriot 5, $20. Cris 8, $40. Nanny 4, $10.	
Wheeler, Leonard		Saratoga St			Priscilla 16, $80.	
White, George (Estate of)		Howard St		Cooper	Jerry 16, $125.	
Winchester, William		Wagon Alley			Phil 20, $125.	
Wolf, Dr. George		Pratt St			Mary 14, $80.	
Woodward, Abraham		North St		Proprietor of the Fountain Stables	Sandy 16, $125. Judy 19, $80. Mary 11, $40.	
Worley, Joseph		Howard St			Charles 21, $125. Harry 8, $40. Jesse 17, $125. Clara 17, $80. Sophia 10, $40. Bridget 45, $30.	
Worrell, Mrs.	Widow	Howard St			Perry 20, $125. Catherine 40, $20.	Catherine is infirm.
Young, William L.		Sharp St			Henny 17, $80. Diana 15, $80.	

Free Blacks and Slave Owners in Baltimore City Tax Assessor's Ledger, 1818, Ward 2

NAME	RACE/ STATUS	RESIDENCE	REAL PROPERTY	OCCUPATION	ENSLAVED PROPERTY Name, Age, Value	COMMENTS
Allison, Mrs. Ann		Pratt St			Henny 23, $80.	
Appleby, Mr.		Market St			Louisa 8, $40.	
Armstead, Mrs.	Widow of the colonel	Forest St			Yorick 18, $125. Obenson 21, $125. Ida 11, $40.	
Batturs, Richard		Hanover St			Charles 18, $125. Harriot 16, $80. Maria 9, $40.	
Birkhead, Hugh		King Tammany St			Milford 18, $125. Teeney 40, $40.	
Boughan, Augustine		Pratt St			Sarah 45, $40.	
Breston, Jacob	C	Honey Alley	Lot $20, Imp $15, Furn $5			
Briscoe, James	C	Timber Neck Lane	Lot $40, Imp $25			
Brown, Charles		Sharp St		Brick maker	Isaac 18, $125. Jane 8, $40.	
Browning Mrs.	Widow	Conway St			Ben 2, $5. Ann 18, $80.	
Brundige, William		Conway St			Washington 17, $125.	
Burges, Rachel		Camden St			Kit 12, $40.	
Carter, Peter	C	Hill St	Lot $40, Imp. $20			
Casey, Robert		Hanover St			Ben 19, $125.	
Cheers, William	C	Goodman St	Lot $50, Imp $50			
Cheston, James		Sharp & Lee Sts			Agnes 30, $80. Harriet 2, $5.	
Clark, John		Sharp St			Charles 25, $125.	
Cole, John		Chatham St			Flora 25, $80. Alis 15, $80.	
Collins, James W.		Barnitz St			Milky 50, $30.	
Conner, Hanibal	C	Montgomery St	Lot $20, Imp. $15, Furn $5			

Free Blacks and Slave Owners in Baltimore City Tax Assessor's Ledger, 1818, Ward 2

NAME	RACE/ STATUS	RESIDENCE	REAL PROPERTY	OCCUPATION	ENSLAVED PROPERTY Name, Age, Value	COMMENTS
Constable, Charles		Charles St			Charles 17, $125. Thomas 25, $125. Susan 12, $40.	
Cooper, Samuel B		Hanover St			Ann 24, $80. Louisa 6, $20.	
Cooper, Sarah J.		Coniwago			James 10, $40. Jenny 40, $40.	
Count, Mr.		Coniwago			Aron 40, $125. Augustine 35, $125. Fanny 22, $80.	
Croutch, William		Barre St			Bill 30, $125. Ned 8, $40. Rachel 20, $80. Ruth 10, $40. Sally 6, $20. Maria 8, $40.	
Cummings, John	C	Honey Alley	Lot $25, Imp $30			
Curton, Mrs. M.		Pratt St			William 6, $20.	
Dagan, Mary		Charles St			Clarrisa 27, $80. Peggy 17, $80.	
Dall, Eleanor Mrs.	Widow	Hanover St			Thomas 35, $125. Ephraim 18, $125.	
Dare, Nathaniel C.		Hanover St			Will 37, $125. Jim 22, 125. Janey 35, $125. Ben 15, $125. Sam 18, $125. Toney 18, $125. Jim 12, $40. Nelson 8, $40. Washington 5, $20. Aron 6, $20. Jinny 47, $30. Denuf 25, $80. Sarah 17, $80. Kitty 13, $40. Sarah 14, $80. Barbara 2, $5.	
Delozier, Mrs.	Widow	Charles St			Mary 14, $80.	
Donaldson, Dr. William		Coniwago			Beck 10, $40.	
Dorsey, Julia	C	Hill St	Lot $75, Imp $30			

Free Blacks and Slave Owners in Baltimore City Tax Assessor's Ledger, 1818, Ward 2

NAME	RACE/ STATUS	RESIDENCE	REAL PROPERTY	OCCUPATION	ENSLAVED PROPERTY Name, Age, Value	COMMENTS
Dugas, Lewis J.		German Lane			George 9, $40. Nancy 35, $80. Mary 12, $40.	
Duncan, Rev. James M.		Market St			Flora 25, $80.	
Durham, John		Market St			Maria 18, $70.	
Edmondson, T & J		Market St			Asburg 30, $125. Clara 30, $80. Sally 28, $80.	
Eichelberger, Martin		Hanover St			James 4, $10. William 25, $125. Nelly 25, $80. Peggy 15, $80.	
Ennis, Benjamin	C	Honey Alley	Lot $25, Imp $15			
Essender, John		Coniwago			Stephen 15, $125.	
Evans, Mrs. Elizabeth	Widow	Sharp St			John 14, $125.	
Everett, Rebecca		Market St			Emiline 25, $80. Milly 2, $5.	
Fisher, John		Charles St		Currier	James 10, $40. Eliza 12, $40.	
Fosbenner, Daniel		Sharp St			Elizabeth 5, $20.	
France, Joseph		Market St			Joe 17, $125. Hannah 40, $40. Margaret 9, $40. Levin 13, $40.	
Frieze, Philip R.J.		Hanover St			Jordan 17, $125. Anthony 21, $125.	
Fuller, Ann		Market St			Nace 20, $80	
Furguson, Capt. John		Forest St			Ann 14, $80. Sukey 21, $80. Jane 21, $80.	

Free Blacks and Slave Owners in Baltimore City Tax Assessor's Ledger, 1818, Ward 2

NAME	RACE/ STATUS	RESIDENCE	REAL PROPERTY	OCCUPATION	ENSLAVED PROPERTY Name, Age, Value	COMMENTS
Gadsby, John		Market St			James, Thomas, Jerry, Sam, James, Edward, James, William, Benjamin, Nace, Mingo, Ceaser, Zach @ $125 each. Gowan & Robert over 50, $120. John & James $20 each. Rainey, Jane & Liddy over 50, @ $30 each. Maria, Eve, Mary & Henny @ $80 each. Margaret, Kezia, Anna, Priscilla, Betsy, & Milly @ $80 each. Louisa, Emaline, Maria, Julia & Harriot @ $20 ea.	
Garrett, Henry	C	Honey Alley	Lot $30, Imp $30			
Gertz, Mrs. Catherine	Widow	Hanover St			Henry 14, $125. Mary 13, $40.	
Goames, Nathan	C	Honey Alley	Lot $40, Imp $40			
Godfroy, Maxmillion		Hanover St			Fredk 4, $10. Mary 27, $80.	
Goodwin, Melcah		Vulcan Alley			Juliet 25, $80. Maria 23, $80.	
Goudon, Ferdinand		Market St			Lydia 8, $40.	
Grafton, Nathan		Charles St			Ann 18, $80.	
Graham, Robert		Sharp & Lee Sts		Carter	Charles 26, $125.	
Grant, Elizabeth		Hanover St			William $125.	
Gray, Sarah	C	Timber Neck Lane	Lot $40, Imp $10			
Guiese, Lewis		Hanover St			Sally 17, $80.	
Gwinn, Caleb D.		Market St			Harry 28, $125. Clarissa 33, $80.	

Free Blacks and Slave Owners in Baltimore City Tax Assessor's Ledger, 1818, Ward 2

NAME	RACE/ STATUS	RESIDENCE	REAL PROPERTY	OCCUPATION	ENSLAVED PROPERTY Name, Age, Value	COMMENTS
Hackett, Henry W.		Pratt St			Fanny 19, $80. Jude 9, $40.	
Hall, Richard W.		Coniwago		MD	Jack 20, $125. Jacob $125. Priscilla 44, $40. Fanny 17, $80.	
Harmange, Anthony (Estate of)		Market St			Ann 35, $80.	
Hewitt, Eli		Forest Lane			Dick 25, $125. Jacob 22, $125. Perry 27, $125. Hanson 15, $125. Peg 23, $80. Caroline 9, $40. Peggy 6, $20.	
Hildon, Abraham	C	Bussy Alley	Lot $30, Imp $10			
Hoffman, George		Charles St			William 45, $125. Frank 12, $40. Nimrod 16, $125. Charlotte 33, $80.	
Hollingsworth, Samuel		Charles St			Dennis 35, $125. Benedick 33, $125. Pompey 40, $125. Hannah 36, $80. Jane 27, $80. Clara 30, $80. Agnes 12, $40. Dan 4, $10. Edward 2, $5.	
Hope, Daniel		King Tammany St.			Eliza 16, $80.	
House, Samuel		Camden St			Jane 40, $30. Mary 13, $40.	Jane is infirm.
Howard, Rebecca	Widow of Dr. Henry Howard	Lombard St			Sarah 22, $80. Hetty 23, $80. Harriot 4, $10.	
Hubbell, Josiah		Hanover St			Rose 34, $80. Louisa 17, $80.	
Hughe, Mrs. Jane		Charles St			Frisby 34, $125. Suter 7, $20. William 6, $20. Rachel 4, $30. Pat 11, $40.	

Free Blacks and Slave Owners in Baltimore City Tax Assessor's Ledger, 1818, Ward 2

NAME	RACE/STATUS	RESIDENCE	REAL PROPERTY	OCCUPATION	ENSLAVED PROPERTY Name, Age, Value	COMMENTS
Hughes, Christopher Sr.		Charles St			Jubra 42, $125. Landeen 43, $125. Harry 23, $125. Gibson 20, $125. Nero 32, $125. Bill 15, $125. Ceasar 40, $125. Duffer 32, $125. Beck 55, $30. Leah 36, $80. Dinah 29, $80.	
Hunter, Rebecca		Goodman St			Lloyd 5 & John 2, $25. Peggy 35, $80.	
Jarvis, Ormand		Goodman St			Joshua 19, $125. Easter 35, $40.	Easter is infirm.
Johnson, George	C	Goodman St	Lot $20, Imp $40,			
Johnson, Samuel	C	Bussy Alley	Lot $30, Imp $30			
Kelty, Catherine		Sharp St			Charles 21, $125. Marier 21, $125. John 3, $10. Bill 5, $20. Ann 18, $80. Melvina 16, $80.	
Knight, Isaac		Pratt St			Lloyd 19, $125. Pompey 9, $40. Minty 10, $40. Mary 15, $80.	
Kyle, Adam B.		Camden St			Edward 20, $125.	
Lemmon, Mrs.	Widow	Goodman St			Maria 21, $80. Charlotte 18, $80. Harges 14, $80.	

Free Blacks and Slave Owners in Baltimore City Tax Assessor's Ledger, 1818, Ward 2

NAME	RACE/ STATUS	RESIDENCE	REAL PROPERTY	OCCUPATION	ENSLAVED PROPERTY Name, Age, Value	COMMENTS
Leonard, Joseph		Conway St		Brewer	Sam 50, $40. Thomas 30, $125. Daniel 27, $125. David 23, $125. Myles 14, $125. Bill 25, $125. Ned 3, $10. Michael 18, $125. Colonel 22, $125. Merey 18, $80. Augustine 11, $40. Grig 7, $20. Henry 13, $20. Tom 4, $10. Fanny 36, $80. Dacy 5, $10. Johanna 50, $30. Milly 30, $80. Susanna 20, $80. Minty 5, $10. Jenny 5, $10. Kitty 3, $5. Charles 9, $40.	Sam is infirm.
Levering, Nathan		Hanover St			Henry 10, $40.	
Levering, Peter		Hanover St			Edward 25, $125. George 12, $40. Hannah 30, $80.	
Lindenberger, Jacob		Hanover St			Mary 25, $80.	
Littlejohn, M. (Estate of)		Hanover St			Caroline 20, $80. Mary 9, $40.	
Long, Reubin		Hanover St			Than 18, $125. Ann 18, $80.	
Low, Cornelius		Hanover St			Jonas 22, $125.	
Lyles, David		Hanover St			William 25, $125. Sule 22, $80.	
Malden, Mrs.		Sharp St			Beck 14, $80.	
Marshal, Francis		German Lane			Kitty 16, $80.	
Martin, William	C	Hill St	Lot $40, Imp $25			
Mayer, Lewis		King Tamany St			Samuel 20, $125.	
McCreery, Mrs.	Widow of William	Conway St			Ariadne 10, $40.	

Free Blacks and Slave Owners in Baltimore City Tax Assessor's Ledger, 1818, Ward 2

NAME	RACE/ STATUS	RESIDENCE	REAL PROPERTY	OCCUPATION	ENSLAVED PROPERTY Name, Age, Value	COMMENTS
McGill, Mary		Hanover St			James 23, $125. Frank 19, $125. Frank 17, $125. Jeff 40, $125. Hannah 30, $80. Sall 15, $80. Lindy 10, $40.	
McKean, John		McClellan Alley			Edmund 4, $10. Elizabeth 16, $80. Pakens 25, $80. Amey 2, $5.	
McLaughlin, Matthew		Hanover St			Moses 16, $125.	
Middleton, Richard		Sharp St			Clemm 21, $125.	
Moale, Ellen	Widow	Pratt St			Charles 27, $125. Henny 35, $80. Lydia 44, $40.	
Moore, Samuel		Charles St			Elijah 22, $125. Redeld 20, $125.	
Morehead, Turner		Conewago St			Emily 12, $40.	
Neal, Hannah	C	Goodman St	Lot $50, Imp $25			
Nelson, Richard C.		Charles St			Cornelius 16, $125. Sam 9, $40. Leige 7, $20. Rachel 14, $80. Nell 12, $40. Nance 10, $40.	
Nettis/Neutes, Jack	C	Timber Neck Lane	Lot $40, Vacant			
Norman, Capt. T. W.		Charles St			James 18, $125. Anthony 11, $40. Clarke 40, $125. Polly 30, $80.	
Norris, William		Hanover St		Dry goods store	Riston 19, $125. Kitty 18, $125.	
Norris, William Jr.		Chatham St			Nichols 27, $125. Merdigo 15, $125. Hetty 45, $40. Rachel 19, $80. Wency 20, $80. Cecilia 7, $20.	

Free Blacks and Slave Owners in Baltimore City Tax Assessor's Ledger, 1818, Ward 2

NAME	RACE/ STATUS	RESIDENCE	REAL PROPERTY	OCCUPATION	ENSLAVED PROPERTY Name, Age, Value	COMMENTS
Norton, Frank	C	Honey Alley	Lot $20, Imp $20			
Norwood, Mrs.		Sharp St			David 10, $40. Kitty 9, $40.	
Orrick, Capt. John W.		Honey Alley			Darky 25, $80.	
Osborn, Christopher	C	Honey Alley	Lot $20, Imp $15, Furn $5			
Osburn, William		York St			Harry 15, $125. Abbe 35, $80. Charity 11, $40.	
Osgood, Robert H.		Barnett St			Emeline 18, $80. Rason 16, $80.	
Palmer, Edward		Howard St			James 9, $40. Maria 11, $40. Margaret 30, $80. Juno 18, $80.	
Patten/Potter, Dr. Nathaniel		German Lane			Maria 12, $40.	
Patterson, Joseph		German Lane			Robert 25, $125.	
Payson, Henry		Hanover St			John 12, $40. Susan 9, $40. Kitty 25, $80.	
Peck, Henry		Pratt St			Susan 25, $80. Artage 21, $80.	
Poleny, Mary	C	Coniwago	Lot $150, Imp $100			
Poumairat, John		Camden St			Lewis 7, $20. Alfred 5, $20. Maria 28, $80.	
Pressman, Mrs.	Widow	Goodman St			Alec 45, $125. Cecealia 50, $30. Anna 19, $80. Margaret 12, $40.	
Priffith, Samuel G.		Hanover St			Charles 29, $125. James 45, $125. Henry 2, $5. Dian 33, $80. Ruth 37, $80.	
Purviance, Robert		Howard St			Harriot 35, $80. Harriet 10, $40.	
Queen, Stephen	C	Hill St	Lot $50, Imp $25			

Free Blacks and Slave Owners in Baltimore City Tax Assessor's Ledger, 1818, Ward 2

NAME	RACE/STATUS	RESIDENCE	REAL PROPERTY	OCCUPATION	ENSLAVED PROPERTY Name, Age, Value	COMMENTS
Repold, Mrs. Metta		Pratt St			Frank 10, $40.	
Ricaud, Mrs.	Widow of Benjamin	Hanover St			Darky 45, $40. Hetty 22, $80. Jude 20, $80. Kitty 18, $80.	
Ridgely, Noah		Pratt St			Catherine 20, $80. Hannah 12, $40.	
Riley, William		Forest St			Bill 10, $40.	
Ringold, Benjamin		Camden St			Moses 21, $125. Charles 14, $125. Henry 9, $40. John 3, $10. Mint 50, $30. Sukey 35, $80. Ruth 30, $80. Filly 21, $80. Emany 27, $80. Eliza 17, $80. Maria 16, $80. Ann 16, $80. Jane 12, $40. Aranthe 9, $40. Rose 9, $40. Susan 8, $40.	
Riston, George		Market St			Henry 16, $125.	
Ruckle, John		Market St			Rachel 20, $80.	
Russell, James		Honey Alley			Lloyd 18, $125. Diana 18, $80. Cornelius 18, $125.	
Sampson,	Colored man	Hill St	Lot $50, Imp $50			
Schwartze, A. J.		Hanover St			Lewis 10, $40. Sam 3, $10. Henny 30, $80. Dolly 35, $80. Rachel 15, $80. Mary 13, $40.	
Seankins, Clem	C	Timber Neck Lane	Lot $40, Imp $15			
Shanley, James		Hanover St			Minty 10, $40.	
Sherrer, George		Sharp St		Carpenter	Fan 10, $40.	

Free Blacks and Slave Owners in Baltimore City Tax Assessor's Ledger, 1818, Ward 2

NAME	RACE/ STATUS	RESIDENCE	REAL PROPERTY	OCCUPATION	ENSLAVED PROPERTY Name, Age, Value	COMMENTS
Shorter, Ann	C	Hill St	Lot $100, Imp $150 Lot $40, Imp $20			
Simmons, Matthew W.		Pratt St			Francis 4, $10. Nace 30, $60. Evan 8, $40. Hopewell 27, $80. Sena 10, $40.	Nace is infirm.
Simonson, James		Camden St			Eliza 12, $40.	
Small, Jacob		Conway St			Juliet 17, $80. Matilda 9, $40. Bill 7, $20.	
Smith, Robert (Honorable)		Pratt St			Richard 27, $125. Dick 15, $125. Henny 17, $80.	
Spicknell, John		Pratt St			Cedos 15, $125. Betty 24, $80.	
Stewart, Richardson		Vulcan Alley			Ben $30, $125. Vincent 30, $125. Sam 15, $125. Harry 16, $125. John 30, $125. Tamar 50, $30.	
Stump, Samuel		Hanover St			Charlotte 20, $80. Jane 8, $40. Juliet 7, $20.	
Summerwelt, Elizabeth		Lee St			Ingo 26, $125. Charles 24, $125. Jim 14, $125. Isaac 12, $40. Jesse 12, $40. Nell 45, $40. Kitty 16, $80. Sam 10, $40.	
Sumwalt, George		Welcome Alley			Fan 15, $80.	
Sutherland, John		Hanover St			Mary 20, $80. Henrietta 16, $80. Josephene 3, $10.	
Swaes, Basil	C	Timber Neck Lane	Lot $40, Imp $50			
Thomas, Allen MD		Camden St			Henry 45, $125. Phill 20, $125. Debby 25, $80.	
Thomas, Philip	C	Hill St	Lot $50, Imp. $100			

Free Blacks and Slave Owners in Baltimore City Tax Assessor's Ledger, 1818, Ward 2

NAME	RACE/STATUS	RESIDENCE	REAL PROPERTY	OCCUPATION	ENSLAVED PROPERTY Name, Age, Value	COMMENTS
Thompson, Ann	C	Honey Alley	Lot $20, Imp $50, Furn $5			
Tiernan, Luke		Charles St			Sarah 35, $80.	
Tyson, Nathan		Pratt St			Richard 28, $125.	
Uhler, Barbara	Widow of George	Hanover St			Hess 18, $80. Dolly 7, $20.	
Uhler, Erasmus		Pratt St			Warrick 40, $125. Roger 21, $125. Jess 12, $40.	
Uhler, Philip		Pratt St			Catherine 12, $40.	
Vail, Mr.		King Tammany St		Teacher of Music	Sarah 22, $80.	
Wallis, John Jr.		Coniwago			Eliza 9, $40.	
Warfield, Charles		Vulcan Alley			Columbus 2, $5. Cate 26, $80. Maria 8, $20.	
Warfield, Charles		Lee St			Clem 20, $125. Maria 23, $80. Harriot 15, $80. Mary 10, $40.	
Watkins, Tobias		Coniwago		MD	Henry 7, $20. Harriet 9, $40.	
Webster, William		York St			John 10, $40. Cate 20, $80.	
Wells, Nelson	C	Sugar Alley	Lot $75, Imp $25			
Wetherall, William		Sharp St			Tobias 35, $125. Samuel 20, $125. John 8, $40. Juliet 15, $40.	Juliet is infirm.
Whelan, Thomas		Charles St			Rachel 13, $40. Sarah 19, $80.	
Wilkins,	Col	Bussy Alley	Lot $30, Imp $10			
Wilkins, Joseph		Hanover St			Charlotte 18, $80.	

Free Blacks and Slave Owners in Baltimore City Tax Assessor's Ledger, 1818, Ward 2

NAME	RACE/ STATUS	RESIDENCE	REAL PROPERTY	OCCUPATION	ENSLAVED PROPERTY Name, Age, Value	COMMENTS
Williams, Thomas	C	Sugar Alley	Lot $200, Imp $20			
Wills, Joseph		Forest St			Jude 22, $80.	
Wilmer, John W.		Hanover St			Charlotte 21, $80. Rya 13, $40.	
Wilson, James C.		Howard St			Louisa 19, $80. Eliza 12, $40.	
Wilson, Nixon		Lombard St			Sukey 12, $40.	
Wilson, William		Sharp St			Nance 15, $80. Jenny 25, $80.	
Winchester, Charles		Hanover St			Sarah 35, $80.	
Witmor, Mrs.		Hanover St			Phoebe 8, $40	
Woodland, William		Coniwago			Lewis 6, $20.	
Woods, William		Pratt St			James 15, $125.	
Woodward, William W.		Vulcan Alley			Henderson 12, $40.	
Wyant, Peter (Estate of)		Hanover St			Allesder 12, $4.	
Yellott, George (Estate of)		Pratt St			Eliza 10, $40. Venus 8, $40.	
Young, Hugh		Coniwago			Nell 22, $80.	
Young, Mrs.	Widow	Howard St			Harriot 44, $40. Hamimia 22, $80. Henry 5, $20.	

Free Blacks and Slave Owners in Baltimore City Tax Assessor's Ledger, 1818, Ward 3

NAME	RACE/STATUS	RESIDENCE	REAL PROPERTY	OCCUPATION	ENSLAVED PROPERTY Name, Age, Value	COMMENTS
Aisquith, John		Bank St			Isaac 30, $125. Ralph 21, $125. Bill 7, $20. Sarah 29, $80. Jane 24, $80. Ann 6, $15. Maria 3, $15.	
Alexander, Ashton		Chatham St		M.D.	Lavi 25, $125. Ephraim 20, $125. Charles 7, $20. Joseph 4, $10. Charlotte 24, $80. Ledia 30, $80. Sarah 13, $40. Ellen 3, $5.	
Alexander, Isabella		St. Paul's Lane			Ceres 12, $40. Mary 50, $30. Hetty 20, $80.	
Armstrong, John		Market St		Shoe Man	Sarah 15, $80.	
Baker, Dr. Samuel		Light St			Joseph 46, $125. David 11, $40.	
Bear, William		Pratt St		Blacksmith	Leonard 20, $125. Susan 26, $80.	
Benson, Robert		Market St			Reuben 12, $40.	
Berry, Robert		Charles & Chatham Sts			Ervin 14, $125. Sally 27, $80. Nancy 10, $40. Anny 9, $40.	
Betts, Solomon		Market St			Abram 27, $125. Sam 15, $125. Samuel 36, $125. Lidia 40, $40. Hester 33, $80. Caroline 9, $40.	
Birckhead, Solomon		Chatham St		M.D.	Levin 27, $125. Charles 25, $125. Nelly 50, $30. Eliza 14, $80.	
Bohme, Charles G.		Market St			Arthur 18, $125. Lemon 30, $125. Emery 23, $80.	
Boyd, Alexander H.		Calvert St			Nancy 50, $40. Julian 17, $80.	
Boyd, Elizabeth & Mary		Market St			Lewis 11, $40. Jacob 4, $10. Ann 12, $40.	
Branson, William		Market St			Jack 20, $125.	
Brice, John		Calvert St			Letty 18, $80.	
Brice, Nicholas		Church St			Sam 28, $125. Matthew 25, $125. John 8, $40. Lida 20, $80. Charlotte 17, $80.	

Free Blacks and Slave Owners in Baltimore City Tax Assessor's Ledger, 1818, Ward 3

NAME	RACE/STATUS	RESIDENCE	REAL PROPERTY	OCCUPATION	ENSLAVED PROPERTY Name, Age, Value	COMMENTS
Brown, Alexander		Market St			Edward 19, $125. Polrae 28, $125. Charles 23, $125. Ellen 50, $30. Elliza 11, $40. Jane 22, $80.	
Brown, Samuel		Chatham St		Teacher	Agnes 21, $80. Priscilla 36, $80.	
Buchanan, James A.		Calvert St			Prince 50, $40. Robert 50, $40. Reese 26, $125. David 26, $125. Abram 16, $125. Lucy 30, $80. Peggy 22, $80. Caroline 4, $10. Jane 30, $80. Charlotte 3, $8. Rachel 2, $5.	
Calhoun, Lydia		East St			Henry 25, $125. Charlotte 45, $40. Venus 41, $40. Jane 21, $80.	
Campbell, James		Charles St			Jack 60, $20. Plesant 55, $20. Henry 18, $80.	
Cannon, Mary M.		Market St			Hannah 20, $80. Charlotte 10, $40.	
Chamillon, Joseph		Primrose Alley		French cook	Rose 18, $80. Rachel 15, $80.	
Coale, Edward J.		Calvert St			Maria 22, $80. Susan 24, $80.	
Cochran, William G. (Estate of)		Chatham St			Frisby 20, $125. Charlotte 30, $80.	
Coe, William		Calvert St			Thomas 33, $125. William 20, $125. York 25, $125. Jim 23, $125. Nelly 22, $80.	
Colter, Alexander		Market St			Sophia 17, $80. Kitty 40, $40.	
Cooke, George		Public Alley			Jack 12, $40.	
Cox, James		Market		Cashier, Bank of Baltimore	Henry 21, $125. Dolly 7, $20.	

Free Blacks and Slave Owners in Baltimore City Tax Assessor's Ledger, 1818, Ward 3

NAME	RACE/STATUS	RESIDENCE	REAL PROPERTY	OCCUPATION	ENSLAVED PROPERTY Name, Age, Value	COMMENTS
Cox, Joseph		Pubic Alley			Kitt 22, $125. Perry 20, $125. Tom 15, $125. Hetty 40, $60. Rachel 20, $80. Harriot 3, $10.	
Cromwell, John		Church St		M.D.	Elijah 10, $40. Benjamin 36, $125. Nance 36, $80. Mary 13, $40.	
Davidge, John B.		Church St.		M.D.	Abraham 30, $125.	
Didier, Henry Jr.		Church St.			Nace 15, $125. James 10, $40. Eliza 19, $80. Patty 16, $80.	
Donaldson, Samuel J.		St. Paul's Lane			John 20, $125. Adam 22, $125. Ann 18, $80.	
Dorsey, Walter (Esq.)		Church St			Richard 16, $125. Prudence 45, $60. Louisa 13, $40. Maria 11, $40. Jane 9, $40.	
Douglas, George	Colored Man	Light St	Lot $400, Imp $500. Lot $30, Imp $10. Lot $40, Imp $30. Lot $40, Imp $30. 4 horses @ $10 each, 3 drays $18, Furn $10, Plate $11	Drayman		
Egerton, Charles		Calvert St			Priscilla 16, $80. Harriot 20, $80.	
Emery, Thomas L. Jr.		St. Paul's Lane			David 20, $125. Lidia 18, $80.	
Evatt, Edward		Light St			Grace 20, $80.	

Free Blacks and Slave Owners in Baltimore City Tax Assessor's Ledger, 1818, Ward 3

NAME	RACE/STATUS	RESIDENCE	REAL PROPERTY	OCCUPATION	ENSLAVED PROPERTY Name, Age, Value	COMMENTS
Farnandis, Walter		Charles St			Susan 14, $80. Harriot 8, $40.	
Fowler, Benjamin		Calvert St			Charlotte 19, $80	
Frick, William		St. Paul's Lane			William 17, $125.	
Fulford, William		Chatham St			Sarah 33, $80. Venus 27, $80. Milcha 4, $10.	
Gates, Mrs.		Calvert St			Jack 13, $40. Charlotte 15, $80.	Charlotte is property of C. Jackson.
Golder, Robert		Market St			Henry 10, $40. Sall 30, $80.	
Goodwin, Elizabeth		St. Paul's Lane			Charles 25, $125. Natt 16, $125. Tom 12, $40. Harriot 33, $80. Hannah 20, $80. Ann 14, $80. Pegg 13, $40. Repega(?) 13, $40. Margarett 6, $20. Lidney 8, $40.	
Gould, Capt. Peter		Charles St			George 11, $40. Henry 8, $40. David 5, $20. Nancy 30, $80.	
Gowan, Lloyd		Church & Calvert Sts			Philip 19, $125. Sally 10, $40.	
Griffith, Susanna		Market St			John 25, $125. Thomas 9, $40. John 7, $20. Edward 5, $20. Flora 45, $40. Betty 25, $80.	
Griffith, Thomas W.		Church St			James 40, $125.	
Gwynn, William of John		St. Paul's Lane			Henry 17, $125.	
Hall, Benjamin W.		Calvert St			James 20, $125. Jerry 30, $125.	
Hall, Richard M.		Market St			Jack 20, $125. Rebecca 13, $40.	
Hammond, Miss Harriot		Market St			Henry 18, $125. Thomas 17, $125. Maria 50, $30. Charlotte 2, $80. Dafiny 20, $80.	
Harris, John F.		Chatham St.			Nance 17, $80.	

Free Blacks and Slave Owners in Baltimore City Tax Assessor's Ledger, 1818, Ward 3

NAME	RACE/STATUS	RESIDENCE	REAL PROPERTY	OCCUPATION	ENSLAVED PROPERTY Name, Age, Value	COMMENTS
Heide, George		Pratt St north side			Thomas 16, $125. Maria 30, $80. Margarete 10, $40.	
Hodges, Benjamin M.		Chatham St			Talbott 29, $125. Frederick 15, $125. John 25, $125. Eliza 24, $80. Flora 22, $80. Mary 16, $80. Maria 16, $80. Rachel 20, $80.	
Hoffman, John		Market St			Barnet 35, $125. Henry 18, $125. Lucy 40, $40. Rachel 43, $40.	
Hoffman, Peter		Church St			Charles 33, $125. Stephen 20, $125. William 10, $40. Grace 2, $80. Charity 20, $80. Margaret 40, $40.	
Hollins, John		Calvert St			David 53, $40. Henry 30, $125. Edward 23, $125. Jim 8, $40. Eliza 10, $40.	
Howard, Henry		Market St		Tailor	Levin 12, $40. Ann 17, $80. Matilda 10, $40.	
Jenkins, Michael		Light St			Phebe 12, $40.	
Jenkins, Thomas C		Charles St			Henry 7, $20. Rose 16, $80.	
Jones, Thomas S.		Market St			William 13, $40. Rachel 45, $30. Charlotte 28, $80.	Rachel is infirm.
Kaminskey, John C.		Market St			Wilkes 23, $125. Maria 32, $80. Nance 30, $80. Harriot 6, $20.	
Keener, David		Chatham St			Martha 25, $80. Selby 5, $10.	
Kelly, Thomas		Public Alley		Cooper	Peck 20, $80.	
Lansdale, William M.		Charles St			Andrew 33, $125. Richard 5, $20. Henry 30, $80. Ann 10, $40.	
Latimer, James P.		Calvert St			Eliza 12, $40.	

Free Blacks and Slave Owners in Baltimore City Tax Assessor's Ledger, 1818, Ward 3

NAME	RACE/ STATUS	RESIDENCE	REAL PROPERTY	OCCUPATION	ENSLAVED PROPERTY Name, Age, Value	COMMENTS
Latimer, Mrs.		Calvert St			James 6, $20. Charles 3, $10. Sarah 32, $80. Ann 28, $80. Jenny 10, $40. Harriot 8, $40. Peggy 2, $5.	
Lettig, Philip		Market St			Abram 18, $125. Ceasar 25, $125. Polly 27, $80.	
Librou, Anthony		Calvert St		Barber	Nelly 26, $80. Rachel 11, $40.	
Linville, James M.		Market St			Jacob 21, $125. George 4, $10. Hagar 22, $80.	
Lorman, William		Church St			Abegale 30, $80.	
Mactier, Alexander		Charles & Chatham Sts			Jerry 21, $125. Brutus 13, $40. Abby 28, $8. Milly 40, $40. Maria 2, $5.	
Maris, George		Charles St			Simon 20, $125.	
Martin, Luther		Charles St			Fanny 5, $30. Rachel 35, $80. July 20, $80.	
McCulloh, James W.		Church St			Mary 28, $80.	
McHenry, James		Calvert St		M.D.	Unnamed slave 12, $40.	
Merryman, Elizabeth		Calvert St			Mary 45, $40.	
Merryman, John		Calvert St			Susan 42, $40.	
Merryman, Sarah R.		Calvert St			Ann 27, $80.	
Messersmith, Mrs.		Washington Square			Edward 9, $40.	
Moore, Stephen H.		Washington Square			Lucy 13, $40.	
Mosher, James		Chatham St			Milly 30, $80. Peggy 9, $40. Linday 8, $40.	
Mullikin, Basil		Light St			Ben 15, $125. Judy 15, $80. Sophia 7, $20.	
Neal, Abner		Market St			Julia 12, $40.	

Free Blacks and Slave Owners in Baltimore City Tax Assessor's Ledger, 1818, Ward 3

NAME	RACE/ STATUS	RESIDENCE	REAL PROPERTY	OCCUPATION	ENSLAVED PROPERTY Name, Age, Value	COMMENTS
Patridge, James		St. Paul's Lane			Thomas 25, $125.	
Perry, Jeremiah		Charles St			Rody 24, $80.	
Pontier, M.		Market St			Marony 35, $80.	
Pue, Peggy		Calvert St			Sam 4, $10. Henny 15, $80. Mary 33, $80.	
Pue, Rebecca		Calvert St			James 16, $125.	
Quail, Robert		Public Alley			Philis 26, $80.	
Queen, Henry	Colored Man	Public Alley	Lot $125, Imp $20			
Queen, Stephen	Colored Man	Public Alley	Lot $125, Imp $15			
Redding, John		Pratt St			Benjamin 35, $125. Frederick 27, $62. Spence 10, $40. Washington 11, $40. Henny 38, $80. Nancy 28, $80. Adaline 2, $5.	
Repold, George (Estate of)		Market St			Tom 26, $125. Frank 11, $40. Maria 20, $80. Ann 42, $40. Silvia 9, $40.	
Rescaniere, Peter		Primrose Alley			Colmo 25, $125. Joseph 30, $125. Kay 30, $125. Neptune 30, $125. Angle 35, $80. Laura 35, $80. George 30, $80. Lucy 12, $40.	
Ricaud, Thomas P.		Market St			Eliza 14, $80.	
Robinson, Joseph		Market St			Robert 14, $125. Rachel 20, $80.	
Scott, John		St. Paul's Lane			Alexander 21, $125.	
Seller, Abraham		Calvert St			Martha 22, $80.	
Short, John		South St			George 14, $125. Abby 14, $80.	

Free Blacks and Slave Owners in Baltimore City Tax Assessor's Ledger, 1818, Ward 3

NAME	RACE/ STATUS	RESIDENCE	REAL PROPERTY	OCCUPATION	ENSLAVED PROPERTY Name, Age, Value	COMMENTS
Skinner, John S.		Calvert St		Postmaster	Sam 27, $125. Willilam 4, $10. Samuel 3, $10. Fany 50, $30. Marian 23, $80.	Sam is property of Clopper.
Sloan, James		Washington Square			George 18, $125.	
Small, John		Calvert St			Jim 22, $125. Alley 25, $80. Jane 16, $80.	
Smith, Ralph		Charles St			Sarah 34, $80.	
Stapleton, Joseph K.		Market St			John 15, $125. Artimus 50, $30.	
Stewart, David C.		Lovely Lane			William 2, $5. Charlotte 20, $80. Rachel 18, $80.	
Stiles, Mrs.	Widow of Capt.	Calvert St			Eliza 16, $80. Larel 11, $40. Onusia 9, $40.	
Stricker, John		Charles St			Butler 37, $125. Mary 40, $40.	
Summercamp, Mr.		Calvert St			Benjamin 12, $40. Betty 6, $20.	
Swan, Gen. John		Market St			Fanny 18, $80. Sall 10, $40.	
Taylor, Lemuel		East St			Charles 30, $125. Isaac 30, $125. Henny 45, $40. Keziah 26, $80. Eliza 6, $20.	
Thomas, Ebenezer S.		Chatham St			Mary 35, $80.	

Free Blacks and Slave Owners in Baltimore City Tax Assessor's Ledger, 1818, Ward 3

NAME	RACE/ STATUS	RESIDENCE	REAL PROPERTY	OCCUPATION	ENSLAVED PROPERTY Name, Age, Value	COMMENTS
Thomas, John		Chatham St			Elias 16, $125. Charlotte 40, $40. Eliza 15, $80.	
Thompson, Stephen J.		Market St			Prince 50, $60. Lewis 50, $60. Jane 27, $80. Maria 7, $20.	
Tilghman, Mary Lloyd		Church St			Jenny 13, $40.	
Towson, Rebecca		Market St			Comfort 26, $80.	
Usher, Mary	Widow	Calvert St			Nancy 20, $80. Lydia 17, $80.	
Vance, William		Charles St			Jim 13, $125.	
Walker, Samuel P.		Market St			Stephen 25, $125. Essep 15, $125. Luce 50, $30. Fanny 11, $40.	
Walsh, Robert		Church St			Isaac 30, $125.	
Ward, Elizabeth	Widow	Calvert St			Thomas 14, $125. Feby 20, $80. Betty 45, $40.	
Watson, Robert		Church & Calvert Sts			Mary 18, $80.	
Welford, Robert		Charles St			William 11, $40. Mary 11, $40.	
Wells, Rev. Joshua		Light St			Thomas 21, $125.	
White, Jane		Charles St			Letty 16, $80.	
Wilkins, Dr. Henry		Light St			James 45, $125.	
Williams, James		Charles St			Matilda 25, $80.	
Williamson, Basil		Fountain Inn			Sprig 25, $125. Moses 38, $125. Richard 22, $125. David 22, $125. Hannah 25, $80. Kitty 22, $80. Mary 27, $80.	

Free Blacks and Slave Owners in Baltimore City Tax Assessor's Ledger, 1818, Ward 3

NAME	RACE/ STATUS	RESIDENCE	REAL PROPERTY	OCCUPATION	ENSLAVED PROPERTY Name, Age, Value	COMMENTS
Wilson, Thomas		Church St			Hannah 22, $80.	
Wilson, William Sr.		Market St		Merchant	Prisy 50, $30.	
Winchester, George		Church St			Sterley 50, $40. Richard 21, $125. Henny 18, $80.	
Winder, Gen. W. H.		Chatham St			James 32, $125. Mary 14, $80.	
Wirgman, Peter		Calvert St			Milly 33, $80.	
Woods, William H.		East St			Priscilla 31, $80.	

Free Blacks and Slave Owners in Baltimore City Tax Assessor's Ledger, 1818, Ward 4

NAME	RACE/ STATUS	RESIDENCE	REAL PROPERTY	OCCUPATION	ENSLAVED PROPERTY Name, Age, Value	COMMENTS
Allison, Mrs. Mary	Widow	Gay St			William 24, $125. Sarah 31, $80.	
Ayres, Jacob		Commerce St			Betsy 12, $40.	
Barnes, Levin P.		South St			Charlotte 23, $80. & child 4 yrs. old, $10.	
Beal, John W.		South St			David 9, $40. Henny 40, $40. Daley 11, $40.	
Benson, Samuel		Baltimore St		Tailor	Henry 12, $40. Henny 20, $80.	
Boggs, Harmanus		Baltimore St		Dry goods merchant	Peg 25, $80. Mary 7, $20.	
Boyd, Ann		Holliday St			Ellen 10, $40.	
Bradenbaugh/Breidenbach, John		Fish St			Lucy 16, $80.	
Brown, Dr. George		Holliday St		M.D.	Jim 44, $125. Essex 24, $125. Suck 32, $80.	
Buchanan, Misses Sidney & Margaret		Gay St			Abraham 23, $125. Matilda 33, $80.	
Buchanan, Mrs.	Widow	Gay St			Eli 15, $125. Female Slave 35, $80. Fanny 35, $80 & child 6, $20.	
Bull, Elisha		Orange Alley		Carpenter	Isaac 16, $125. Little Isaac 10, $40.	
Campbell, William		Water St & South St		Tailor	Jenny 53, $20. Mary 10, $40.	
Canon, Mary	Tenant to Anthony Favier	South St			Female slave 20, $80.	
Carrere, John		East St		Merchant	Jeremiah 45, $125. Nicholas 42, $125.	

Free Blacks and Slave Owners in Baltimore City Tax Assessor's Ledger, 1818, Ward 4

NAME	RACE/STATUS	RESIDENCE	REAL PROPERTY	OCCUPATION	ENSLAVED PROPERTY Name, Age, Value	COMMENTS
Clark, Stephen		Commerce St			Abraham 12, $40. Harry 6, $20. Sarah 44, $40. Grace 4, $10.	
Creery, Jonathan		Lovely Lane			Peter 15, $125. Ann 50, $30.	
Crowl, Henry		Commerce St		Proprietor of livery stable	George 16, $125. Rollins 12, $40. Mary 16, $80.	
Dickinson, William		Baltimore St			Jacob 22, $125. Dick 11, $40. Moses 2, $5. Nan 22, $80. Kitty 8, $40. Mary 14, $80.	
Donnell, John		Water St		Merchant	Norris 15, $125. John 25, $125. Sarah 18, $80.	
Dunwoody, Robert		Pratt St			James 18, $125. Gracy 19, $80. Betsy 9, $40. Eliza 9, $40.	
Fairbairn, Thomas H.		Holliday St			Peter 17, $125. Ellick 4, $10. Charlotte 26, $80. Mary 12, $40.	
Farquharson, Charles		Fish St		Carpenter	Female slave 10, $40.	
Fisher, Henry M.		Commerce St		Guilder	William 30, $125.	
Fitzhugh, Mrs. Elizabeth		Gay St			Siddy 15, $80. Mary 45, $40.	
Frelet, Augustus		Second St			Romay 31, $125.	

Free Blacks and Slave Owners in Baltimore City Tax Assessor's Ledger, 1818, Ward 4

NAME	RACE/STATUS	RESIDENCE	REAL PROPERTY	OCCUPATION	ENSLAVED PROPERTY Name, Age, Value	COMMENTS
Gatchell, Increase		Baltimore St		Dry goods merchant	Hett 25, $80. Rose 18, $80.	
Gilmor, Robert		Water St		Merchant	George 31, $125.	
Gilmor, Robert Jr.		Water St		Merchant @ house of Robert Gilmor & Sons	John 30, $125. Frank 15, $125. Nelly 25, $80. Isabella 17, $80.	
Giraud, Dr. John J.		South St		M.D.	Jack 50, $60. Charlotte 44, $40. Susan 29, $80.	
Gregg, John		Pratt St		Grocer	Jane 40, $40. Kitty 15, $80.	
Griffith, Henry B.		Baltimore St		Dry goods merchant	Harriett 11, $40.	
Gwinn, Charles		McClure's Wharf			Henry 7, $20. Lucy 24, $80.	
Hamilton, Dr. Thomas		Gay St		M.D.	Rachale 21, $80.	
Hawkins, James L		Baltimore St		Cashier	Harry 26, $125. Henry 8, $40. Nancy 21, $80.	
Hollingsworth, Mrs. Ann		South St			Robert 30, $125. Polydore 27, $125. Phillis 23, $80. Prudence 21, $80.	
Jenkins, Edward		South St		Saddle & harness maker	Jim 12, $40. Jane 35, $80. Sarah 15, $80.	

Free Blacks and Slave Owners in Baltimore City Tax Assessor's Ledger, 1818, Ward 4

NAME	RACE/STATUS	RESIDENCE	REAL PROPERTY	OCCUPATION	ENSLAVED PROPERTY Name, Age, Value	COMMENTS
Jenkins, William		Water St		Currier	George 14, $125. Dennis 9, $40. Harry 7, $20. Sally 35, $80.	
Keener, John		Water St		Gunsmith	Jim 4, $10. Male slave 2, $5. Caty 36, $80.	
Key, Abner		Pratt St		Grocer	Harriett 15, $80.	
Kurtz, Rev. Daniel		Holliday St		Rector of the German Lutheran Church	Charlotte 12, $40.	
Lewis, Abraham J.		Holliday St			Elisha 30, $125.	
Leypold, Frederick		Gay St		Grocer	Jacob 28, $125. Elizabeth 48, $30. Kitty 17, $80. Ellen 10, $40.	
Lovell, William		Gay St		Baker	Richard 16, $125. Rice 23, $80.	
Maggs, Jane	Widow	Gay St			Molly 40, $40.	
Marks, William		Baltimore St		Shakespeare Tavern	Jack 18, $125.	
Maroste, D.	French Lady	Gay St			Rose 45, $40. Ronna 12, $40.	
Martin, James		Baltimore St		Grocer	Joe 22, $125. Edward 19, $125. Priscilla 70, no value. Juliet 28, $80. Maria 18, $80.	
Matthews, William		Water St			James 25, $125. Edward 23, $125.	
McClellan, Samuel		Lovely Lane			Joseph 19, $125. Rachel 17, $80. Agnes 11, $40. Louisa 10, $40.	
McDowell, George		Baltimore St		Blank book & stationary store	Ann 10, $40.	

Free Blacks and Slave Owners in Baltimore City Tax Assessor's Ledger, 1818, Ward 4

NAME	RACE/ STATUS	RESIDENCE	REAL PROPERTY	OCCUPATION	ENSLAVED PROPERTY Name, Age, Value	COMMENTS
McFerrin, John		Second St		Baker	Laid 17, $125. Caty 22, $80.	
McKenzie, George		Water St			Adam 11, $40. David 9, $40. Male slave 2, $5. Milly 35, $80.	
McKim, John Jr.		Holliday St			Richard 45, $125. David 28, $125. John 12, $40. Penlab 50, $30.	
Moale, Samuel		Gay St			Charles 44, $125. Harry 15, $125. Milley 40, $40. Sarah 27, $80. Jane 12, $40. Sophia 10, $40.	
Moore, William S.		Bowley's Wharf			Philip 30, $125. Simon 38, $125. Richard 28, $125. Henry 16, $125. Perry 22, $125. Anna 28, $80. Nancy 33, $80.	
Myers, Godfrey		Second St			Rachael 26, $80.	
Myers, Jacob		McClure's Wharf		China Merchant	Jack 30, $125. Mary 18, $80. Polly 15, $80.	
Myers, John		Water St		Merchant	Lewis 23, $125.	
Nicholson, John		South St			Female slave 70, no value.	
Oldham, John		South St		Chair factory	Enoch 22, $125. Sidney 28, $80. Darky 25, $80.	

Free Blacks and Slave Owners in Baltimore City Tax Assessor's Ledger, 1818, Ward 4

NAME	RACE/ STATUS	RESIDENCE	REAL PROPERTY	OCCUPATION	ENSLAVED PROPERTY Name, Age, Value	COMMENTS
Owens, Joseph		Baltimore St			Jack 19, $125. Mary 12, $40.	
Pannell, Edward		South St		Gent.	Bina 50, $30. Ann 24, $80.	
Patterson, John		South St		Tailor	Andrew 12, $40. Stephen 3, $10. Nancy 12, $40.	
Patterson, William		South St		Merchant in House of William Patterson & Sons	William 50, $60. David 22, $125. Bill 10, $40. Sucky 27, $80. Young Rena 25, $80. Anny 20, $80. Mary 3, $10.	
Pennington, Joshua		South St			Henrietta 6, $20.	
Pool, Rezin		South St		Cordwainer	Eve 9, $40.	
Raborg, Christopher (Estate of)		Water St			Frank 40, $125. Sevy 33, $80. Sall 7, $20.	
Readel, John		Gay St			Nelson 12, $40. Charlotte 32, $80. July 6, $20.	
Reigart, Philip		Baltimore St		Gent.	Harriett 15, $80.	
Rogers, Jacob		South St		Hatter	Anthony 27, $125. Bill 18, $125. Nat 12, $40. David 25, $125. Sophia 32, $80. Fanny 24, $80. Nancy 18, $80.	
Ross, Reuben		South St			Eliza 15, $80.	

Free Blacks and Slave Owners in Baltimore City Tax Assessor's Ledger, 1818, Ward 4

NAME	RACE/STATUS	RESIDENCE	REAL PROPERTY	OCCUPATION	ENSLAVED PROPERTY Name, Age, Value	COMMENTS
Roy, John		Baltimore St			Willis 24, $125. Julia 32, $80.	
Schaeffer, Frederick G.		Holliday St		Printer, Proprietor of *The Federal Republican & Baltimore Telegraph*	Female Slave 15, $80.	
Singleton, Mrs. Elizabeth		Gay St			Susan 16, $80. Beck 6, $20.	
Sinners, Elijah R.		Water St		Proprietor of the Globe Hotel	Deborah 30, $80. Minty 21, $80. Adaline 24, $80.	
Slater, Hannah	Widow	Baltimore St			Rosina 45, $40. Esther 36, $80.	
Smith, Gen. Sam		Water St			William 12, $40. Rebecca 50, $30. Rossetta 50, $30. Lydia 18, $80.	
Starr, William		Calvert St		Tobacconist	Harriett 25, $80.	
Stenson, William		Baltimore St			Female slave 50, $30.	
Sterett, Joseph		Holliday St			Clem 50, $60. Eliza 11, $40.	
Tharp, George		Gay St		Silver Plater	Mable 22, $80. Harriet 3, $10.	
Vallette, Charles		Baltimore St			Paul 11, $40. John 5, $20. Mary 36, $80. Louisa 16, $80. Caroline 8, $40.	

Free Blacks and Slave Owners in Baltimore City Tax Assessor's Ledger, 1818, Ward 4

NAME	RACE/ STATUS	RESIDENCE	REAL PROPERTY	OCCUPATION	ENSLAVED PROPERTY Name, Age, Value	COMMENTS
Walker, Isaiah		Water St			Hannah 25, $80. Mary 7, $20.	
Weise, S.L.	Widow	Baltimore St			Stev 17, $125. Mary 14, $80.	
White, Dr. John C.		East St		Merchant in the House of John C. White & Sons	Harry 25, $125. Robbins 14, $125.	
White, John		Gay St			Fan 28, $80.	
Williams, Capt. William N.		Gay St			Maria 25, $80.	
Williamson, James		South St			James 13, $40. Stephen 10, $40. John 7, $20.	
Wilson, James		Holliday St		Merchant in the House of William Wilson & Sons	Phelan 32, $125. Clarey 29, $80.	
Wilson, Robert		South St		Cashier	Joe 13, $40. Mary 20, $80.	
Wintkle, Elizabeth	Widow	McClure's Wharf		Proprietor of the Union Hotel	Andrew 18, $125. Jefferson 10, $40. Polly 33, $80. Hetty 21, $80. Ruth 20, $80. Agnes 7, $20.	
Worrall, Margaret	Widow	Holliday St		Boarding House	Charlotte 22, $80. Ann 10, $10.	Ann is infirm.

Free Blacks and Slave Owners in Baltimore City Tax Assessor's Ledger, 1818, Ward 5

NAME	RACE/STATUS	RESIDENCE	REAL PROPERTY	OCCUPATION	ENSLAVED PROPERTY Name, Age, Value	COMMENTS
Bangs, John		Baltimore St			Ellen 8, $40.	
Baque, Margaret	Widow	Pratt St			Mary 18, $80. Theodore 1, $5.	
Bingham, Gordon		Frederick St			George 7, $35. Emaline 6, $30.	Emaline is property of Robert Bingham.
Bolgino, Francis		Frederick St			Ann 27, $80.	
Bonefono, John		N. Gay St			Stafford 26, $125.	Stafford is property of John Sprosler.
Bonner, John		Frederick St			Suckey 11, $40.	
Bosley, Daniel & James		Market Space			Abraham 24, $125.	
Bosley, James B.		Market Space			Minty 28, $80. Stephen 12, $40.	
Buck, Jacob		Market Space			Daniel 13, $40.	
Callender, John		Market Space			Jack 12, $40.	
Camp, William		Water St			Lambert 30, $125. Mary 16, $80.	
Carnigham, James		Frederick St			Juliet 21, $80. Fanny, no age given, $40.	Fanny is property of William Gragian.
Carr, Thomas		Baltimore St N side			Becky 33, $80. Harriet 8, $40. William 18, $125.	William is property of John Carr.
Coale, William H.		Cumberand Row			Maria 23, $80.	
Cole, William		S. Gay St		Merchant	Joe 15, $125. Beck 11, $40.	

Free Blacks and Slave Owners in Baltimore City Tax Assessor's Ledger, 1818, Ward 5

NAME	RACE/ STATUS	RESIDENCE	REAL PROPERTY	OCCUPATION	ENSLAVED PROPERTY Name, Age, Value	COMMENTS
Cooke, William	Cooke live in Gen. Redgely's house	Frederick St			Hetty 10, $40.	
Cox, Peter		Dugan's Wharf			Silvey 16, $80. Dick only 6 weeks, no value.	
Darden, Henry		Harrison St			Richard 19, $125. Carlos 19, $125. Suckey 17, $80. Charlotte 17, $80. Susan 11, $40.	
Dew, Ann		Frederick St			Pheby 30, $80. Hezekiah 10, $40. Nate 28, $125. Luzerene 13, $40.	
Diffendall, John		Frederick St		Stone cutter	Jack 5, $25.	
Diffenderffer, Peter		Frederick St			Sarah 29, $80. Charles 4, $20. Saul 18, $125. Charlotte 13, $40.	Charlotte is the property of W.H. Winder.
Dobson, Priscilla	Widow of Joseph	Baltimore St			Margaret 16, $80. Mary 7, $35. Nathan 6, $30. Charles 8, $40.	
Ducatel, Edme		Harrison St			Annett 35, $80. Agnes 35, $80.	
Dugan, Cumberland		Dugan's Wharf			Ned, Jacob,& Dick 60 plus. Pheby 30, $80. Allen 17, $125. Airy 3, $15. Phebe 2, $10. John Charley 3, $15.	Value not stated for Ned, Jacob & Dick.
Eunick, Thomas		Gay St			Maria 16, $80.	

Free Blacks and Slave Owners in Baltimore City Tax Assessor's Ledger, 1818, Ward 5

NAME	RACE/ STATUS	RESIDENCE	REAL PROPERTY	OCCUPATION	ENSLAVED PROPERTY Name, Age, Value	COMMENTS
Faure, Blanche	French Lady	Water St			Mary Ann 16, $80. Nancy 23, $80. Henry 1, $5. Alford 4, $20.	
Femister, Alexander		Baltimore St south side			Priscilla 20, $80.	
Finlay, Hugh		Gay St			Joe, No age given.	Property of W. White at John Aisquith, Esq. who is agent
Foreman, Elijah (Estate of)		Dugan's Wharf			Clara 11, $40. James 17, $125.	
Fowler, William		Harrison St			Milly 22, $80.	
Franciscus, John		N. Gay St			Kitty 17, $80.	
French, Ebenezer		N. Gay St			Mary 24, $10.	Mary is infirm.
Frick, Peter		N. Gay St			Harriot 25, $80. Leah 21, $80. Mary 15, $80. Ann 4, $20.	
Galland, John B.		N. Gay St		Tailor	John 20, $125. Sidney 22, $80.	
Gill, John		South St		Notary	Sally 42, $50. Becky 19, $80.	Becky is property of Richard Tilman.
Gilmore, William		S. Gay St			Thomas 50, $100. James 14, $125. Ambrose 14, $125.	James is property of R. Gilmore, Jr. Ambrose is property of B.C. Howard.
Ginnar, Francis		Water St			Mariline 22, $80.	
Godfroid, William (Estate of)		Water St			Dick 14, $125.	

Free Blacks and Slave Owners in Baltimore City Tax Assessor's Ledger, 1818, Ward 5

NAME	RACE/ STATUS	RESIDENCE	REAL PROPERTY	OCCUPATION	ENSLAVED PROPERTY Name, Age, Value	COMMENTS
Gooding, John		Harrison St			Sophia 20, $80. Ruth 25, $80. Jim 1, $5. One Negro girl 2, $10.	
Green, Armisted		N. Gay St			Susan 25, $40.	
Hammonds, John L.		Market Space			Priss, age unknown, $35.	
Harper, Robert G.		S. Gay St			Jerry 37, $125. John 21, 125. William 15, $125. Joseph 9, $40. Nance 39, $65. Polly 27, $80. Julia 13, $40. Maria 15, $80. Betty 13, $40. Henry 2, $10. Harriot 3, $15. Hetty 5, $25. Harriot 39, $65.	
Haskins, Govert		Second St			James 25, $125. Dafney 25, $80. Delia 7, $35.	
Heslip, John		N. Gay St		Shoemaker	Rosetta 26, $80. Sarah 7, $35.	
Hollins, John S.		Water St			David 25, $125. Mary Ann 30, $80. Maria 8, $40. Edward 1, $5. Susan 18, $80.	
Horton, William L.		N. Gay St			Hetty 18, $80. Kitty 16, $80. Riichard 18, $125. Patty 13, $40. William 8, $40.	
Hutchings, Elizabeth		Frederick St			Charity 18, $8.	At R. Gorsuch's.
Hutton, James		Baltimore St N side			Marshall 24, $125. Sophey 24, $80.	

Free Blacks and Slave Owners in Baltimore City Tax Assessor's Ledger, 1818, Ward 5

NAME	RACE/ STATUS	RESIDENCE	REAL PROPERTY	OCCUPATION	ENSLAVED PROPERTY Name, Age, Value	COMMENTS
Ireland, Edward (Estate of)		Baltimore St. S side			Joseph 13, $40. Ginny 12, $40.	
Jamison, Joseph		Frederick St			Mary 27, $80. Richard 3, $15. Child 8 months, no value.	
Johns, Hosea		Frederick St			Francis, no age, no value given.	Francis is property of Jonathan Harris of Fells Point.
Jones, Aubray (Estate of)		Cumberland Row			Hannah 34, $80. Elizabeth 8, $40.	
Kaylor, George		Cumberland Row			Kitty 15, $80.	
Keys, John		Dugan's Wharf			Jacob 16, $125.	
Larsh, Margaret		S. Gay St			Charlotte 15, $80.	Charlotte is property of Sarah Dorsey.
Lavaly, Mary	Mary is living in the Larsh house.	Baltimore St			Phily 21, $80.	
Legrand, Samuel D.		Market Space			Hannah 15, $80. Harriot 14, $80.	
Mackenzie, Colin		N. Gay St		M.D.	Bill 39, $125.	
Marche, John		Second St			Polly 35, $80. Joseph 5, $25. Andrew 2, $11.	
McConnell, Miss Elizabeth		Frederick St			Julia 7, $35.	
McKim, Samuel		Frederick St			Beck 10, $40	
McMechen, William		Frederick St			Michael & Kitty, 50, no value James 19, $125. Patience 17, $80. Jane 14, $80.	Michael & Kitty are infirm.

Free Blacks and Slave Owners in Baltimore City Tax Assessor's Ledger, 1818, Ward 5

NAME	RACE/ STATUS	RESIDENCE	REAL PROPERTY	OCCUPATION	ENSLAVED PROPERTY Name, Age, Value	COMMENTS
Miller, Catherine	Widow of John	Market Space			Henrietta 18, $80.	
Mills, William P.		Harrison St			Nancy 18, $80.	
Mills, Ezekiel		N. Frederick St		Tailor	Priss 31, $80. Louisa 1, $5.	
Mitchell, Alexander		Frederick St			Rachael 20, $80.	
Munroe, Isaac		Frederick St		Printer	Dolly 38, $70. Didea 3, $15.	
Newton, Anthony		Baltimore St			James 7, $35.	
Ninde, James		S. Gay St			Jacob 11, $40.	Jacob is property of W. Mills.
Olliver, Robert		S. Gay St			George 36, $125. Archey 26, $125. Suckey 45, $40.	
Owens, William		Dugan's Wharf		Grocer	Nance 16, $80. Grace 14, $80. Aaron 38, $125.	
Patterson, Edward of William		Frederick St			Charlotte 15, $80. James 7, $35. Robert 24, $125.	Robert is property of C. Hughes, Jr.
Perkins, John		Baltimore St S side		Dry goods store	Joe 9, $40.	
Philippe, Joseph		S. Gay St			Betty 22, $80. John 2, $10.	
Poncet, Lewis		Baltimore St north side			Armin 25, $80. Candis 40, $60. Dick 11, $40. Rachael 14, $80.	
Presbury, George G. III		N. Gay St			Milcah 23, $80. Dutchy 25, $80. Maria 14, $80.	
Ridgely, Greenbury, Jr.		Baltimore St S side			George 8, $40. Molly 11, $40.	
Salmon, Charles		Baltimore St			Prudence 11, $40. Nelly 30, $80. Lucy 18, $80.	Nelly is property of Caleb Johnson.

Free Blacks and Slave Owners in Baltimore City Tax Assessor's Ledger, 1818, Ward 5

NAME	RACE/STATUS	RESIDENCE	REAL PROPERTY	OCCUPATION	ENSLAVED PROPERTY Name, Age, Value	COMMENTS
Schaeffer, William A.		Baltimore St			Patty 5, $25.	
Smith, Arnold (Estate of)		Gay St			Peter 33, $125. Jack 16, $125.	
Smith, Elizabeth	Widow of William	Baltimore St N side			Christianna 12, $40.	Property of Lloyd Rogers.
Smith, George		S. Gay St		Carver & Guilder	Sarah 20, $80.	Sarah is property of P. R. I. Freieze.
Smith, George C.		S. Gay St			Susan 21, $80. Reman 19, $125.	
Smith, Job		Frederick St			Caroline 12, $40.	
Smith, William		S. Gay St		Wood corder	Sarah 12, $40.	
Smythe, James		Frederick St		M.D.	Nathan 28, $125.	Property of Susan White.
Sollers, Basil		Baltimore St north side		Hatter	Sally 28, $80. Sophia 22, $80. Gabriel 7, $35. Patsy 5, $25. Mary Ann 3, $15. Henry 1, $5. Eliza, under 1, no value.	
Spear, Barbara	Widow of Joseph	S. Gay St			Sophia 29, $80. Ben 4, $20. Elizabeth 2, $10.	
Sprigg, Thomas		Dugan's Wharf			Charles 22, $125.	Charles is property of W. Schriver of Calvert County.
Sprole, William		Second St			Nathan 16, $125. Betsy 18, $80.	
Spurrier, William		Baltimore St N side		Painter	Louisa 10, $40.	

Free Blacks and Slave Owners in Baltimore City Tax Assessor's Ledger, 1818, Ward 5

NAME	RACE/ STATUS	RESIDENCE	REAL PROPERTY	OCCUPATION	ENSLAVED PROPERTY Name, Age, Value	COMMENTS
Sterrett, James		S. Gay St			Maria 23, $80. Charlotte 23, $80. Betty 14, $80. Davy 22, $125. Ben 2, $10.	
Stewart, David (Estate of)		S. Gay St			Charity 21, $80. Sophia 17, $80.	
Sutliff, Thomas		Market Space		Innkeeper	Mary 14, $80. Susan 16, $80.	Susan is property of John Martiacq, tailor.
Tenant, Thomas		Frederick St			Chaney 30, $80. Ann 35, $80. Hester 25, $80. Henry 30, $125. Vincent 50, $100. Theodore 35, $125. George 16, $125. Henry 6, $30. One infant, no value.	
Torrance, Charles		Harrison St			Mary 43, $40. Fanny 28, $80. Levin 27, $125.	
Towson, Philemon		S. Gay St			Nancy 47, $35. Fanny 42, $50. Jacob 13, $40. Marqa 12, $40. Ann 8, $40. Anthony 27, $125. Resin 19, $125. Philip 19, $125.	Anthony is property of H. Warren. Resin is property of Benjamin Hutchings. Philip is property of Elizabeth Troop.
Van Wyck, William (Estate of)		S. Gay St			Bristol 39, $125. George 15, $125. Sally 41, $55. Milly 25, no value.	Milly is subject to fits.
Vintkler, John		Dugan's Wharf		Tailor	Rachael 22, $80.	

Free Blacks and Slave Owners in Baltimore City Tax Assessor's Ledger, 1818, Ward 5

NAME	RACE/ STATUS	RESIDENCE	REAL PROPERTY	OCCUPATION	ENSLAVED PROPERTY Name, Age, Value	COMMENTS
Volunbrun, Jean M.	Volunbrun is a female.	Harrison St			Irene 1, $5. Loveque 32, $125. Mago 41, $125. Tronquilla 42, $125. Bishop 32, $125. Prudence 35, $80. Adale 21, $80. Sanite 35, $80. Popote 35, $80. Saline 31, $80. Tresoline 11, $40. August 12, $40. Charles 35, $125. Bael 30, $125. Bazile 37, $125.	
Wall, John E.		Water St		Tavern	Peter 21, $125. Caroline 10, $40.	
Warner, William		N. Gay St			Samuel 20, $125. Nelly 40, $60. James 12, $40.	
Weise, Felix		Harrison St			Nele 18, $80.	
Welmore, Margaret		Baltimore St S side			Fanny 12, $40.	Fanny is property of Andrew Aldridge.
Wesley, Thomas		Second St		Tavern	John 9, $40.	John is property of James Gunn.
West, John		Cumberland Row		Tailor	Peggy 35, $80. Joe 10, $40.	
West, Maria	Widow of James	S. Gay St			Weickley, 30, $125. Nace 14, $125.	Nace is property of W. Summerville.
Wilson, Joseph		N. Gay St		Cabinetmaker	Mary 8, $40.	

Free Blacks and Slave Owners in Baltimore City Tax Assessor's Ledger, 1818, Ward 5

NAME	RACE/ STATUS	RESIDENCE	REAL PROPERTY	OCCUPATION	ENSLAVED PROPERTY Name, Age, Value	COMMENTS
Wyvill, Marmaduke		Frederick St			Ariel 14, $80.	
Zollers, Dr. Charles, (Estate of)		Frederick St			Susan 11, $40.	

Free Blacks and Slave Owners in Baltimore City Tax Assessor's Ledger, 1818, Ward 6

NAME	RACE/ STATUS	RESIDENCE	REAL PROPERTY	OCCUPATION	ENSLAVED PROPERTY Name, Age, Value	COMMENTS
Amos, John		High St E Side		Hatter	Dinah 25, $80 Toby 8, $40	
Armstrong, James		McElderry's Wharf		Grocer	Sarah 35, $80 Caroline 9, $40 Harry 25, $125	
Armstrong, James C.		High St E Side			Henry 26, $80 Jenny 30, $80 Nelson 5, $25 Ann 2, $10 Margarett 10, $49	Henry D. to H.T. Armstrong 1822. Jenny abated 1821. Nelson H.T. Armstrong. Ann H.T. Armstrong. Margarett is property of Thomas Barney.
Ashbaw, Francis		Front St E Side		Tavern	Moses 21, $125. William 5, $25. Mary 11, $40.	
Baker, Providence & Betsey Baker		Jones S W Side			Flora 25, $80. Bet 25, $80 James 21, $125 Matilda 4, $20. Rachel 2, $10	
Ball, Elizabeth	Widow of William	Temple St			Hannah 8, $40. Hagar 6, $30.	Hagar released being in the country for 1821.
Ball, William		Sty's Lane N Side		Constable	Harriot 13, $40.	

Free Blacks and Slave Owners in Baltimore City Tax Assessor's Ledger, 1818, Ward 6

NAME	RACE/ STATUS	RESIDENCE	REAL PROPERTY	OCCUPATION	ENSLAVED PROPERTY Name, Age, Value	COMMENTS
Barney, John H.		Pitt St N Side			Alice 45, $40. Tom 40, $125. Jane 16, $80. Rachel 18, $80. Tom 60, no value given.	Rachel and Richard are released; deduct for slave Rachel $80 and slave Richard $125. Tom is infirm.
Barrickman, Hannah		Bridge St N Side		Hard ware store	Fanny 16, $80	
Barry, Lavallin		Bridge St N Side		In Bank of Baltimore	Peggy 39, $65 Cassey 12, $40	
Bateman, Benjamin		High St E Side		Clerk in the City Bank	Louisa 12, $40	
Beal, Evan		High St W Side		Grocer	Susan 33, $80. Ned 11, $40 Maria 11, $40. Harriett, 9 $40. Orick or Brick 7, $35.	Beal is tenant. Susan abated in 1822. Ned abated in 1822.
Bivins, Baker		Jones St E Side		Slater	Amey 4, $20 Ann 3, $15	
Black, James		Fish market		Oyster House	Susan 17, $80 Ann 12, $40	Released slave Ann 1822. Released Susan 1821.
Blake, Ruth		Bridge St N Side			Mary 25, $80 Ann 2, $10	Blake lives at Ensors.
Bolte, John		High St W Side		Broker	Susan 28, $80. Thomas 8, $40 Sam 6, $30. Jane 4, $20. Patience 18, $80	Susan abated, transferred 1821. Patience abated out of town for 1821.

Free Blacks and Slave Owners in Baltimore City Tax Assessor's Ledger, 1818, Ward 6

NAME	RACE/STATUS	RESIDENCE	REAL PROPERTY	OCCUPATION	ENSLAVED PROPERTY Name, Age, Value	COMMENTS
Bond, Peter		High St E Side		Merchant	Rachel 33, $80 George 11, $40	
Bonnett, Joseph		St. Patricks Row		Mattress maker	Modest 45, $40. Zemer 55, $20 Louisa 26, $80. Charity 15, $80. Grace 10, $40. Arone 62, $20. Philipene 52, $60. Ferdinand 3, $15. Josephine 1, $5. Jane 60, $30.	
Bowen, Catherine	Widow	High St E Side			Alice 46, $20. Rosetta 10, $40 Delinda 5, $25.	
Briscoe, Alexander		St. Patricks Row		Constable	Tom 15, No value Kitty 20, $80 Nancy 22, $80	Tom has only one leg. Kitty and Nancy property of Ruth Urlson.
Briscoe, James Alexander		Pitt St S Side		Shoemaker	James 9, $40. Maria 8, $40.	Tenant
Briscoe, Samuel		Trent St		Merchant	John 28, $125. Jonas 17, $125. Willis 15, $80.	
Bromwell, William		Pitt St S Side			John 22, $125. Matilda 9, $40	
Bromwell, William Jr.		McElderry St		Lumber yard	Tom 15, $125	Tom property of T. D. Lang?her.
Brown, Jehu		Sty's Lane S Side		Pile Driver	June 12, $40	June property of Josiah Green in the Neck.

Free Blacks and Slave Owners in Baltimore City Tax Assessor's Ledger, 1818, Ward 6

NAME	RACE/ STATUS	RESIDENCE	REAL PROPERTY	OCCUPATION	ENSLAVED PROPERTY Name, Age, Value	COMMENTS
Brown, Mary	Widow	High St W Side			Tom 23, $125	Tom property of Elizabeth Hinson. Abated slave Tom at Orleans $125 for 1821.
Bruscup, John		Front St E Side		Storekeeper	Ann 11, $40	Ann property of Dick Mitchell on Duke St.
Bryson, Nathan G.		Bridge St N Side			Jarvis 26, $125 James 12, $40	
Buchanan, Elizabeth		Front St W Side			Priss 25, $80. John 8, $40. Eliza 3, $15.	
Busch, Henry		Pitt St S Side		Tailor	Lose 10, $40.	
Caldwell, Thomas		Great York N Side		Merchant	Stephen 12, $40	Tenant
Carson, Andrew (estate of)		Great York N Side			Eve 12, $40	Property of Hawkins.
Carthouse, Charles W.		Great York N Side			Harry 16, $125	
Casey, Mary	Widow	High St E Side			Mary 26, $80	
Chambers, Daniel		Bridge St N Side		Rope store	Harriott 12, $40 Dennis 10, $40	Release all ??? to country for 1822.

Free Blacks and Slave Owners in Baltimore City Tax Assessor's Ledger, 1818, Ward 6

NAME	RACE/ STATUS	RESIDENCE	REAL PROPERTY	OCCUPATION	ENSLAVED PROPERTY Name, Age, Value	COMMENTS
Chenoweth, Richard B.		Front St W Side		Blacksmith	Harry 20, $125. Liven 23, $125. Daniel 30, $125. Harry 18, $125. Alpha 16, $80.	Harry released free for 1821. Liven property of Haddenton; released sold out of city 1821. Daniel property of Briscoe; released in 1822. Harry 18, yrs., .property of Joan Norris; released for 1821. Alpha property of Marge Home.
Cobb, Lyman H.		Bridge St S Side		Formerly blacksmith	Sally 18, $80	Sally property of Susan Peaker.
Cockey, Thomas		Addison St		Constable	Ann 16, $80	
Colvin, Ann	Widow of Samuel	Front St W Side			Dinah 7, $35	
Conn, William		Pitt St N Side		Franklin Bank	Mary 40, $60.	
Constable, John		High St W Side		Carpenter	Mary 14, $80	Mary property of Richard Patterson. Mary released out to W.P. who lives on the E. Shore. $80 for 1821.
Conway, William		St. Patricks Row		Blacksmith and grocer	Harriot 19, $80	

Free Blacks and Slave Owners in Baltimore City Tax Assessor's Ledger, 1818, Ward 6

NAME	RACE/ STATUS	RESIDENCE	REAL PROPERTY	OCCUPATION	ENSLAVED PROPERTY Name, Age, Value	COMMENTS
Crock, Charles		St. Patricks Row		Store on Cheapside	Jude 35, $80	
Crook, Walter		Pitt St N Side		Cabinet Maker	James 30, $150. Nelly 13, $40. Sarah 7, $35.	James is cabinet maker.
Cross, William		High St E Side		Carpenter	Esther 20, $80. Daniel 2, $10. Bill 12, $40.	
Curlett, John		Union St W Side		Coach maker	Mahaley 11, $40	
Dalrymple, James		High St E Side		Bricklayer	Fred 36, $125 Joe 23, $125	Both slaves released and sold out of state.
Dangirord, Mary	Widow	Harrison St E Side			Laured 20, $80. Eliza 18, $80. John 2, $1.	
Davidson, Margaret	Widow of James	Baltimore St S Side			Rebecca 12, $40 Kitty 10, $40	James was a cooper.
Dawes, Mary	Widow	Dulany St N Side			Sarah 12, $40	
Diffenderfer, John		Great York N Side		Grocer	Thomas 20, $125. Paul 32, $125. Jude 29, $80. Milky 38, $70. Ann 10, $40.	
Diffenderffer, Charles		Market Space		Grocer	Bill 15, $125 Julia 17, $80	Julia released free for 1822.
Donaldson, Jane	Widow of Lowry	Front St E Side			Sophy 25, $80	
Elderkin, William G.		Lives on Green St		Wholesale & retail dry goods store	Harriet 16, $80	Harriet property of James Maggs on Gay St.
Ellery, Eppes		Pitt St S Side		Spectacle Manufacturer	Christina 10, $40	Christina property of Thomas Stone, Baltimore Co.

Free Blacks and Slave Owners in Baltimore City Tax Assessor's Ledger, 1818, Ward 6

NAME	RACE/ STATUS	RESIDENCE	REAL PROPERTY	OCCUPATION	ENSLAVED PROPERTY Name, Age, Value	COMMENTS
Elliott, John		Straight Lane		Plasterer	Charles 22, $125	
Evans, Griffith		Water St N Side		Cooper	Caroline 24, $80 Henry 2, $10	
Fitgzhugh, George		North St N Side		In the Bank of Maryland	Henry 16, $80 Comfort 10, $40	Henry property of Mary Fitzhugh. Comfort property of Margaret Martin.
Forrister, Ralph E.		St. Patricks Row		Cabinet maker	Sophia 20, $80	
Frazier, Richard		High St E Side		Custom House Officer	Ellen 21, $80 Louisa 9, $40	Ellen released for 1823.
Gauline, John B.		Great York N Side		Music Master	Hagar 10, $40	Hagar is property of Wm. Mechin.
Gilbert, Harry		Jones St E Side		Market yard	Lindy 60, $20 Joshua 25, $125	Joshua is property of Sarah Amos.
Giles, Jacob W.		Great York N Side			John 10, $40. Delia 30, $80. Ann 18, $80. Samuel 40, $125	Delia being sold in the county.
Gill, John		Caroline St W Side			Harriot 14, $80	
Gillard, Jacob	Col'd. man	Green St W Side	Lot $120, Imp $30, Furn $2, Horse $10, Dray $6	Drayman		
Goldthwait, Mary	Widow of Samuel	Front St W Side			Darkey 30, $80 Mary 2, $10	Valued at same amount in 1822.
Gorsuch, Joshua		Bridge St S Side		Store keeper	Susan 19, $80 Rose 6, $30	
Gorsuch, Nicholas		Front St E Side		Tavern Keeper	Richard 25, $125. Harry 8, $40. Sam 3, $15.	

Free Blacks and Slave Owners in Baltimore City Tax Assessor's Ledger, 1818, Ward 6

NAME	RACE/ STATUS	RESIDENCE	REAL PROPERTY	OCCUPATION	ENSLAVED PROPERTY Name, Age, Value	COMMENTS
Gough, Prudence		Front St. W Side			Milly 21, $80. Sarah 70, $80. Lydia 20, $80. Perry 18, $125. Maria 23, $80. Philip 60, $10.	Perry to H.D. Carroll for 1821. Maria released for 1820.
Gouiran, Isadore		Baltimore St N Side		Dry goods store	August 17, $125 Henny 35, $80 Lewis 2, $10	
Gouldsmith, Sarah	Widow	Pitt St N Side			Rachel 38, $70. Acquilla 25, $125. Elisha 20, $125. Matilda 18, $80. Lucy 17, $80. Abraham 10, $40. Zack 9, $40.	
Gover, Ephraim G.		Pitt St N Side			Josiah 37, $125. Clarey 35, $80	Tenant
Graham, Dr. William. L.		Dulany St N Side		Physician	Fanny 30, $80. William 5, $25. Henry 3, $15. James 18 mos. $10	
Grasham, Margaret		Pitt St S Side			Maria 30, $80. James 5, $25. Jane 2, $10.	At Louis Richards.
Green, Benjamin		Green St E Side		Carpenter	Caroline 6, $30 Sarah 28, $80	
Green, Charles R.		Swan St S Side		Livery stable	Emery 10, $40	
Guildener, Charles		Petticoat Alley			Teaney 19, $80.	
Hall, Richard		High St W Side		Shoemaker	Nelly 18, $80	Nelly abated for 1823.
Hamilton, Robert		High St E Side		Captain	Libby 35, $80 Jess 8, $40 Joseph 1 1/2, $10	

Free Blacks and Slave Owners in Baltimore City Tax Assessor's Ledger, 1818, Ward 6

NAME	RACE/STATUS	RESIDENCE	REAL PROPERTY	OCCUPATION	ENSLAVED PROPERTY Name, Age, Value	COMMENTS
Hammon, William L.		Pitt St N Side		Dry Goods Store on Market St	Nancy 11, $40. Eliza 5, $25.	
Hanson, William		Front St W Side		Tailor	Harriot 14, $80	
Haslam, John		High St W Side		Furrier or farrier	Patience 13, $40	
Hay, Martha	Widow	High St W Side			William 10, $40	William released to Henry Armstrong.
Hays, William		Jones St E Side		Carpet store	Minty 24, $80. Harriot 20, $80. Maria 4, $20. Rachel 1, $5.	
Heddinger, Michael		Sty's Lane S Side			Isaac 21, $125	
Henshaw, James		Front St E Side			Violet 31, $80. Sam 11, $40. Diana 9, $40. Rose 7, $35. Jewel 4, $20. Arch 2, $10.	
Hickley, Sebastian		Addison St		Stone Cutter	James 21, $125 Jack 15, $125	
Hicks, John		Pitt St S Side		Carpenter	Henney 25, $80.	Henney property of Edward Griggs.
Hillen, John		Pitt St S Side			Easter 21, $80. Joe 28, $25.	Joe disabled
Hobson, George		Great York N Side		Sea Captain	Henry 22, $80.	Tenant. Henry is property of Mr. Clanagan.
Hopkins, Sarah	Widow	High St W Side			James 16, $125. Eliza 8, $40. Hannah 15, $80	
Horlon, James		Pitt St S Side		Auctioneer	Batties 10, $40	
Horne, Thomas		Commet St		Bricklayer	Tom 16, $125	
Howard, John		Pratt St N Side			Isaac 14, $125	

Free Blacks and Slave Owners in Baltimore City Tax Assessor's Ledger, 1818, Ward 6

NAME	RACE/ STATUS	RESIDENCE	REAL PROPERTY	OCCUPATION	ENSLAVED PROPERTY Name, Age, Value	COMMENTS
Hunt, Barbara	Widow	High St E Side			Rachael 15, $80.	Rachel is property of Henry Hunt.
Hurst, Shadrach		Bridge St N Side		Butcher	Maria no age given, $40	
Hyde, Samuel G.		High St W Side		Soap factory	Neomy 23, $80 Ann 2, $10	Neomy abated for 1823.
Jacobs, Samuel		Baltimore St S Side		Grocer	Fanny 17, $80 Moses 14, $125	Slave Fanny abated for 1822.
Jacquin, Paul		St. Patricks row		Broker	Susan 20, $80 Gracey 16, $80	Gracey property of Capt. Charles A. Chalmo.
Jamart, Michael		Fish market			Eagar 80, no value. Christine 16, $80. Isaac 13, $40. Kitty 6, $30. Edmond 5, $25. Charity 3, $15.	
Jamison, Joseph		Great York N Side			Scipio, $50	Scipio from Thomas Kell. Scipio to Robert Gorsuch.
Kell, Thomas		Commett St N Side			Scipio 50, $50 George 13, $40 Castileo 28, $125	Deduct for slave Scipio transferred to Col. Jamison.
Kincaid, James		Bridge St N Side		Storekeeper	Nancy 25, $80	? to Mathias B. Edgar, slave Nancy $80, 1822.
King, Samuel		High St E Side		Tavern and market yard	Tom 25, $125	Tom is property of John Waters.

Free Blacks and Slave Owners in Baltimore City Tax Assessor's Ledger, 1818, Ward 6

NAME	RACE/ STATUS	RESIDENCE	REAL PROPERTY	OCCUPATION	ENSLAVED PROPERTY Name, Age, Value	COMMENTS
Klinefelter, Michael		North St N Side		Tavern	Bill 12, $40 Luke 43, $125	Luke property of Ann Hall. Released Luke free for 1819.
Lamb, Joshua		Pitt St N Side			Jane 14, $80	Tenant
Lanney, Peter		Harrison St E Side		Varnish leather manufactury	Rosetta 40, $60. Rosetta 20, $80. Paul 1, $5.	
Letter, Thomas		High St E Side		Porter in the U. States Bank	Ann 15, $80	
Long, Henry		Jones St W Side		Soap factory	Fanny 35, $80. Mary An 10, $40. Thomas 5, $25. Darby 2, $10.	
Lowry, Samuel		St. Patricks Row		Dry goods store, corner	Charlotte 19, $80 Kitty, no age, $5	
Lusby, Henry		High St E Side		Cabinet Maker	Milly 10, $40	Milly is property of Patty Wheeler
Maher, Martin F.		High St W Side		Merchant	Ned 8, $40	Ned released for 1821-dead.
McAllister, John		Fish market		Tavern	Dinah 47, no value. Ann 28, $80. Rhode 12, $40. Jacob 60, no value. Vachel 25, $140.	Vachel is mechanic brass founder. Ann & Vachel abated for 1822.
McCauslen, James		St. Patricks Row		Merchant	Charlotte 14, $80	Charlotte property of Mrs. Bock. Released to C. Buck hire for 1822.

Free Blacks and Slave Owners in Baltimore City Tax Assessor's Ledger, 1818, Ward 6

NAME	RACE/ STATUS	RESIDENCE	REAL PROPERTY	OCCUPATION	ENSLAVED PROPERTY Name, Age, Value	COMMENTS
McComas, Elizabeth	Widow	High St near the corner of French St			Maria 19, $80	
McGinnes, John		Fish market		Livery stable	Rachel 19, $80. Ann 9, $40. Sam 40, $125.	Sam property of Henry Hale.
Meeteer, Samuel & William		Baltimore St. S Side		Paper maker	Charlotte 27, $80	
Merryman, Micajah Sr.		Front St W Side			Henry 6, $30. Ester 90, $30.	Henry released for 1821.
Miller, George W.		Fish market		Tavern	Jenny 25, $80. Esher 14, $80. Harry 14, $125. Milly 8, $40. Horace 2, $10. Eliza, a young child, no value.	
Miller, Jacob		Bridge St N Side		Tanner	Toby 36, $125. Elijah 36, $125. Charlotte 25, $80. Child 3 months old, $0.	Release Toby & Elijah set free and Charlotte dead for 1829.
Miller, Sarah		Trent St			Sam 22, $125. Zack 16, $125. Matilda 19, $80.	
Mo??in, James		High St E Side		Supt. Of Streets	Sylvia 27, $80. Harry 3, $15. Harriot 1, $5.	
Mohler, Peter		Harrison St E Side		Brass founder	Julia 14, $80	
Morgan, Edward		Pitt St N Side		Auctioneer	Charlotte 22, $80. Harriot 1, $5. Oysten 19, $125	
Morin, Francois		St. Patricks Row			Mary 55, $20. Virginia 20, $80. Edward 20, $125.	Morin lives with Bonnett.

Free Blacks and Slave Owners in Baltimore City Tax Assessor's Ledger, 1818, Ward 6

NAME	RACE/ STATUS	RESIDENCE	REAL PROPERTY	OCCUPATION	ENSLAVED PROPERTY Name, Age, Value	COMMENTS
Mousnier, Lacouste/Laurent		Great York N Side			Polly 18, $80. Ann 50, $10. Cicely 2 mos.	Tenant
Murphy, Thomas		High St E Side		Printer	Lydia 30, $80	
Myers, Andrew		Pratt St N Side		Brass founder	Scott 25, $140. Ned 19, $125. Emery 2, $10.	Scott is a brass founder.
Myers, Elizabeth	Widow	Bridge St S Side			Nelly 15, $80	Nelly released for 1823.
Neild, Richard		Pratt St S Side		Nield "goes by water."	Galloway 16, $125 Peter 6, $30	
Neilson, James		Forrest St E Side		Agent for Carrol	Maria 11, $40	Maria property of C. Carrol.
Nesbit, Alexander		Great York N Side		Judge C. Court	Nicholas 22, $125. Rose 30, $80. Easther 12, $40. Lindy 9, $40.	
Ogden, Nathan		Petticoat Alley at Spring St		Constable	Edward 9, $40	Edward property of Clarissa Harrison.
Page, Daniel		McElderry's Wharf		Ship joiner	Venus 28, $80 Harriet 4, $20	
Parker, Samuel		High St E Side		Tavern and market yard	Charette 30, $80. Nancy 25, $80. Steven 19, $125. Sampson 3, $15. Cass 10, $40.	Cass is property of John McGaw.
Pentz, Joseph		Pitt St		Butcher	Hetty 13, $40	Hetty property of Chisley of the house of Dave Chisley Pratts.
Petherbridge, John		Great York N Side		Dentist	Betsy 14, $80	Property of Miss Polly Nellums.

Free Blacks and Slave Owners in Baltimore City Tax Assessor's Ledger, 1818, Ward 6

NAME	RACE/ STATUS	RESIDENCE	REAL PROPERTY	OCCUPATION	ENSLAVED PROPERTY Name, Age, Value	COMMENTS
Phoenix, Thomas		Commet St N Side		Of the firm of Phoenix and McElderry	Hannah 30, $80. Betty 25, $80. Basil 40, $125. Tom 35, $125. George 30, $125. John 11, $40. David 3, $15 Solomon 1, $5	George released for 1822. John released for 1822. David released for 1822. Solomon released for $1822.
Pierce, Israel		High St W Side			James 22, $125. Jack 20, $125. Fanny 40, $60. Dorcas 22, $80. Peter 18, $125. Rachel 12, $15. Charlotte 11, $15. Rosetta 11 and Emily 3, $55. Ann 1 and Toby 0 years, $5.	
Pitt, William		Great York N Side		Store Keeper	Nancy 38, $70. Lucretia 13, $40	
Porter, William		Great York N Side		Merchant	Catherine 22, $80	
Priestly, Edward		Great York N Side		Cabinet Maker	Brooks 45, $100	
Randall, Elisha		Front St W Side		Carpenter	Rachel 16, $80	Rachel property of Richard Gelling.
Raney, William		Great York N Side		Grocer	Louisa 15, $80	
Rice, Thomas K.		Front St W Side		Auctioneer	James 21, $125	James property of Eliss Troup.
Richardson, Daniel		Milk Lane		Carpenter	Louisa 8, $40	Louisa property of William H. Linch.

Free Blacks and Slave Owners in Baltimore City Tax Assessor's Ledger, 1818, Ward 6

NAME	RACE/STATUS	RESIDENCE	REAL PROPERTY	OCCUPATION	ENSLAVED PROPERTY Name, Age, Value	COMMENTS
Richardson, Mary	Widow of Arnold	High St W Side			Sarah 45, $35. Nelson 7, $35. Priss 16, $80.	Priss property of Susan Hutchins.
Ridgely, Greenbury		Pitt St S Side		Store in Market St	George 16, $125. Sam 6, $30.	
Robb, John		Great York N Side			Jacob 8, $40. Eliza 10, $40.	Rob is a tenant. Jacob is property of Wm. Ball, Western precincts. Eliza is property of Allen Warfield near Annapolis.
Rogers, William C.		High St W Side		Storekeeper	Hannah 30, $80	Hannah property of Perry Welmore on the E. Shore.
Roney, William		Harrison St E Side		Turner	Mary 15, $80	Mary released for 1820, Sept. 13.
Ross, William		Pitt St N Side		Grocer	Maria 12, $40. Peter 10, $40.	Estate of B.C. Ross.
Rusk, William		Sty's Lane N Side		Butcher	Matilda 47, $10.	Matilda is infirm.
Ryan, Thomas for the heirs of Andrew Hanna		Great York N Side		Cast iron founder	Charlotte 21, $80	
Scharf, William		Jones St E Side		Cordwainer	Abraham 15, $125	
Sewel, Elizabeth	Widow of John	Pratt St N Side			Betty 50, $12	
Sewell, Richard		Bridge St S Side		Shoemaker	William 10, $40	William property of Benjamin Sewell.
Slade, Elizabeth		Front St W Side			Rachel 16, $80	

Free Blacks and Slave Owners in Baltimore City Tax Assessor's Ledger, 1818, Ward 6

NAME	RACE/ STATUS	RESIDENCE	REAL PROPERTY	OCCUPATION	ENSLAVED PROPERTY Name, Age, Value	COMMENTS
Smith, Elizabeth	Widow of Capt. Joe Smith	Pitt St S Side			Eliza 15, $80. Bill 16, $125. Joe 11, $40. Rachel 10, $40. Susan 4, $20.	
Smith, James		Milk Lane		Capt. Bridge St	Mary 4, $20. Rose 19, $80.	Rose property of D. Dare, Calvert Co.
Smith, Job Jr.		Front St W Side			Charles 24, $125	
Spencer, Robert		Pitt St			Mary 8, $40	Mary property of Richard Spencer, abated for 1821 and 1822.
Stansbury, Darius		High St E Side		Carpenter	Lydia 42, $50	Lydia property of Josiah J. McComas.
Stansbury, William (of Abraham)		High St W Side			George 17, $125	
Stevens, Capt. Richard		Dulany St N Side			Ann 9, $40. Sarah 17, $80.	Sarah is property of Henry Greenfield at L. G. Albers.
Stevenson, Josiah		Front St W Side		Tobacco inspector	Caleb 60, $10. Peter 60, infirm. Sarah 40, $60. Maria 21, $80. Henry 13, $40.	
Swear, Joseph		Milk Lane			Sophy 12, $40.	Sophy property of Mrs. Miles.

Free Blacks and Slave Owners in Baltimore City Tax Assessor's Ledger, 1818, Ward 6

NAME	RACE/STATUS	RESIDENCE	REAL PROPERTY	OCCUPATION	ENSLAVED PROPERTY Name, Age, Value	COMMENTS
Sykes, John		Pitt St S Side		Storekeeper on High St	Ned 35, $125	
Taylor, Joseph		Bridge St		Grocer	Negro Solomon, 10 years old, $40	
Thomas, Daniel L.		North South St N Side		Sugar refiner	Charity 17, $80 Judith 17, $80	Charity property of Miss Prudence Gough of Harford Co. Judith property of Mary Thomas.
Thompson, John R.		Fish Market		Blacksmith	Luke 17, $80	Luke released to Wallace William.
Tool, John		Front St W Side		Sugar Refiner	Susan 10, $40	Susan property of Richard Gelling.
Tupper, Mary	Widow	Pitt St S Side			Lucy 43, $45. Lydia 18, $80.	To Mrs. Hendrick
Vincent, Samuel		Pitt St S Side			Mary 14, $80.	This to ???? Gough
Ware, John		Bridge St N Side		Butcher	Charity 18, $80	Released to Jonathan Hancock.
Watson, Thomas		Water St N Side		Tavern	Stephen 27, $125	Stephen property of Nancy Pearce, released for 1822.
Westwood, John		Corner of Bridge & Union Sts		Grocer	Slave girl 12, $40	Slave girl is property of Mrs. Scott, widow of Judge Scott.
Whitaker, Thomas		Green St W Side		Carpenter	Hetty 15, $80	
Wilhelm, John		North St N Side		Innkeeper	Charity 45, $20	

Free Blacks and Slave Owners in Baltimore City Tax Assessor's Ledger, 1818, Ward 6

NAME	RACE/ STATUS	RESIDENCE	REAL PROPERTY	OCCUPATION	ENSLAVED PROPERTY Name, Age, Value	COMMENTS
Williamson, Basil		Front St W Side			Richard 20, $125.	Richard from Tom Barney
Wilson, James (estate of)		Bridge St N Side			James 5, $25	James abated for 1822.
Wilson, John		Baltimore St S Side		Grocer	Henny 25, $80. Ann 25, $80. Dinah 25, $80. Patty 10, $40. Washington & Jefferson, under 6 mos. no value	
Woodyear, Edward		Pitt St N Side			Ann 28, $80. Charity 19, $80. Charles 14, $125. Ellen 10, $40.	
Worthington, Henry		Bridge St N Side		Sadler	Bob 18, $125	
Wright, John		Great York N Side			Archibald 31, $125. Elijah 19, $125. Aaron 17, $125. Barbara 28, $80.	At the Widow Carsons York St.
Young, Ann T.		Bridge St N Side			Fanny 8, $40	Young at Peter Bonds.
Young, John		Temple St		Carpenter	Mary 16, $80.	
Zane, Peter		McElderry's Wharf		Cooper	Alice 19, $125. Jack 19, $125 Harry 16, $125	Alice released for 1822. Harry released for 1823.

Free Blacks and Slave Owners in Baltimore City Tax Assessor's Ledger, 1818, Ward 7

NAME	RACE/STATUS	RESIDENCE	REAL PROPERTY	OCCUPATION	ENSLAVED PROPERTY Name, Age, Value	COMMENTS
Adams, Capt. Alexander		E side Market St			Pamela 45, $30 Grace 13, $40	
Aitkin, Hannah	Coloured Woman	E Strawberry Alley	Lot $50. Imp. $5			
Allen, Hugh		W side of Gramby St		Coppersmith	Maria 16, $80	
Allen, Robert D.		W side of Gramby St		Bricklayer	Ann 16, $80	
Almeda, Capt. Joseph		N side of Duke St			Jim 16, $125. Yorl 16, $125. Julia 16, $80.	
Austin, Capt. Purnel		E side Gramby St			Sol 9, $40	
Bandell, George		E Petticoat Alley		Supt. of chimney sweeps	Tom 14, $125	
Barker, William		N side Aliceanna St		Shipwright	John 19, $125 Old Jane 50, $20 Young Jane 14, $80	
Barton, Thomas		N side of Duke St		Drayman	Hannah 25, $80	
Bateman, Catherine		E side Eden St			Emanuel 27, $80 Charles 19, $125	Emanuel is hand crippled.
Benelant, Stephen		N side Fleet St		Shipwright	Azan? 55, $25 (male) Jeunton 50, $20(female)	
Betts, Enoch		N side of Queen St		Nailer	Eliza 14, $8	
Biev, Jacob		N side Aliceanna St		Cashier, Marine Bank	Eliza 16, $80	
Bosley, Daniel		E side of Gramby St		Dry goods merchant	Joseph 12, $40 Grace 40, $80	
Bosley, William		N side of George St			Richard 30, $125. John $16, no value. Edward 11, $40. Jenny 40, $40. Maria 11, $40.	Tenant to Mons. Desmoulin. John is crippled.

Free Blacks and Slave Owners in Baltimore City Tax Assessor's Ledger, 1818, Ward 7

NAME	RACE/ STATUS	RESIDENCE	REAL PROPERTY	OCCUPATION	ENSLAVED PROPERTY Name, Age, Value	COMMENTS
Bowen, Richard		S side of George St		Cordwainer	John 12, $40. Eliza 16, $80. Dorcas 50, $25.	
Bowser, Rebecca	Coloured Woman	W Petticoat Alley	Lot $50. Imp. $25			
Boyd, Peter		W side of Albemarle St		Candle Manufacturer	Frederick 21, $125	
Boyer, Jacob		E side of Albemarle St		Merchant	Ann 13, $40	
Buck, Benjamin		S side Queen St		Sailmaker	Sam 11, $40. Rebecca 27, $80. Ellen 24, $80. Mary 3 and Eliza 3, $14.	
Buck, Christopher (Heirs of)		W side Exeter St			Rose 25, $80 Ann 10, $40	
Burgoyne, Cheston	Col'd. Man	N side Fleet St	Lot $50. Imp brick $120. Lot west side of Wolfe St $75, Imp, $75	Gardener		
Burke, Henry	Coloured Man	E side Caroline St	Lot $70. Imp. $30			
Caduc, John		W side Albemarle St		Tobacconist	Tom 13, $30. Lloyd 10, $40. Margaret 20, $80.	Tom lost one eye.
Canby, Hannah	Widow	N side Fleet St			Adeline 11, $40	
Carroll, Acquilla		E side of Gramby St		Constable	Abraham 9, $40	
Cathell, Capt. Clement		W side Ann St			Leah 50, $20 Ehster 20, $80	

Free Blacks and Slave Owners in Baltimore City Tax Assessor's Ledger, 1818, Ward 7

NAME	RACE/STATUS	RESIDENCE	REAL PROPERTY	OCCUPATION	ENSLAVED PROPERTY Name, Age, Value	COMMENTS
Caton, Richard		N side of George St			Luke, 40, $40. Edward 30, $125. William 30, $125. Richard 21, $125. Henny 40, $30. Henny 18, $80. Mary 19, $80. Ellen 14, $80.	
Chapman, Christopher		E side Bond St		Ropemaker	Harry 18, $125. Susan 28, $80. Harriet 10, $40.	
Chayter, Capt. James		W side Market St			Phoebe 20, $80	
Chevolleaux, Alice		E side Albemarle St			Perry 16, $125	
Claggett, Eli & Co.		S side of George St		Brewers	Ben 40, $40	
Clare, Thomas	Coloured Man	W side Bond St	Lot $50. Imp. $25			
Clark, James		S side Little York St			Curtis 25, $125 Ann 8, $40	Clark is tenant to William West.
Coates, William	Colored Man	E side Eden St	Lot W side Petticoat Alley $50. Imp $20			
Cole, Dr. Skipwith H.		W side Gramby St			John 7, $20 Elizabeth 12 months, No value	Cole is tenant to Gen. John Swann.
Colvin, Rachel (Miss)		S side of Great York St			Ishmael 20, $125. Edward 14, $125. Eliza 19, $80. Nancy 17, $80	
Connell, Priscilla M.		E side Wolfe St			Elizabeth 15, $80	Connell is tenant to E. Chatfield.
Cook, Capt. Robert		N side Little York St			Nan 18, $80	
Coombs, Capt. Solomon		N side Aliceanna St			Sal 19, $80	

Free Blacks and Slave Owners in Baltimore City Tax Assessor's Ledger, 1818, Ward 7

NAME	RACE/ STATUS	RESIDENCE	REAL PROPERTY	OCCUPATION	ENSLAVED PROPERTY Name, Age, Value	COMMENTS
Corner, James		W side Market St		Sailmaker	Rezin 20, $125 Ennels 15, $125	
Coulson, George		S side of Duke St		Housewright	Phoebe 15, $80	
Coulter, John Dr.		W side of Stillhouse St		Physician	Cyrus 51, $50 Rachel 55, $20	
Courtenay, William		W side of Albemarle St		U.S. Bank	Sophia 11, $40	
Craig, Henry		S side Queen St		Merchant	Caroline 14, $80	
Cross, Andrew (Heirs of)		S side Wilke St			Harriet 10, $25	
Currie, John	Coloured Man	E side Caroline St	Lot $100. Imp. $10			
Dalrymple, John, heirs of		N side of George St			Ann 13, $80 Mary 30, $50	
Dalrymple, William P.		S side of George St		Merchant	Bazil 50, $40. Susan 22, $80. Jenny 10, $35.	
Davis, Capt. Peter		W side Wolfe St			George 13, $40	
Davis, Samuel	Coloured Man	S side Smith St	Lot $40. Imp. $10			
Dean, Capt. Henry		W Strawberry Alley			Maria 21, $80	
Denees/Dewees, Andrew		W side of Gramby St			Suke 15, $80	Denees is tenant to Bosley.
Denson, John		S side Fleet St			Peg 12, $40	
Deshon, Christopher		N side of George St		Merchant	Lucy 40, $40 Priscilla 17, $80	
Dobbin, Catherine Mrs.	Widow	W side of Albemarle St			Alfred 2, No value. Nelly 30, $80. Louisa 4, $10.	Dobbin is tenant to William Bates, Clerk.
Doda/Dode, Julian		S side of George St		French Gent.	Muffee 45, $30	

Free Blacks and Slave Owners in Baltimore City Tax Assessor's Ledger, 1818, Ward 7

NAME	RACE/STATUS	RESIDENCE	REAL PROPERTY	OCCUPATION	ENSLAVED PROPERTY Name, Age, Value	COMMENTS
Dooley, Capt. James		E side Ann St			Charlotte 17, $80	
Dunham, Jacob		W Strawberry Alley		Shipwright	Priss 16, $80	
Durkee, Pearl Capt.		N side of Duke St		Sea captain	Wat, 13, $50	
Elbert, Dr. Laudman		E side Market St			John 3, $5. Susan 30, $80. Ann 10 mos., No Value	Elbert is tenant to Jacob Graff, tailor.
Ennis, Joshua		W side Market St		Lumber Measurer	Cato 25, $125 Phill 23, $125	
Ensor, Luke & William		N side Prince or Voince St		Brickmakers	Abram 20, $125. Bristow 18, $125. Nat 26, $125. Jim 4, $10.	
Fadon, John M.		N side of George St			Linus $50 Fanny $80	
Feigare, Mrs. Louisa		N side Fleet St			Claris 16, $80 Alisan 10, $40	
Fitch, Capt. Daniel		W side Wolfe St			Sarah 11, $40	Fitch is tenant to Joseph Watts.
Flanagan, William		W side Wolfe St		Shipwright	John 21, $125	
Folkes, Henry	Coloured Man	W side Bond St	Lot $60. Imp. $20			
Ford, Joseph T.		N side of Queen St		Wheelwright	Bill 11, $40. William 15, $125. Rosina 19, $80. Dolly 30, $80.	Ford is tenant to the Perine heirs.
Frazier, Capt. James		N side Fleet St			Henney 17, $80	
Gay, Deborah	Coloured Woman	W side Bond St	Lot $50. Imp. $10			
Gettings, Mrs. Mary		S side Little York St			Henry 10, $40 James (No age or value given) Susan 30, $80. Louisa 3, No value	

Free Blacks and Slave Owners in Baltimore City Tax Assessor's Ledger, 1818, Ward 7

NAME	RACE/STATUS	RESIDENCE	REAL PROPERTY	OCCUPATION	ENSLAVED PROPERTY Name, Age, Value	COMMENTS
Gibson, Capt. James		E side Ann St			Bonaparte 4, $10. Grace 50, $20. Eliza 20, $80 Margaret 1, No value	
Giles, James	Coloured Man	E side Happy Alley	Lot $30, Imp $25			
Graham, Hamilton		W side of Albemarle St		Clerk @ the Bank of Maryland	Nathan 10, $40 Ann 21, $80	
Graves, Robert		E Petticoat Alley		Housewright	Maria 14, $80	
Gray, Joseph	Coloured Man	W Petticoat Alley	Lot $60. Imp. $25			
Griggs, James		W side Exeter St		Pilot	Abram 19, $125. Joe 17, $125. Isaac 14, $125. Ellen 23, $80. Eliza 21, $80.	
Guestier, P. A.		W side of Albemarle St		Merchant	Peter 15, $125 Betty 25, $80 Rom 25, $80	Guestier is tenant to Thomas Usher's heirs. Deduct male slave Peter, sold out of state.
Haley, Mary Mrs.		W side of Albemarle St			Tom 13, No value Bridget 26, $80	Tom is blind
Hall, Capt. John		W side Ann St			Henry 12, $40. Susan 10, $40. Ann 18, $80.	Hall is tenant to Patrick Bennett.
Hall, Don Carlos	Coloured Man	S side of Salsbury St	Lot $100, Imp $75			
Hall, George		E side Market St		Lumber measurer	Daniel 65, $25 Charles 5, $20	
Hall, Sophia		N side Aliceanna St			Ned 13, $40 Rhoda 20, $80	Hall is tenant to John Smith.
Hall, Teresa		N side German St			Harry 17, $125	
Hall, Thomas		N side Aliceanna St		Shipwright	Jesse 25, $125	

Free Blacks and Slave Owners in Baltimore City Tax Assessor's Ledger, 1818, Ward 7

NAME	RACE/ STATUS	RESIDENCE	REAL PROPERTY	OCCUPATION	ENSLAVED PROPERTY Name, Age, Value	COMMENTS
Hancock, Capt. Robert		W side Market St			Emily 11, $40	
Hanna, Alexander B.		S. side of Great York St		Bootmaker	Caroline 18, $80	
Hanson, William H.		S side of George St		Custom House	William 9, $40. Charity 25, $80 Julia 6, $15. Mary 2, No value.	
Hargrove, John		W side Exeter St		Minister	Jack 16, $125 Sidney 14, $80	Sidney is female.
Harrison, Hall		S side of Great York St		Merchant	George 4, $10 Fanny 20, $80	Harrison is tenant to Mr. McNeil.
Hart, Capt. Robert		N side Gough St			Ann 15, $80 Julian 7, No value	Hart is tenant to Frederick Shaffer. Julian is an invalid.
Hart, Joseph		S side Great York St		Innkeeper	Nice 40, and son Will, 2, $70	Hart is tenant of Brian Philpot heirs.
Heddricks, Thomas		S side Queen St		Sailmaker	Kitty 17, $80	
Herring, Henry		N side of Queen St		Lumber merchant	Joe 45, $125	
Herring, Ludwig (Heirs of)		W side Albemarle St		Lumber merchant	Jack 12, $80 Mint 20, $80	"Abated in valuation Slave Jack $70"
Hewitt, William		S side Little York St			Harry 20, $125. Ehster 25, $80. Mary 1, No value.	Hewitt is tenant to L. & W. Ensor.
Higson, George Esq.		E side Caroline St		Attorney	Margaret 17, $80	
Hill, George		S side Dulany St		Veneering sawmill	Sally 8, $40	
Hodgkin, Mrs. Susan/Susanna	Widow	E side of Gramby St			Lavinia 67, No value Female slave 15, $40	Female slave is defective in sight.
Holbrook, Joseph Capt.		S side of Great York St			Peggy 29, $80	
Holmes, Thomas		E side Caroline St			Harry 15, $125 Nimrod 10, $40	Holmes is tenant to James Holmes' heirs.

Free Blacks and Slave Owners in Baltimore City Tax Assessor's Ledger, 1818, Ward 7

NAME	RACE/ STATUS	RESIDENCE	REAL PROPERTY	OCCUPATION	ENSLAVED PROPERTY Name, Age, Value	COMMENTS
Hooper, William		E side of Albemarle St		Sail maker	Maria 22, $80	
Hooper, William	Coloured Man	W side Bond St	Lot $50. Imp. $15			
Horsey, Mrs. Sarah	Widow	E side Brandy St			Bill 35, $125. Bob 12, $40. Ehster 15, $80.	Horsey is tenant to Mrs. Shreves.
Houlton, William		S side Wilke St			John 19, $125. Tom 12, $40. Sol 12, $40. Quill 13, $40. Jacob 11, $40.	Houlton is tenant to T. Ford.
Howell, William		E side Albemarle St			Kitty 50, $20	Howell is tenant to John Hannon.
Hoy, (No first name given)	Coloured Man	E side Strawberry Alley	Lot $40. Imp. Old Workshop $10			
Hughes, George M.		W side of Albemarle St		Cordwainer	Isaac 10, $40 Maria 9, $30	
Hynson, Nathaniel		S side Dulany St			Cato 30, $125. William 25, $125. John 14, $125. Joshua 6, $20 Sukie 30, $80. Milly 10, $40. Mary 6, $15.	Hynson is tenant to Ducheman.
Inloes, William		N side Aliceanna St		Ship joiner	Ann 26, $80 Joe 6 mos., No value	Inloes is tenant to Philip Towson.
Isaacs, Mrs. Elizabeth		E side Wolfe St			Ben 20, $125. Dick 20, $125. Amanda 10, $40. Willey 7, $25.	
Johnson, David	Coloured Man	S side of Salsbury St	Lot $100, Imp $25	Carter		
Johnson, Edward Esq.		W side of George St		Attorney	Beck 50, $30. Teresa 25, $80. Rosetta 20, $80.	
Kempton, Samuel		S side Queen St		Merchant & Farmers Bank	Nancy 30, $80. Hetty 20, $80. Caroline 1, No value.	

Free Blacks and Slave Owners in Baltimore City Tax Assessor's Ledger, 1818, Ward 7

NAME	RACE/ STATUS	RESIDENCE	REAL PROPERTY	OCCUPATION	ENSLAVED PROPERTY Name, Age, Value	COMMENTS
Kerns, Capt. John		N side Fleet St			Matilda 13, $40	
Kilbourne, Capt. Russell		W side Ann St			Tilly 15, $80	
Kinnard, Nicholas	Coloured Man	S side Smith St	Lot $50. Imp. $10. 2 horses $25. 2 drays $10			
Konkey, William M.		E side Exeter St		Housewright	Alexander 7, $20. Dolly 23, $80. Ann 11, $40.	
LaFaranier, Mrs.		S side Wilke St			Pompey 30, $125. Frances 50, $50.	
Leeke, Nicholas		W side Ann St		Teacher	Eliza 16, $80	
Lomax, David	Coloured Man	W side Strawberry Alley	Lot $40. Imp. $10			
Loney, Phoebe	Coloured Woman	W Petticoat Alley	Lot $60. Imp. $25			
Long, Thomas		S side Dulany St			Nat 50, $25. Nick 10, $40. Lydia 30, $80. Reuben, Lydia's child, 3, No value	Long is tenant to M. King, Chairmaker.
Lowrey, John		W side Market St			Joshua 3, $5. Phillis 35, $80. Becca 24, $80. Susan 10, $40.	Lowrey is tenant to Capt. William Pitterkin's heirs.
Martin, Dr. Samuel B.		W side Ann St			Delia 6, $20	Martin is tenant to L. Kiersted.
Mays, George	Coloured Man	E Strawberry Alley	Lot $40. Imp. $10			
McDonnald, William Col.		S side of Great York St			George 35, $125. Milly 35, $80. Ruth 10, $40.	
Merriott, Mary D.		N side of Duke St			John 30, $125 Eliza 12, $40	

Free Blacks and Slave Owners in Baltimore City Tax Assessor's Ledger, 1818, Ward 7

NAME	RACE/ STATUS	RESIDENCE	REAL PROPERTY	OCCUPATION	ENSLAVED PROPERTY Name, Age, Value	COMMENTS
Mezick & Johnson		@ Patterson's Ropewalk			Ned 45, $40. Scott 40, $125. Anthony 40, $125. Peter 40, $125. Jo 26, $125. Levin 29, $125. Isaac 27, $125. Davy 26, $125. Cato 25, $125. Bob Green 35, $125. Sam Green 30, $125. Essex 23, $125. Jacob 20, $125. Sam 24, $125. Bob 21, $125. Nat 22, $125. Harry 13, $40. Prince 9, $25. Bob 5, $20. John 2, No value. Caty 30, $80. Ellen 3 mos, No value.	
Mezick, Capt. Joshua		N side Aliceanna St		Sea captain	Jim 17, $125	Mezick is tenant to Capt. Coward.
Miles, Jane Mrs.		S side of George St			Phillis 13, $40	
Miles, John		N side of Queen St		Merchant	Richard 40, $125	
Mills, Capt. George		N side Fleet St		Sea captain	Jane 18, $80	
Mince, Joseph		N side Bank St		Grocer	Jenny 35, $80. Dorcas 6, $15.	
Mitchell, Richard		S side of Duke St		Shipwright	Eliza 17, $80. Ann 11, $30.	
Mondell, William, Esq.		S side Fleet St		Attorney	Teresa 23, $80	
Monker, William		N side Aliceanna St		Lumber measurer	Beck 10, $80	
Montgomery, Amos	Coloured Man	W side Bond St	Lot $80. Imp. $30. Furn. $5			

Free Blacks and Slave Owners in Baltimore City Tax Assessor's Ledger, 1818, Ward 7

NAME	RACE/ STATUS	RESIDENCE	REAL PROPERTY	OCCUPATION	ENSLAVED PROPERTY Name, Age, Value	COMMENTS
Montgomery, Martin	Coloured Man	E side Petticoat Alley	Lot $50. Imp. $50			
Moore, Philip Esq.		W side Market St		Pres. of the Franklin Bank & Clerk of U.S. District Court	Phil 17, $125 Fan 50, $20	
Morton, John		N side Fleet St		Cabinetmaker	Lloyd 70, $25	
Murray, Alexander	Coloured Man	S side of Salsbury St	Lot $60, Imp $60			
O'Connor, Dr. John		E side Argyle Alley			Phoebe 10, $80	
Page, James		S side of Great York St		Physician	Sophia 19, $80 Fanny 18, $80	Page is tenant of Robert Oliver, Merchant.
Parker, Walter S.		W side of Albemarle St			Moses 30, $125 Sarah 28, $80	Parker is tenant to William Patterson, cabinet maker.
Parks, Abraham		S side Gough St		Carter	Grace 25, $80	
Parks, William		N side Bank St		Grocer	Kezia 17, $80	
Peck, Frank	Coloured Man	E Strawberry Alley	Lot $40. Imp. $10. Horse $15. Cart $10.			
Pendleton, Daniel		E side Gramby St		Auctioneer	Jim 11, $40. Missy 20, $80. Ann 15, $80. Henny 1, No value.	Pendleton is tenant to Capt. Henry Dashiell.
Penrice, Capt. Thomas		W side Happy Alley		Sea captain	Lucy 28, $80 Susan 9, $40	
Periel, Alexander		S side of George St		French Gent.	Harriet 25, $80	
Phillips, James Capt.		E side of Albemarle St		Sea captain	Kitty 25, $80	
Pullett, Nehemiah		S side Fleet St			George 3, $5. Charlotte 9, $40.	

Free Blacks and Slave Owners in Baltimore City Tax Assessor's Ledger, 1818, Ward 7

NAME	RACE/STATUS	RESIDENCE	REAL PROPERTY	OCCUPATION	ENSLAVED PROPERTY Name, Age, Value	COMMENTS
Quinn, William M.		E side President St		Lumber merchant	Belle 14, $80. Maria 12, $40	
Reese, Elizabeth	Widow	E side Bond St			Mint 35, $80	
Rice, Shields	Coloured Man	E side Caroline St	Lot $100. Imp. $75			
Roberts, George	Coloured Man	E side Ann St	Lot $20, Imp $25			
Robinson, Charles		S side of George St		Custom House	Peter 35, $125. Gideon 15, $125. Robin 11, $40. Lydia 22, $80. Nancy 21, $80.	
Robinson, Joseph		N side Fountain St		Shipwright	Joseph 15, $125	
Rogers, Edward	Coloured Man	S side Smith St	Lot $200. Imp. $40. Furn. $5. Horse $15. Cart $10			
Rogers, Thomas		S side of Great York St		City Collector	Bristane 15, $125. Harry 16, $125. Nancy 40, $40. Hannah 30, $80. Caroline 18, $80.	
Rowles, Rezin		S side Queen St		Custom House Officer	George 2, No value. Rosetta 25, $80. Matilda 14, $80. Bet 7, $40.	
Sewell, James H.		E side of Albemarle St			Joe 12, $40. Ann 10, $40. Sall 35, $80.	Sewell is tenant to Jacob Winchester.
Sexton, Charles		S side Wilke St		Cordwainer	George 10, $40. Ann 10, $30.	
Shaffer, Frederick Esq.		E side Harford St			Harry 15, $125. Nell 70, No value	
Sharp, James	Coloured Man	N side Bond St	Lot $70. Brick Imp. $40. Furn $10			

Free Blacks and Slave Owners in Baltimore City Tax Assessor's Ledger, 1818, Ward 7

NAME	RACE/STATUS	RESIDENCE	REAL PROPERTY	OCCUPATION	ENSLAVED PROPERTY Name, Age, Value	COMMENTS
Shaw, John		W Petticoat Alley		Bricklayer	Jim 16, $125 Jack 15, $125	
Sinclair, William		W side Caroline St		Grocer	Nell 20, $80 Nerva 10, $40	
Smith, John	Colored Man	E side Strawberry Alley	Lot $40, Imp $40			
Smith, Pamela	Widow of Caleb	Plowman St			George 6, $40 Henrietta 16, $80	
Smith, Richard W.		E side Bond St		Copper refiner	William 23, $125	
Speck, Capt. Cornelius		S side Wilke St			Chloe 20, $80 Mastine 30, $80	Speck is tenant to Charles Stansbury.
Stansbury, Solomon	Coloured Man	E Strawberry Alley	Lot $50. Imp. $10			
Steuart, Col. William		S side Queen St		Stonecutter	Diane 30, $80. Hannah 25, $80. Cassandra 12, $40.	
Steuart, James Dr.		W side of George St		Physician	Charles 20, $125. Jim 12, $40. Abram 8, $25. Hanna 18, $80. Maria 16, $80. Sophia 10, $40.	
Steuart, Robert St. John		S side of Duke St		Stonecutter	Erth 17, $80	
Steuart, Robert, Esq.		N side of George St			Vinney 51, $20	
Stevens, Capt. J.H.		W side Ann St			Fanny 20, $80	Stevens is tenant to L. Kiersted.
Stevens, Mrs. Ann		W side Ann St			Milly 25, $80	Stevens is tenant to P. Bennett.
Stiles, Hon. George		S side Queen St			Edward 30, $125. John 25, $125. Jane 45, $30. Ann 30, $80. Betty 13, $40.	Stiles is tenant to Capt. William West.
Stockett, William Capt.		W side of Albemarle St			Philip 21, $125 Susan 18, $80	Stockett is tenant to Elias Brewer.

Free Blacks and Slave Owners in Baltimore City Tax Assessor's Ledger, 1818, Ward 7

NAME	RACE/ STATUS	RESIDENCE	REAL PROPERTY	OCCUPATION	ENSLAVED PROPERTY Name, Age, Value	COMMENTS
Sultzer, Sebastian		E side President St			Fanny 17, $80	Sultzer is tenant to William Quinn.
Sumwalt, Philip		N side Fleet St		Brickmaker	Noah 30, $125	
Sunderland, Elizabeth		E side Burk St			John 22, $125	
Taylor, Lemuel G.		N side of George St			Rachel 20, $80	Taylor is tenant to John Dalrymple's heirs.
Taylor, Vincent	Coloured Man	E Strawberry Allen	Lot $50. Imp. $25. Horse $15. Cart $10	Carter		
Thomas, Barton		E side Ann St		Pilot	Tabitha 20, $80	
Thompson, Capt. John		E side Wolfe St		Sea captain	Mahala 12, $40	
Vickers, Capt. Joel		W side Gramby St		Merchant	Beck 17, $80. Perry 12, $40	Vickers is tenant to Gen. John Swann.
Waltham, Mary	Widow	N side Fleet St			Leander 12, $40. Richard 9, $40. Fanny 6, $20.	
Waters, Joshua	Coloured Man	W Petticoat Alley	Lot $60. Imp. $25			
Waters, Peter		W side of Albemarle St		Grocer	Milly 16, $80. Mary 9, $25	
Waters, Richard		S side of George St			Robert 18, $125. George 12, $40. Hannah 50, $30. Ann 6, $15.	Waters is tenant to James Williams, Sr.
Watts, Dickson B.		S side Wilke St		Custom House	Eliza 12, $25	
Weems, Capt. Charles		W side Market St		Sea captain	Georg 3, $5. Fanny 23, $80	
Welch, Jacob Jr.		E side of Albemarle St			Isaac 50, $40. Charles 30, $125. Martha 50, $20. Matilda 25, $80. Margaret 45, $30.	Welch is tenant to the Thomas Yates heirs.

Free Blacks and Slave Owners in Baltimore City Tax Assessor's Ledger, 1818, Ward 7

NAME	RACE/ STATUS	RESIDENCE	REAL PROPERTY	OCCUPATION	ENSLAVED PROPERTY Name, Age, Value	COMMENTS
Welch, Peter	Coloured Man	E side Petticoat Alley	Lot $40. Imp. $30			
Welks, Benjamin Capt.		N side of George St			Fanny 36, $80. Nancy 25, $80. Lucy 9, $40.	Welks is tenant to John Kelso.
West, William		S side Little York St		Blockmaker	Grace 30, $80 Louisa 12, $40	
White, John J.		W side of Gramby St			Daniel 23, $125. Abel 25, $125. Milbee 25, $125. Nat 22, $125. Peter 19, $125. Mitchell 17, $125. Pleasant 50, $20. Matty 12, $40.	White is tenant to William Robinson, merchant.
Williams, Ezekiel	Coloured Man	E side Caroline St	Lot $100. Imp $40. Furniture $5. Horse $15. Cart $10			
Williams, Mrs. Catherine		W side of Albemarle St			Tabitha 25, $80. Harriet 7, $20. Louisa 6, $15. Mary 3, No value.	Williams is tenant to the Dalrymple heirs.
Willis, Joshua		E side Market St		Shipwright	Joe 30, $125. Aaron 29, $125. Milly 4, $10.	
Winchester, Jacob		E side of Albemarle St		Housewright	Harriet 16, $80	
Winstanley, William H.		S side Dulany St		Dry goods store	Maria 19, $80	Winstanley is tenant to Mrs. Ashwell.
Woodward, Capt. Abraham		N side Wilke St			Charlotte 30, $80 Julia 9, $40	
Worrell, Thomas		N side Aliceanna St		Blacksmith	Richard 42, $125. Simon 31, $125. Nero 29, $125. Joe 35, $125. Frederick 18, $125. Hannah 33, $80. Patty 31, $8. Charity 13, $40.	

Free Blacks and Slave Owners in Baltimore City Tax Assessor's Ledger, 1818, Ward 7

NAME	RACE/ STATUS	RESIDENCE	REAL PROPERTY	OCCUPATION	ENSLAVED PROPERTY Name, Age, Value	COMMENTS
Yearly, Henry Capt.		E side of Gramby St			Amy 25, $80 Margaret 6, $20	
Young, John S.		N side of George St		Nailer	Jo 18, $125. Sidney 18, $80. Eliza 14, $40.	Sidney is female

Free Blacks and Slave Owners in Baltimore City Tax Assessor's Ledger, 1818, Ward 8

NAME	RACE/ STATUS	RESIDENCE	REAL PROPERTY	OCCUPATION	ENSLAVED PROPERTY Name, Age, Value	COMMENTS
Allender, Joseph Dr.		S side Fell St		Physician	Frank 19, $125. Charlotte 45, $30. Louisa 9, $40.	
Anderson, Capt. William J.		S side Aliceanna St		China store	Charlotte 6, $40	
Atkinson, Isaac		N side Lancaster St		Housewright	Perry 2, No value. Annie 19 $80	
Auld, Capt. William		E side Happy Alley		Sea captain	Fo_ _ n 15, $80	
Baarstcher, William		S side Thames St		Rigger	Lydia 27, $80. Ann 25, $80.	
Barnes, Capt. James		W side Ann St			Perry 21, $125	Barnes is tenant to Kiersted.
Barnes, William P.		S side Fell St		Market Master	Tom 17, $125. Harry 12, $10. Jo 9, $40. Lemon 45, $30.	Harry is infirm.
Beacham, James		W side Pitt St			Vincent 22, $125. Rose 10, $40	Beacham is tenant to James Belt & Co.
Belt, James Jr.		W side Pitt St		Ship Chandler	Judy 45, $30	
Biays, Col. Joseph		S side Fell St		Merchant	Jack 35, $125. Edmund 14, $125. Ben 12, $40. Fanny 40, $40. Eliza 12, $40.	
Bond, Mrs. Margaret		N side Thames St			Fanny 10, $40	
Bonfiel, John (Heirs of)		N side Shakespeare St			George 27, $125. Sam 4, $10. Martha 17, $80.	
Bounds, Capt. Joseph		N side Philpot St		Sea captain	Rachel 10, $40	
Brewer, Nicholas		S side Fell St		Taylor	Delia 18, $80. Winifred 8, $40.	

Free Blacks and Slave Owners in Baltimore City Tax Assessor's Ledger, 1818, Ward 8

NAME	RACE/ STATUS	RESIDENCE	REAL PROPERTY	OCCUPATION	ENSLAVED PROPERTY Name, Age, Value	COMMENTS
Brown, Dixon		S side Philpot St		Shipwright	Edinburgh 25, $125. George 24, $125. James 23, $125. Harry 19, $125. Perry 14, $125. Lloyd 4, $10. Sam 3, No value. Sarah 45, $30. Matilda 22, $80. Rachel 1, No value.	
Burk, David Esq.		S side George St		Boat builder	Harry 12, $40. Mary 24, $80. Maria 15, $80. Jane 5, $15.	
Burke, Thomas	Coloured Man	E side Happy Alley	Lot $30, Imp $30			
Bush, William		W side Bond St			Maggy 8, $40	Bush is tenant to James Farrell.
Caughan, Davis M.		N side George St		Plumber	Thomas 3 mos., No value. Ehster 30, $80. Polly 6, $15. Jane 3, No value.	
Chappell, John G.		S side Philpot St			Caleb 36, $125	Chappel is tenant to Capt. Wise's heirs.
Chase, Capt. John		S side Aliceanna St			James 2, No value Hetty 25, $80	Chase is tenant to Mrs. Jenne.
Chase, Capt. Thorndick		S side Thames St			Jacob 20, $125. Eliza 18, $80. Hanna 38, $40.	
Clendenin, Dr. William H.		E side Ann St		Physician	Lydia 45, $30 Polly 10, $40	
Cloney, James		Lancaster St		Grocer	Aaron 4, $10. Louisa 15, $80.	
Cockrill, Thomas (Heirs of)		S side Philpot St			Robert 35, $125. Perry 25, $125. George 1, No value. Avy 25, $80. Molly 4, $10.	
Cooper, Robert		W side Wolfe St		Shipwright	Eliza 17, $80	
Cordery, James		S side Philpot St		Shipwright	Charles 20, $125. Abram 20, $125. Harry 22, $125. Lydia 20, $80. Sophia 18, $80.	

Free Blacks and Slave Owners in Baltimore City Tax Assessor's Ledger, 1818, Ward 8

NAME	RACE/ STATUS	RESIDENCE	REAL PROPERTY	OCCUPATION	ENSLAVED PROPERTY Name, Age, Value	COMMENTS
Cork, Matthew T.		E side Ann St		Shipwright	Rachel 28, $80	
Craig, John		N side George St		Grocer	Cyrus 25, $125. Cyrus 1, No value. Priscilla 23, $80.	
Cunyngham, Capt. John		E side Queen St			Lilly 18, $80	
Curtis, Capt. James		E side Wolfe St		Sea captain	Lloyd 10, $40. Lora 17, $80. Ann 12, $40.	
Dashiell, Capt. Henry		W side Market St			Julia 23, $80. Betty 13, $40.	
Davis, Joseph		E side Queen St		Boat builder	Henry 10, $40	
Davy, Capt. Hugh		W side Pitt St			Sophia 24, $80. Dinah 2, No value.	Davy is tenant to George Stiles.
Deale, Mrs. Hannah	Widow	E side Market St			Betty 18, $80	
Despeaux, Joseph		S side Philpot St		Shipwright	Jack 55, $25. Jerry 35, $125. John Louis 25, $125. George 14, $125. Lou Fleur 9, $40. Gabriel 9, $40. Florence 60, $20 Release 40, $30. Mary 30, $80. Mary Louise 16, $80.	
Dorry, Dr. Henry		N side Fell St		Druggist	Priscilla 15, $80	Dorry is tenant to William Trimble.
Doxcy, Joseph		N side Philpot St		Boarding house	Isaac 27, $125. George 6, $25. Agnes 26, $80. Sarah 27, $80. Ann 7, $20. Harriet 4, $10. Richard 1, No value.	Doxcy is tenant to David Burke.
Farrell, James		S side Fell St			Hannah 20, $80. Mary 7, $20.	
Fenby, Peter		W side Wolfe St		Cooper	Rachel 20, $8	
Fitze, John		N side Philpot St		Cooper	Charlotte 15, $80	

Free Blacks and Slave Owners in Baltimore City Tax Assessor's Ledger, 1818, Ward 8

NAME	RACE/ STATUS	RESIDENCE	REAL PROPERTY	OCCUPATION	ENSLAVED PROPERTY Name, Age, Value	COMMENTS
Fry, James		N side Lancaster St		Grocer	Levi 20, $125. Ben 15, $125. John 10, $40. Milly 36, $80. Rachel 34, $80. Beth 16, $80. Eliza 10, $40.	
Gallaway, Ezekiel		N side Lancaster St		Innkeeper	Flora 20, $80	Gallaway is tenant to William Trimble.
Galt, Peter Esq.		S side Fell St		Watch & clock maker	Celia 40, $30 Moll 13, $20	Moll is deficient in sight.
Hagthrop, Edward		W side Bond St		Bootmaker	Lare 20, $80	
Hanna, John		N side Thames St		Merchant	Washington 7, $40. Milky 16, $80. Maria 9, $40.	Hanna is tenant to Peter Hoffman's heirs.
Harrison, Jonathan		W side Bond St			Henry 9, $40. Rachel 19, $80. Harriet 9, $40. Margaret 1, No value.	
Harrison, Thomas (Heirs of)		W side Bond St			John 18, $125	
Holmes, Capt. John H.		S side Aliceanna St			Terry 29, $80	
Hooper, James		W side Bond St		Boardinghouse	David 7, $40	
Howe, Capt. Thos. C.		E side Queen St		Sea captain	Peggy 32, $80	
Humphreys, Kerr		N side Lancaster St		Grocer	Ehster 23, $80	
Jackson, William		S side Thames St		Blockmaker	Jack 27, $125. Dennis 22, $125. Abram 20, $125. Peter 9, $40. Jim 8, $40. Chloe 50, $20. Diana 16, $80.	
James, Daniel		W side Bond St		Boardinghouse	Caleb 12, $40. Henny 11, $40.	
James, William		N side Shakespeare St			Daniel 21, $125	

Free Blacks and Slave Owners in Baltimore City Tax Assessor's Ledger, 1818, Ward 8

NAME	RACE/ STATUS	RESIDENCE	REAL PROPERTY	OCCUPATION	ENSLAVED PROPERTY Name, Age, Value	COMMENTS
Johnson, James		S side George St			Bob 13, $40. John 2 mos., No value. Henny 20, $80.	Johnson is tenant to B. Mezick.
Kerr, Capt. Archibald		S side Fell St			Robert 55, $25. John 18, $125. Lydia 35, $80. Teresa 18, $80. Nelly 10, $40.	
Kiersted, Luke		W side Ann St		Sailmaker	Dan 33, $125. Ned 13, $40. Lydia 10, $40. Nance 7, $20.	
Kinnard, Samuel		S side Philpot St		Shipwright	Deb 13, $40	
Lattee, Joseph		E side Pitt St		Boat builder	Jacob 7, $25. Henry 4, $10. Mary 2, No value.	
Laudeman, Mrs.		W side Bond St		Tobacconist	Jonas 19, $125. Old Rachel 60, No value. Young Rachel 20, $80. Sarah 3 mos., No value.	
Lawrence, Richard		S side Aliceanna St		Blacksmith	Elisha 45, $40. Joshua 55, $25. Ehster 25, $80.	
Lewis, Mrs.		S side George St			Kitty 19, $80	Lewis is tenant to Col. Thomas Tenant.
Ling, Robert		E side Bond St		Grocer	Ned 4, $15. Charlotte 28, $80.	
Lovell & Sultzer		E side Queen St		Bakers	Harry 18, $125	
Lovell, William Jr.		S side George St		Baker	Rachell 20, $80. Eliza 16, $80. Mary Ann 6 mos., No value	
Martin, Capt. James M.		E side Ann St			Fanny 20, $80 Eliza 3, No value	
Mezick, Capt. Baptist		S side George St		Sea captain	Arthur 27, $125 Muscat 26, $125	
Millard, Joseph Lee		E side Ann St			Henry 4, $10. Gerard 2, No value. Dinah 24, $80.	
Monsarrat, Capt. David		N side Shakespeare St		Sea captain	Rachel 15, $80	Monsarrat is tenant to Job Smith, Esq.

Free Blacks and Slave Owners in Baltimore City Tax Assessor's Ledger, 1818, Ward 8

NAME	RACE/ STATUS	RESIDENCE	REAL PROPERTY	OCCUPATION	ENSLAVED PROPERTY Name, Age, Value	COMMENTS
Pamphilion, Thomas		S side Aliceann St		Ship carpenter	Ben 13, $40. Dinah 10, $40. Lydia 7, $20. Sidney 3, No value. Agnes 1, No value.	
Peduzi, Peter		W side Market St		Grocer	Jim 2, No value. Betty 36, $80. Harriet 6, $20.	
Peirce, John		E side Market St		Innkeeper	Perry 21, $125. Sal 14, $80.	
Pilch, James		W side Market St		Grocer	Mary 40, $30	
Pilkington, Thomas		E side Bond St		Taylor	Milky 16, $80	
Pitt, Capt. Richard		W side Wolfe St		Sea captain	Sarah 30, $80	
Price, John		E side Wolfe St		Shipwright	Levi 18, $125. Isaac 19, $125. Jo 24, $125. Lloyd 22, $125. Ned Phillips 40, $125. Jim Sudley 50, $25. Jess 35, $125. Lily 24, $80. Mary 4, $10. Milly 2, No value.	

Free Blacks and Slave Owners in Baltimore City Tax Assessor's Ledger, 1818, Ward 8

NAME	RACE/ STATUS	RESIDENCE	REAL PROPERTY	OCCUPATION	ENSLAVED PROPERTY Name, Age, Value	COMMENTS
Price, William		W side Pitt St		Shipwright	Bill Fisher 70, No value. Mingo 60, No value. Charles 54, $25. Bill Watkins 40, $40. Tom Martin 50, $25. Lloyd 33, $125. Harry 20, $125. Dan 13, $40. Andrew 7, $25. Major 45, $125. Dick Rice 35, $125. Horace 7, $20. Dave Brooks 3, $10. Old Bet 55, $20. Young Bet 45, $20. Harriet 35, $8. Charlotte 30, $80. Henny 16, $80. Till 15, $80. Sidney 6, $20. Susan 1, No value.	
Ramsay, James		S side Thames st		Ship chandler	Sol 20, $125. John 12, $40. Sarah 33, $80.	
Ramsay, Joseph		W side Market St		Blacksmith	Minty 19, $80	
Sharpe, Mrs. Ann		S side Philpot St			Ehster 55, $20. Violet 26, No value. Mary 4, $10. George 9, $40.	Violet is deranged.
Sheppard, Major Thomas		S side Fell St			Jesse 47, $40 Hamilton 22, $125. Hannah 40, $40. Betty 16, $80. Katy 20, $80.	
Sinners, Elijah R.		S side Fell St			Harriet 15, $80. Adaline 15, $80.	Sinners is tenant to Biays.
Smith, John		S side Fell St		Blacksmith	Sylph 22, $80	
Speck, William A.		E side Queen St			Henny 15, $80	Speck is tenant to Ramsay's heirs.

Free Blacks and Slave Owners in Baltimore City Tax Assessor's Ledger, 1818, Ward 8

NAME	RACE/ STATUS	RESIDENCE	REAL PROPERTY	OCCUPATION	ENSLAVED PROPERTY Name, Age, Value	COMMENTS
Stansbury, Dr. James		S side Fell St		Physician	Joshua 16, $125	Stansbury is tenant to Col. Biays.
Stansbury, Nicholas		W side Bond St		Ship chandler	Harry 21, $125. Charles 7, $25. John 4, $10. Lydia 30, $80. Bridget 12, $40. Effy 4, $10.	
Steel, Capt. John, Heirs of		E side Pitt St			Jack 80, No value. Richard 35, $125. Caesar 34, $125. Perry 31, $125.	
Stewart, Mrs. Ann	Widow	S side Fell St			Nelly 20, $50	Nelly is infim.
Thompson, Capt. Alexander		E side Ann St			Ezekiel 30, $125 Jane 30,	
Tyler, Mrs.		N side Thames St			Evaline 17, $80	Tyler is tenant to Mrs. Prendeville.
Waggner, George		N side George St		Block maker	Rachel 10, $80	
Waters, Hezekiah Esq.		E side Wolfe St			Frank 15, $125 Jane 30, $80	
Weavy/Weary, Peter		E side Pitt St		Measurer of wood	Bristow 28, $125 Siky 35, $80	
Weems, Capt. George		S side Philpot St		Sea captain	Gerard 14, $125	
Wilson, Benjamin		S side Shakespeare St		Grocer	Norah 25, $80	

Free Blacks and Slave Owners in Baltimore City Tax Assessor's Ledger, 1818, Ward 9

NAME	RACE/ STATUS	RESIDENCE	REAL PROPERTY	OCCUPATION	ENSLAVED PROPERTY Name, Age, Value	COMMENTS
Agnew, William		Philadelphia Rd		Keeper of East Potter's Field	James 14, $125.	
Allen, Nancy A.	Widow of James	Britton St			Harriet 8, $40.	Harriet property of Hollingsworth.
Alricks, Harmanus		Aisquith St			David 19, $125. Flora 9, $40.	
Amos, Benjamin	Negro	Union St	Lot $24, Imp dwelling $25, Horse & Dray $8, Furn $2	Drayman		
Bailey, Thomas		Pitt St		Assessor of the U.S. for the fourth collection of Maryland	Abraham 25, $125. Mary 22, $80.	"Property of W.H. Winder but T. Baily will pay."
Bandell, Michael		Liberty St		Superintendent of Sweeps	Charlotte 15, $80. Nick 10, $40. Sam 7, $30. Joe 6, $30. John 16, $125. Dick 11, $40.	John is property of Peddiman Eastervan. Dick is property of George Wolfnagle
Barry, Dinah	Negro	Union St	Lot $16, Imp Dwelling $9, Furn $1			
Barry, Elizabeth	Widow of John	Green St			Jane 45, $35. Abraham 8, $40. David 5, $25.	
Bennett, Peter	Colored Man	Friendship St	Lot $45, Imp $120, Furn $5	House Carpenter		
Bennett, Peter	Colored Man	Holland St	Lot 30 by 175, $22 Imp Frame $50	Carpenter		

Free Blacks and Slave Owners in Baltimore City Tax Assessor's Ledger, 1818, Ward 9

NAME	RACE/ STATUS	RESIDENCE	REAL PROPERTY	OCCUPATION	ENSLAVED PROPERTY Name, Age, Value	COMMENTS
Bond, Mary	Widow of Richard	Bridge St			Female slave 18, $80.	Property of J. Hardesty, Eastern Shore.
Brown, Alexander		New Harford Rd		Merchant	Charlotte 50, $100. Ellen 35, $80.	
Brown, William	Negro	New Harford Rd	1 acre of land $30 Imp $10, Horse $3			
Bryden, Capt. William		New Harford Rd		Sea Captain	Sarah 23, $80. Susan 12, $40. Henry 2, $10. Harry 1, $5.	
Cappeau, Ann	Widow	Green St			Zamo 60, & Zabot 45, $35. Adelle 12, $40. Eliza 9, $40. Lain 60, no value.	
Carter, John S		Aisquith St		Bricklayer	Jerry 7, $35	
Carter, William B.		Britton St		Baker	Maria 25, $80. Eliza 2, $10.	
Chalk, Mordecai	Negro	New Harford Rd	1 acre of land $25 of P. Rogers, 1 horse & cart $10	Gardener		
Chalmers, James		Harford Rd		In custom house	Rosetta 30, $80. Ellen 9, $40. Ephraim 6, $30. Sophy 4, $20. Thomas 2, $10.	
Chalmers, William		Old Harford Rd		Rope maker	Abraham 22, $125. Dennis 16, $125.	Dennis property of Sarah Pew.
Churchman, Enoch		Green St		In Franklin Bank	Charity 48, $20. Eliza 26, $80. John 12, $40. Henry 11, $40. James 9, $40.	
Coats, Jeremiah	Negro	Friendship St	Lot $20, Imp frame $30	Laborer		

Free Blacks and Slave Owners in Baltimore City Tax Assessor's Ledger, 1818, Ward 9

NAME	RACE/STATUS	RESIDENCE	REAL PROPERTY	OCCUPATION	ENSLAVED PROPERTY Name, Age, Value	COMMENTS
Conn, Daniel		Aisquith St		Carpenter	Samuel 44, $125. Baril 13, $40. Mary 50, No value.	Mary is infirm.
Cox, David	Colored	Union St	Lot on Friendship St, $10 Imp frame dwelling $10	Shoemaker		
Creamer, Joshua		Britton St		Carpenter	Rachel 18, $80.	Rachel property of James Hooper.
Cry, Frederick		Mill St		Paver	Henry 18, $125.	
Curtain, Thomas		Pitt St		Butcher	Robert 30, $125. Easter 23, $80. Young Esther 14, $80.	
D'Arcey, John N.		Harford Rd		Merchant	Ben 45, $120. Rachel 11, $40.	
Deale, Capt. James		New Harford Rd		Sea captain	Pleasant 50, $20. Angelino 17, $80. Anderson 13, $40.	
Delsher, George		York Rd		Meal Seller	Nell 40, $60. Mahala 10, $40. John 15, $125.	John property of William Lawrence.
Delsher/Delcher, Jemima	Widow of George	York Rd			Bet 20, $80. Rachel 1, $5.	
Delsher/Delcher, John		York Rd		Mealseller	Maria 13, $40. Mitchell 20, $125.	Mitchell property of Mr. White, Granby St.
Denmead, Adam		Green St		Measurer	Daphne 46, $30.	
Dew, James C.		Harford St		Merchant	Priscilla 32, $80. Charlotte 7, $35. Betsy 37, $75. Isaac 4, $20.	

Free Blacks and Slave Owners in Baltimore City Tax Assessor's Ledger, 1818, Ward 9

NAME	RACE/STATUS	RESIDENCE	REAL PROPERTY	OCCUPATION	ENSLAVED PROPERTY Name, Age, Value	COMMENTS
Dorsey, Lucinda	Colored Woman	McElderry St	Lot $25, Imp $20	Laundress		
Douglas, George		Aisquith St			Maria 20, $80. Sam 18, $125.	Maria property of Matilda Douglass. Sam property of Doc. Allender of Fells Point.
Duppin, James	Negro	New Harford Rd	1 acre of land $30, Imp frame $12. Horse $5. Furn $2			
Ensor, William		Britton St		Brick maker	Rachel 22, $80. Chase 1, $5.	
Fitch, Gideon		Harford St		Lime & feed store	Elizabeth 14, $80.	Gideon, son of William. Elizabeth property of W. K. Lynch.
Fitch, William		Bridge St		Carter	Zach 35, $125.	Property of Mrs. Brown.
Floyd, Thomas		Old Harford Rd		Shoe maker	Margaret 23, $80. Matilda 1, $5.	
Ford, Samuel	Negro	Union St	Lot $17, Imp $15. Lot on Friendship St $20, Imp $30. Furn $20. ray $5. Horse $10.	Drayman		
Frazier, Joseph		Short St		Carpenter	Esther 19, $80. Jane 5 mos.	Jane, no value.

Free Blacks and Slave Owners in Baltimore City Tax Assessor's Ledger, 1818, Ward 9

NAME	RACE/ STATUS	RESIDENCE	REAL PROPERTY	OCCUPATION	ENSLAVED PROPERTY Name, Age, Value	COMMENTS
Gale, Joseph	Black Man	New Harford Rd	1 acre of land $25, Imp frame $10 of P. Rogers	Carpenter		
Gallaway, James		Union St		Carpenter	Deal 20, $80.	
Gantt, Capt. Christian		Green St		Mariner	Patty 47, $25. Molly 12, $40. Margaret 14, $80.	
Garretson, Benjamin		Harford St		Store	Charlotte 15, $80.	
Gilliard, Jacob Sr.	Colored Man	Old Harford Rd	Lot 70 by 130, $35, Imp brick $100, plate $1, Furn $3	Blacksmith		
Gladden, Samuel		Potter St		Shoemaker	Leah 9, $40.	
Gott, Ruth	Widow of Richard	Aisquith St			Charles 20, $125. Rachel 17, $80. Maria 7, $35. George 6 mos, no value.	
Gouing, James	Colored Man	Friendship St	Lot $25, Imp dwelling $20, horse & cat $13, Furn $2	Carter		
Govens, Daniel	Negro	Bridge St	Lot on Aisquith St $30, Imp frame $80	Grocery & feed store		
Gray, Henry W.		Green St		Merchant at Cheapside	Nancy 17, $80.	
Grayham, Charles	Colored Man	Pitt St	Lot 40 by 120, $30. Imp $15 2 horses $12 Cart $3, Furn $4	Butcher		

Free Blacks and Slave Owners in Baltimore City Tax Assessor's Ledger, 1818, Ward 9

NAME	RACE/ STATUS	RESIDENCE	REAL PROPERTY	OCCUPATION	ENSLAVED PROPERTY Name, Age, Value	COMMENTS
Griffin, Luke		Liberty St			Amy 20, $80. Solomon 18, $125. Isaac 1, $5.	
Gudgeon, Jesse		Liberty St		Auctioneer @ Market	Betsy 40, $60. George 20, $125. Isaac 5, $25. Ann 1, $5.	
Gudgeon, Providence		Liberty St		Seamstress	Seret 19, $125. Emaline 4, $20.	Providence lives with Jesse Gudgeon.
Hackett, Margaret	Negro	Bridge St	Lot 80 by 150, $60, Imp dwelling $30, Furn $2			
Hadkis, Samuel H.		Point Rd		Rope maker	Ben 50, $100. George 20, $125. Charlotte 14, $80. Sam 8, $40. Henry 5, $25.	
Hall, Don Carlos	Negro	New Harford Rd	2 acres of land $50, of P. Rogers	Bootblack & varnish manufactory		Works in cellar of 124 Baltimore St..
Hamilton, Jacob	Negro	Bridge St	Lot 40 by 100 $20, Imp $10, Furn $2			
Harker, John		Liberty St		Meal Seller	Charlotte 6, $30. Horace 3, $15.	
Harris, Robert	Black man	Low St	Lot $25, Imp $15	Laborer		
Harvey, Polly	Negro	Britton St	Lot $24, Imp brick $50			
Herter, Ignatius		York Rd		Grocer	Fanny 18, $80.	

Free Blacks and Slave Owners in Baltimore City Tax Assessor's Ledger, 1818, Ward 9

NAME	RACE/ STATUS	RESIDENCE	REAL PROPERTY	OCCUPATION	ENSLAVED PROPERTY Name, Age, Value	COMMENTS
Hooper, William		Harford St		Carpenter	Dolly 24, $80.	
Howard, Diana	Negro	Britton St	Lot $19. Imp old $15			
Hynson, Joseph	Colored	Liberty St	Lot $13, Imp dwelling $15, Furn $2	Blacksmith		
Jackson, Ann	Negro	Neighbor St	Lot $20, Imp $15, Furn $1			
Jackson, Stephen	Colored Man	New Harford Rd	½ acre of land $10, Imp old $10, 2 old horses $4			
Jenkins, Henry		Green St		Hatter	Trecey 18, $80.	
Johnson, Jane	Colored Woman	Friend St	Lot $20, Imp $30, Furn $2			
Johnson, Thomas		Green St		John Merryman Trustee	Nancy 36, $75. Edward 10, $40. Sophy 15, $80.	Sophy belongs to Catherine Johnson.
Joice, Charity	Negro	Bridge St	Lot 40 by 100, $20, Imp dwelling $40	Laundress		
Kelso, Thomas		French St		Victualler	Harry 18, $125. Sam 12, $40. Dinah 25, $80. Tom 18, $125.	
Kitts, Barnet		Green St		Plaisterer	Ann 18, $80. Lambert 20, $125.	Ann is property of Ringold of Kent Co. Lambert is property of Ben Worrell of Chestertown.
Laferty, William		Harford St		Meal Seller	Phebe 15, $80. Ben 11, $40.	

Free Blacks and Slave Owners in Baltimore City Tax Assessor's Ledger, 1818, Ward 9

NAME	RACE/ STATUS	RESIDENCE	REAL PROPERTY	OCCUPATION	ENSLAVED PROPERTY Name, Age, Value	COMMENTS
Littlejohn, Thomas		City Line		Grocery, liquor & feed store	Tilda 12, $40.	
Lyons, Nace	Negro	Britton St	Lot $26, Imp brick $75			
Mallory, Capt. John		Hamstead Hill St		Sea captain	Jenny 36, $75. Elliot 9, $40. Fanny 7, $35.	
Mann, Dr. Anthony		Jones Falls		Apothecary	January 50, $80. Sandy 22, $125. Hetty 40, $60 & 2 month old twins @$20.	
Maxwell, John		York Rd		Butcher	Seazor $125.	
McElderry, Elizabeth	Widow of Thomas	Aisquith St			Phebe 25, $80. Henry 17, $80. Mary Ann 2, $10. Bill 16, $125.	Bill may be property of Andrew Aldrich.
McElderry, John		Aisquith St		Lumber merchant in house of Conn & McElderry	Maria 22, $80.	
Meagher, Timothy D		Potter St		Grocer	Clary 23, $80. Matilda 3, $15.	
Miller, Lewis		French St		Blacksmith	Jerry 26, $175. Joe 23, $125. Sarah 19, $80. Louisa 2, $10. Jack 20, $125. James 50, $100. Lornelnly (?) 11, $40.	Jack property of Ann Dorsey in Montgomery Co. James property of Courtney of St. Mary's Co. Lornelnly property of B. Hanson of Kent Co.
Montgomery, John Esq.		York Rd		Mayor of the city of Baltimore	Harry 53, $50. Henry 16, $125. Elijah 11, $40. Agnes 10, $40.	Elijah property of a Gent in town.
Moody, Isaac		Aisquith St		Shoemaker	David 19, $125.	

Free Blacks and Slave Owners in Baltimore City Tax Assessor's Ledger, 1818, Ward 9

NAME	RACE/ STATUS	RESIDENCE	REAL PROPERTY	OCCUPATION	ENSLAVED PROPERTY Name, Age, Value	COMMENTS
Moore, Abbey	Negro	Bridge St	Lot 40 by 100 $20, Imp frame $100, Furn $2			
Moore, William	Negro	Aisquith St	Lot $37, Imp dwelling $50, Furn $5, Horse & Dray $13	Drayman		
Moore, William	Negro	Short St	Lot 30 by 40, vacant $7			
Mycroft, John		McElderry St		Gardener	Harriot 19, $80. Dolly 1, $5.	
Myers, William		Aisquith St		In Custom House	Betsy 30, $80. Sam 5, $25. Jane 3, $15. Peter 12, $40.	
Oliver, Robert		York Rd			Nelly 40, $60.	
Parker, Joseph	Mulatto	York Rd	Lot vacant $50	Carpenter		
Pascault, Francis		Old Philadelphia Rd		Gardener	Rozet 40, $60. Lucy 26, $80.	
Piper, James		Old Harford Rd			Louisa 16, $80.	Louisa property of W. Stake.
Presbury, George G. III		Union St		Trustee of John Talbot	Lucy 80, no value. Tracey 10, $40.	
Presbury, Priscilla	Widow of George	Green St			Fanny 24, $80. Julian 5, $25.	
Price, William		York Rd		Fish seller	Horace 8, $40. Rachel 4, $20.	

Free Blacks and Slave Owners in Baltimore City Tax Assessor's Ledger, 1818, Ward 9

NAME	RACE/ STATUS	RESIDENCE	REAL PROPERTY	OCCUPATION	ENSLAVED PROPERTY Name, Age, Value	COMMENTS
Prout, Richard	Colored Man	Falls St	One lot on alley rear of Jeremiah Cannon, $15 Imp $20. Furn $1. Horse & Dray $10.	Drayman		
Richardson, James	Colored Man	Friendship St	Lot $24, Imp frame $50			
Rogers, Philip		Harford Rd			Powell 15, $125.	Powell property of ???
Rusk, Robert		Pitt St		Butcher	Priscilla 50. Fanny 8, $40. Charity 29, $80. Levy 10, $40.	Priscilla is infirm.
Sale, King	Negro	New Harford Rd	1 acre of land $25, Imp dwelling $10, cow $4, Furn $1	Laborer		
Salnave, James		Harford St			Sarah 47, $30. Milly 8, $40. John 20, $125. William 2, $10.	
Sears, William	Colored	Friendship St	Lot $24, Imp $75, Furn $5	Waiter @ W. Taddow		
Smith, John		Green St		Carpenter	Baril 10, $40. Susan 18, $80.	Susan is property of E. Hooper.
Sparks, Acquila W.		Old Harford Rd		Proprietory of the Old Hay Scale Tavern	Lucy 15, $80. Ben 6, $30.	

Free Blacks and Slave Owners in Baltimore City Tax Assessor's Ledger, 1818, Ward 9

NAME	RACE/ STATUS	RESIDENCE	REAL PROPERTY	OCCUPATION	ENSLAVED PROPERTY Name, Age, Value	COMMENTS
Spencer, Jonathan		Green St		Capt. Of Steamboad	Jerry 22, $125. Harriet 15, $80. Betsy 2, $10. Thomas 7 mos., $10. Ann 15, $80. Solomon 45, $125. James 14, $125. Sukey 24, $80. Mary 14, $80. Abby 30, $80.	
Spiars, Capt. Thomas		New Harford Rd			Jacob 25, $125. Maria 21, $80. Debby 2, $10.	Maria property of Rosanna Partridge.
Spottwood, David	Colored Man	Union St	Lot $22, Imp $20, Plate $3, Furn $4	Rope maker		
Stansbury, Thomas		Green St		Carter	George 18, $125.	George is property of John Wheeler.
Sterling, James		Aisquith St			Peter 45, $120. Jerry 50, $100. Phill 14, $125. Tom 14, $125. Lewis 21, $125. Cloe 30, $80. Elisa 20, $80. Mary 9, $40. Margaret 25, $80.	
Stevenson, Dr. Cosmo		York Rd		M.D.	Joseph 14, $125. Milly 22, $80. Fanny 8, $40. Julian 5, $25.	
Stevenson, Joshua	Colored Man	Union St	Lot $25, Imp frame dwelling $20, Furn $2	Bricklayer		
Taylor, Robert		Bridge St		Cooper	Harriet 21, $35.	
Tittle, Jeremiah		Green St		Tailor	Betty 10, $40.	
Vaughen, Charles		Aisquith St (McElderry's Wharf)		Merchant	Harriet 11, $40.	

Free Blacks and Slave Owners in Baltimore City Tax Assessor's Ledger, 1818, Ward 9

NAME	RACE/ STATUS	RESIDENCE	REAL PROPERTY	OCCUPATION	ENSLAVED PROPERTY Name, Age, Value	COMMENTS
Wallace, Major	Negro	Union St	Lot $25, Imp to dwelling & plate	Bootblack		
Waters, Catherine	Negro	Bridge St	Lot 40 by 100 $20, Imp $15, Furn $5, horse $8, cart $5			
Watts, Jeremiah	Colored Man	Union St	Lot $15, Brick Imp $100, plates $12, furniture $10	Laborer		
White, Abraham, Jr.		French St		Grocer	Emily 23, $80. James 40, $125. Sophy 60, no value.	
White, William		Old Harford Rd		Wheelwright	James 19, $125.	
Whitney, Elizabeth	Widow	Bridge St			Charlotte 18, $80. Mary 10, $40.	
Williams, Jacob		French St		Chair maker	Ellen 23, $80.	
Williams, Matthew	Colored	Liberty St	Lot $25, Imp dwelling $18, 2 horses $20, dray $5, Furn $2	Drayman		
Williams, Richard	Colored	Falls St	Lot Halls Alley $10 Imp $65	Stage driver		
Williams, Samuel		Green St		Merchant	Violet 15, $80. Perry 11, $40.	

Free Blacks and Slave Owners in Baltimore City Tax Assessor's Ledger, 1818, Ward 9

NAME	RACE/ STATUS	RESIDENCE	REAL PROPERTY	OCCUPATION	ENSLAVED PROPERTY Name, Age, Value	COMMENTS
Williams, Spinler/Spinter	Colored Man	Liberty St	Lot runs to Potter St $25, Imp dwelling $25, Furn $5, Horse $10, Cart $3	Carter		
Wilson, Charlotte	Colored woman	Union St	Lot $25, Imp $20			
Wilson, Samuel	Colored Man	Friend St	Lot $25, Imp $10			
Woods, William Jr.		Green St		Grocer	George 50, $100.	George is property of Martha M. Killgon.
Worthington, Thomas		New Harford Rd			Nancy 50, $20. Henry 40, $125. Ben 30, $125. Anthony 20, $125.	

Free Blacks and Slave Owners in Baltimore City Tax Assessor's Ledger, 1818, Ward 10

NAME	RACE/ STATUS	RESIDENCE	REAL PROPERTY	OCCUPATION	ENSLAVED PROPERTY Name, Age, Value	COMMENTS
Adams, Eli		St. Paul's Lane		Merchant	Paul 40, $125. Joseph 12, $40.	Joseph owned by the widow Scott.
Alcock, William		Biddle St			Charles 18, $125. Hanna 18, no value given.	
Appleton, William G.		Mulberry St		Merchant	Plato 12, $40.	
Armstrong, James		Calvert St		Merchant	Jacob 12, $40. Ann 22, $80. Caroline 6, $20. Rachel 4, $10. Patty 12, $40.	Patty owned by Robert Smith.
Arthur, Damarls	Widow	Charles St			Female slave 40, $40.	
Athey, Walter F.		N. Paca St		Bricklayer	Will 14, $125. Toby 40, $125.	
Bailey, Elisha		Eutaw St		Paver	Judah 45, $30. Elisa 18, $80. Harriot 14, $80.	
Bailey, George Jr.		Eutaw St		Paver	Provy 14, $80.	
Barklie, Thomas		Reicestertown Rd		Broker on Dawson's land	Will 5, $20. Ellen 12, $40.	
Barol, James		New Lane		Merchant	Sol 25, $125. Betsy 25, $80. Ann 4, $10.	
Betts, Solomon		Windsor Mill Rd		Merchant	Sam 15, $125. Abraham 28, $125. Caroline 15, $80.	
Blair, Michael M.		Franklin St		Merchant	Anthony 24, $125. Harriot 18, $80.	
Bowen, Pitt		Eutaw St		Paver	Wilks 20, $125.	
Bowen, Ruth	Widow of Nathan. Resides in Mrs. Gilling's house	Eutaw St			Fanny 16, $80.	

Free Blacks and Slave Owners in Baltimore City Tax Assessor's Ledger, 1818, Ward 10

NAME	RACE/ STATUS	RESIDENCE	REAL PROPERTY	OCCUPATION	ENSLAVED PROPERTY Name, Age, Value	COMMENTS
Bowen, Susan	Widow of Jehu	Holliday Sr			Male slave 18, $125. Male slave 8, $40.	
Brown, Stewart		Cortland St		Lumber merchant	Even 20, $125.	
Buck, William		Bath St		Millwright	Cecelia 26, $80. Female 11, $40.	
Bucklin, John C.		Wolfe's Land			Sandy 22, $125. Beverly 13, $40.	
Burt, Andrew		St. Paul's Lane		First teller, Union Bank of MD	Henry 20, $125. Sarah 30, $80. Louisa 13, $80.	
Butler, Sarah	Colored Woman	Greenwich St	Lot nw side sw of Reicester Town Rd, $25 Imp dwelling $15			
Carroll, Richard		Pleasant St			Polydore 18, $125. Lucy 18, $80.	
Caughey, Patrick		Reicestertown Rd		Grocer	Kitty 19, $80. Betty 14, $80.	
Chase, Samuel		Falls Turnpike			Frank 40, $125. Levin 47, $60. Gart 40, $125. Bina 36, $80. Charlotte 8, $40.	
Clayton, Philip	Colored Man	Morris St	Lot s corner of Moore's Alley $32 Imp dwelling $50	Laborer		
Clopper, Andrew		Howard St		Merchant	James 35, $125. Nancy 40, $40. Sally 15, $80. Nancy 10, $40.	
Clopper, Edward N.		Windsor Mill Rd		Gentleman	Nick 14, $125.	
Corwine, Jehu		Biddle St		Blacksmith	Betsy 17, $80.	
Craycroft, Sarah	Widow	Holliday St		Mantua maker	Fanny 40, $125. Thomas 17, $125. Nan 30, $80. Dinah 18, $80.	

Free Blacks and Slave Owners in Baltimore City Tax Assessor's Ledger, 1818, Ward 10

NAME	RACE/ STATUS	RESIDENCE	REAL PROPERTY	OCCUPATION	ENSLAVED PROPERTY Name, Age, Value	COMMENTS
Dare, Elizabeth		Falls Turnpike Rd			James 14, $125.	James at Perry Young's, a colored man in Mulberry St.
Delacour, David		Biddle St		Flour merchant	Female 22, $80.	
Didier, Henry Sr.		Cove St		Gent	Charles 18, $125. Frank 7, $20.	
Dilahunt, John		Calvert St		Currier	Betsy 27, $80.	
Distance, William	Colored Man	Morris St	Lot NW side SW of Ross St $50 Imp his dwelling $50			Poor & insane
Donaldson, John		Franklin St		Attorney	Joseph 30, $125. Henry 16, $125. Kitty 25, $80.	
Dorsey, Edward Hill		Charles St		Gent	Nat 35, $125. Ben 32, $125. Sam 29, $125. Saul 23, $125. Tom 21, $125. John 20, $125. Yellow Tom 20, $125. Rachel 25, $80.	Nat hired to Joseph Worley. Ben hired to J. Stouffer. Sam hired to D. Fahnestock.
Evans, Hugh W.		Charles St		Merchant	Male $125. 3 females $240.	
Ferguson, David		Calvert St		Merchant	Jerry 8, $40. Lyda 26, $80.	
Findlay, John		Pearl St		Chair maker	Betsy $15, $80	
Finley, Thomas		Howard St		Merchant	Silas 20, $125. Jean 40, $40. Susan 18, $80.	
Fisher, Robert		Courtland St		Lumber merchant	Gustavus 11, $40.	
Ford, Stephen H.		Mulberry St		Merchant	Charlotte 13, $40. Harriet 9, $40.	
Forsyth, Alexander Jr.		Greenwich St		Victualler with A. Forsyth Sr.	Lydia 4, $10.	

Free Blacks and Slave Owners in Baltimore City Tax Assessor's Ledger, 1818, Ward 10

NAME	RACE/ STATUS	RESIDENCE	REAL PROPERTY	OCCUPATION	ENSLAVED PROPERTY Name, Age, Value	COMMENTS
Forsyth, Alexander Sr.		Reisterstown Rd		Victualler on Pennsylvania Ave.	Thom 20, $125. Harry 13, $40. Doll 14, $80. Ann 12, $40.	
Foster, John		Pleasant St		Of the firm Wilson & Foster	Sam 22, $125. Dorcas 25, $80.	
Francois, Magdaline	Colored Woman	Union St	Lot NW side NE of Reicestertown Rd $23, Imp her dwelling $30			
Freise, John F.		St. Paul's Lane		Merchant	Abraham 25, $125.	
Galloway, William H.		George St		Formerly a Carpenter	Bell 16, $80.	
Gibson, Dr. William		Price St		Physician & surgeon	Frank 18, $125. Lucy 20, $80. Nancy 22, $80.	
Gibson, John		Charles St		Merchant	John 14, $125.	
Gibson, William		Price St		Clerk of the County	Ned 33, $125. Abram 50, $60. Dick 12, $40. Jenny 40, $40. Rachel 10, $40.	
Gittings, Mary	Widow	Eutaw St			Nathan 14, $125. Cornelius 18, $125. Jane 20, $80. Maria 18, $80. Elisa 16, $80. Charlotte 13, $40.	
Glenn, Elias		Hammond St		Attorney	Isaac 50, $60. Ned 12, $40. Phil 18, $125. Fanny 48, $40.	Glenn pays no tax for Isaac because he is a cripple.
Glenn, John W.		Hammond St		Oil & paint store	Lloyd 3, $10. George 5, $20. Sterling 14, $125. Nell 30, $80. Cornelia 8, $40.	
Grace, Redmond		Holliday St		Tobacco merchant	Female 21, $80.	

Free Blacks and Slave Owners in Baltimore City Tax Assessor's Ledger, 1818, Ward 10

NAME	RACE/ STATUS	RESIDENCE	REAL PROPERTY	OCCUPATION	ENSLAVED PROPERTY Name, Age, Value	COMMENTS
Griffith, John		Eutaw St		Carter	Vache 18, $125.	
Grundy, George		Biddle St		Merchant	Tom 50, $60. Harry 40, $125. Henry 22, $125. Dorcas 50, $30. Harriot 14, $80.	
Grundy, Thomas Byrum		Pleasant St			Jacob 22, $125.	
Gunn, James		Charles St		Merchant	Jim 18, $125. Jerry 35, $125. Ralph 18, $125. Jacob 14, $125. Mary 16, $80. Lucy 14, $80.	
Hall, Isabella		Charles St			Jonas 35, $125. James 30, $125. Jessey 25, $125. Judah 27, $80. Hanna 28, $80. Dinah 12, $40. Susan 10, $40. Rosetta 8, $40.	
Hamilton, James		Biddle St		Clerk	Ellen 13, $80.	
Hand, Moses		Howard St		Painter	Eli 22, $125.	
Heighe, James		Cove St		Cordwainer	Juliet 21, $80. Harriet 21, $80. Elisa 9, $40. Jamison 22, $125. Richard 19, $125. Tom 18, $125. Isaac 17, $125. Robert 15, $125. Bill 17, $125. Emma 17, $80. Rosetta 17, $80. Susan 15, $80. Deb 13, $40. Nancy 12, $40. Rachel 49, $30. Jenny 10, $40. Mary 13, $40.	Jamison through Mary are hired out.
Hennely, John H.		Pleasant St		Merchant	Kitty 40, $40.	
Higginbotham, Ralph		Franklin St		Cashier at Union Bank of Maryland	Lucy 25, $80. Rachel 10, $40.	
Hindman, James		Calvert St		Colonel	William 36, $125. Mary 36, $80.	
Hollingsworth, Zebulon		Ireland's Co. Seat			Ben 45, $60. James 30, $125. Robert 6, $20. Rose 30, $80.	
Holmes, James		Bath St		Porter Cellar	Phill 16, $125. Mary 12, $40.	

Free Blacks and Slave Owners in Baltimore City Tax Assessor's Ledger, 1818, Ward 10

NAME	RACE/ STATUS	RESIDENCE	REAL PROPERTY	OCCUPATION	ENSLAVED PROPERTY Name, Age, Value	COMMENTS
Hoppe, Justice		Charles St		Merchant	James 6, $20. Margaret 20, $80.	
Howard, Col. John E.		Cathedral St			Nace 28, $125. John 24, $125. David 7, $20. Adam 21, $125. Becky 41, $40. Maria 19, $80. Caroline 8, $40. Margarett 30, $80.	Adam to serve 8 years. Margaret to be freed this summer.
Howard, Dinah	Colored Woman	LeRue's Alley	Lot E side S of Mulberry St $30, Imp $20			
Ireland, Edward (Estate of)		Cove St			Henry 6, $20. Richard 4, $10. Kate 25, $80. Mary 25, $80. Ellen 4, $10.	
Jackson, William	Colored Man	Chapel Alley	Lot N side E of North St $50, Imp $70			
Jakes, Frederick	Colored Man	North St	Lot ½ of #5 on Poor House Plat $30, Imp $75	Waiter		
James, Edward	Colored Man	Morris St	Lot SE side NE of Ross St, $36, Imp $30			
James, James	Colored Man	Ross St	Lot SW side, NW of Eutaw $40, Imp dwelling $15	Laborer		
Jarvis, Leonard		St. Paul's Lane		Merchant	Maria 25, $80.	
Jefferson, Hanson	Colored Man	Lombardy St	Lot W side of Centre St $60, Imp $65			

Free Blacks and Slave Owners in Baltimore City Tax Assessor's Ledger, 1818, Ward 10

NAME	RACE/ STATUS	RESIDENCE	REAL PROPERTY	OCCUPATION	ENSLAVED PROPERTY Name, Age, Value	COMMENTS
Jefferson, William	Colored	Lombardy St	Lot W side S of Centre St $60, Imp $65, horse $15 & dray $8	Drayman		
Jenkins, Sarah		Bath St			Lewis 22, $125. Basil 17, $125. John 17, $125. Alick 10, $40. Milly 45, $30. Margaret 50, $30. Harriet 19, $80. Caroline 16, $80. Kitty 16, $80. Matilda 12, $40.	
Johnson, Abraham	Colored Man	Greenwich St	Lot NW side, SW of Reicester Town Rd, $25, Imp $15	Laborer		
Keener, Susan	Widow of Christian	Reicester Town Rd			George 7, $20. Peggy 32, $80.	
Kemp, James (D.D.)		Saratoga St		The Rev. Bishop Episcopal	James 6, $20. Lear 5, $20. Bill 3, $10. Margaret 25, $80.	
Kennedy, John		Cove St		Merchant	William 13, $40. Betty 18, $80. Sarah 30, $80. Mary 7, $20.	
Kraber, Martin		Reicester Town Rd		Merchant	Flora 20, $80.	
LeBon, Eliza		Price St			Louis 10, $40. Caroline 40, $40. Mercelino 19, $80.	
LeClaire, Peter Cazeaux V.		Pierce St		Gardener	John 45, $60. Madeline 43, $40. Antoinette 12, $40.	
LeClere, Francis		Price St		Gardener	Oliver 8, $40. Margaret 36, $80. Dauphine 4, $10.	

Free Blacks and Slave Owners in Baltimore City Tax Assessor's Ledger, 1818, Ward 10

NAME	RACE/ STATUS	RESIDENCE	REAL PROPERTY	OCCUPATION	ENSLAVED PROPERTY Name, Age, Value	COMMENTS
Letto, Barbara	Colored Woman	Biddle St	Lot NW side NE of Reicester Town Rd $30, Imp her dwelling $25			
Lindenberger, George		Calvert St		Wholesale hardware merchant	James 14, $125. Kitty 20, $80. Rachel 35, $80.	
Logan, James	Colored Man	Calvert St	2 lots W side S of Centre St $200, Imp his dwelling $60, horse $20	Drayman		
Long, Kennedy		Ross St			Jim 11, $40.	
Martin, John		Courtland St		Carpenter	Matilda 12, $40.	
McCausland, Marcus		Holliday St		Brewer	Sam 12, $40. Will 20, $125. Maria 20, $80. Harriot 24, $80.	
McCulloh, James H.		Price St		Collector customs	Hagar 25, $80. Deily 12, $40.	
McGill, George	Colored Man	Chapel Alley	Lot SW corner of College Alley $30, Imp $100	Teacher of the Methodist Colored School @ The African Methodist Meeting, Sharp St, W side, S of Lombard		
McKim, William D.		Falls Turnpike Rd		Gentleman	Robert 19, $125. Abram 23, $60.	Abram is sickly.
McNulty, John		Calvert St		Carter	Jacques 18, $125. Will 15, $125. Kitt 47, $30.	
Merkle, Jacob		Franklin St		Golden Horse Tavern	Peggy 20, $80. Jean 3, $10.	

Free Blacks and Slave Owners in Baltimore City Tax Assessor's Ledger, 1818, Ward 10

NAME	RACE/ STATUS	RESIDENCE	REAL PROPERTY	OCCUPATION	ENSLAVED PROPERTY Name, Age, Value	COMMENTS
Metzger, William		Keller & Foreman's Yard		Tanner near jail	Will 18, $125. Ann 21, $80.	
Mills, Robert		St. Paul's Lane		Engineer	Peter 20, $125. Elisa 20, $80.	Mills architect of Washington Monument.
Mitchell, Col. George		Reicester Town Rd			Noah 40, $125. Jim 11, $40. Maria 16, $80. Caroline 13, $40.	
Mitchell, Richard B.		Charles St			John 26, $125. Joe 14, $125. Lydia 46, $30. Whima 26, $80.	
Montalibor, Martha	French Lady Widow	Eutaw St			Louisa 30, $80.	
Moore, Anthony	Colored Man	Falls Turnpike Rd	Lot SW off the road leased of Rutter, $45, Imp his dwelling $15			
Moore, William	Colored Man	Calvert St	Lot W side S of Centre St $150			
Morsell, Hetty	Widow	Saratoga St			Maria 14, $80	
Morton, John A.		Mulberry St		Junior Merchant	Stephen 15, $125	
Mullikin, Mary	Widow	Saratoga St			Resin 42, $125. Milly 20, $80. Rachell 42, $40. Mary Ann 16, $80. Eliza 10, $40.	
Murphy, William	Colored Man	Reicester Town Rd	Lot SW side NW of Greenwich St $45, Imp his dwelling $10			
Mushett, Walter		Pleasant St		Merchant	Milly 28, $80.	

Free Blacks and Slave Owners in Baltimore City Tax Assessor's Ledger, 1818, Ward 10

NAME	RACE/STATUS	RESIDENCE	REAL PROPERTY	OCCUPATION	ENSLAVED PROPERTY Name, Age, Value	COMMENTS
Myers, Henry		Reicester Town Rd		Butcher	John 21, $125. Lydia 15, $80.	
Myers, Jacob		New Lane		Butcher	Charlotte 13, $40.	
Neilson, Robert H.		Calvert St		Merchant	David 15, $125. Rachel 30, $80.	
Nelson, Richard		St. Paul's Lane		Merchant	Arthur 17, $125. Sophia 14, $80. Jean 8, $40.	
Norris, Richard		Charles St		Hardware merchant	Lyttleton 15, $125. Abby 16, $80. Letty 3, $10.	
Orme, Archibald E.		Paca St		Bricklayer	Jean 6, $20.	
Owen, Kennedy (Estate of)		Charles St			Daphne 25, $80. Matilda 3, $10.	
Owings, Mary	Widow of Samuel	Reicester Town Rd			Eveline 19, $80. Milla 16, $80.	
Pacolet, Valentine	Colored Man	Reicester Town Rd	Lot NE side on Keener's Lane $35, Imp $10	Cordwainer		
Parker, Thomas		Franklin St		Secretary Universal Insurance Co.	John 21, $125. Flora 14, $80. Anna 8, $40.	
Patterson, Susan	Widow of William	Charles St			Nanny 24, $80.	
Pawley, James		Franklin St		Merchant	Thomas 13, $40.	
Perine, William		Reicester Town Rd		Tailor	Henry 9, $40. Barbara 18, $80.	
Phillips, Isaac		Eutaw St		Merchant	Moses 33, $125. Silvia 50, $30. Louisa 20, $80.	
Phips, Ann	Widow of James, A Colored Woman	New Lane	Lot N side E of Paca St $35, Imp her dwelling $100	Laundress		

Free Blacks and Slave Owners in Baltimore City Tax Assessor's Ledger, 1818, Ward 10

NAME	RACE/STATUS	RESIDENCE	REAL PROPERTY	OCCUPATION	ENSLAVED PROPERTY Name, Age, Value	COMMENTS
Pierce, Levy		Franklin St		Merchant	Toby 50, $60. Charles 30, $125. Sharper 16, $125. Bill 7, $20. Fanny 50, $30. Jenny 35, $80. Proby 35, $80. Harriot 6, $20. Susan 4, $10. Sarah 4, $10. Rose 3, $10.	
Pleasants, John P.		St. Paul's Lane		Merchant	Jack, $125. Charles 12, $40. Ann 14, $80. Margaret 23, $80.	
Ponter, Leonard		Falls Turnpike			Levi 21, $125. Harriot 5, $20.	
Poor, Dudley		Charles St		Merchant	James 4, $10. Harriot 20, $80. Beck 17, $80.	
Price, Hezekiah		Cove St		Lumber merchant	Robert 27, $125. Phoebe 50, $30. Grace 25, $80.	
Price, William		Hammond St		Ship builder	Isaac 30, $125. Lydia 25, $80. Charlotte 20, $80.	
Purviance, William		St. Paul's Lane		Justice of the Peace & Commission Merchant	Mary 22, $80.	
Raphael, Aquila		Franklin St			James 20, $125. Edward 17, $125. Nathan 8, $40. Amelia 30, $80. Venus 18, $80. Prinny 16, $80. Clotilda 12, $40.	
Regnier, Charles L.	French Colored Man	Union St	Lot N side NE of Reicester Town Rd $27, Imp his dwelling $70, Furn $10	Hairdresser		

Free Blacks and Slave Owners in Baltimore City Tax Assessor's Ledger, 1818, Ward 10

NAME	RACE/ STATUS	RESIDENCE	REAL PROPERTY	OCCUPATION	ENSLAVED PROPERTY Name, Age, Value	COMMENTS
Rutter, Thomas (Estate of)		Falls Turnpike Rd			Abraham 30, $125. Joshua 25, $125. Sam 16, $125. Richard 15, $125. Ned 12, $40. Anthony 6, $20. Bob 4, $10. Diana 25, $80. Louisa 15, $80. Rosetta 12, $40. Sidney 11, $40. Charlotte 9, $40.	
Schroeder, Henry		Hammond St		Senior Merchant @ Vansbeck Farm	Milla 12, $40. Daphne 22, $80. Harriot 4, $10.	
Selman, Johnsee		Reicester Town Rd			Jim 21, $125.	
Servary, Peter		Paca St		Segarmaker	Alexander 14, $125. Mary 40, $40.	
Seth, James G.		St. Paul's Lane		Merchant	Perry 16, $125. Cressy 22, $80. Cerilla 3, $10.	
Sewell, Thomas		Reicester Town Rd		Tanner	Milla 17, $80.	
Smith, Jacob G.		Charles St		Gent	Jim 45, $6. Jacob 30, $125. Larry 30, $125. John 25, $125. Fanny 40, $40. Margaret 26, $80. Louisa 12, $40.	
Smith, Samuel R.		Cove St		Gent	Jenny 50, $30. Milla 26, $80. Beck 12, $40.	
Smyth, Samuel		Biddle St			Charlotte 40, $40.	
Smythe, Dr. James		Pleasant St			Henry 7, $40. Doll 14, $80.	
Snuggrass, William		Reicester Town Rd		Grocery & liquor store, Pennsylvania Ave, SW side NW of Windsor Mill Rd	Peter 30, $125.	
Snyder, Peter		Calvert St		Baker	Female slave 25, $80.	
Stephenson, Sater		St. Paul's Lane		Mason	Hagar 25, $80.	
Sterrett, Samuel		Calvert St		Auctioneer	Frank 35, $80. Peter 13, $40.	

Free Blacks and Slave Owners in Baltimore City Tax Assessor's Ledger, 1818, Ward 10

NAME	RACE/ STATUS	RESIDENCE	REAL PROPERTY	OCCUPATION	ENSLAVED PROPERTY Name, Age, Value	COMMENTS
					Sarah 12, $40.	
Stevenson, George P.		St. Paul's Lane		Merchant	Ann 40, $40. Letty 12, $40.	
Stockton, Richard		Reicester Town Rd			Sam 25, $125. John 24, $125. Jacob 8, $40. Eliza 48, $30. Evaline 16, $80.	
Sumwalt, Frederick		Howard St		Stone quarrier	John 14, $125. William 17, $125.	
Swann, William		Charles St			Rhody 15, $80.	
Tate, Alexander		Pleasant St			Emaline 17, $80. Matilda 26, $80.	
Tessier, The Rev. John		Morris St		Of St. Mary's College	John $125. Georgette $80.	
Thomas, Julius	French Colored Man	Union St	Lot NW side NE Reicester Town Rd $27, Imp his dwelling $50			
Tiernan, Patrick		Pleasant St		Merchant	Jacob 12, $40.	
Tonson, Thomas		Saratoga St		Stone cutter	Sam 25, $125. Phil 16, $125. Lewis 9, $40. Alias 8, $40. Frank 5, $20. Belsit 4, $20. Leah 25, $80. Angela 8, $40.	
Troop, Elizabeth		St. Paul's Lane			James 20, $125. Philip 18, $125. Margaret 20, $80. Betsy 9, $40.	
Turrell, John		Reicester Town Rd		Segar maker	James 45, $69. Charity 15, $80.	
Wallace, Joseph		Saratoga St		Merchant	Lydia 15, $80.	
Wallace, William M.		George St		Merchant	Ann 20, $80.	
Wallis, Philip		Charles St		Merchant	2 males between 14 & 45, $250. 1 female between 14-30, $80.	

Free Blacks and Slave Owners in Baltimore City Tax Assessor's Ledger, 1818, Ward 10

NAME	RACE/ STATUS	RESIDENCE	REAL PROPERTY	OCCUPATION	ENSLAVED PROPERTY Name, Age, Value	COMMENTS
Welch, John		Holliday St		Lumber merchant	John 16, $125. Harriot 14, $80.	
Wheeler, John		LeRues Alley near the poor house lots			Sabby 16, $80. Milly 10, $40.	
Whipper, Isaac	Colored Man	Tyson St	Lot NE side NW of Richmond St $5, Imp 4 brick houses $300	Bootblack under 8 N. Charles St		
White, Jacob		Holliday St		Grocer @ the house of Gross & White	Nan 40, $40. Female 9, $40.	
White, John		Holliday St			Female slave 14, $80.	
Wilks, Letty	Colored Woman	Falls Turnpike Rd	Lot SW side off the road leased T. Rutter, $30 Imp her dwelling $10			
Williams, Amos A.		Calvert St		Merchant	Margaret 20, $80.	
Williams, Amos A. & George		North St		Merchant on Bowley's Wharf	Major 30, $125. Felix 30, $125.	
Williams, Caesar	Colored Man	Greenwich St	Lot NW side SW of Reicester Town Rd $25, Imp $15			
Williams, George		Courtland St		Merchant	Judah 50, $30. Bett 7, $20.	
Williams, Nathaniel F.		Franklin St		Merchant	William 18, $125.	
Wilson, John		Eutaw St		Plasterer	Ned 30, $125.	

Free Blacks and Slave Owners in Baltimore City Tax Assessor's Ledger, 1818, Ward 10

NAME	RACE/ STATUS	RESIDENCE	REAL PROPERTY	OCCUPATION	ENSLAVED PROPERTY Name, Age, Value	COMMENTS
Wilson, Lydia	Colored Woman	New Lane	Lot S side W of Eutaw St. $30, Imp $60			
Wirgman, Charles		Franklin St		Merchant	William 30, $125. Larkin 16, $125. Julia 20, $80. Lydia 25, $80.	
Woods, Wesley		St. Paul's Lane		Merchant	Stephen 25, $125. Kitty 20, $8. Elliza 12, $40. Ann 5, $20.	
Woodyard, Neptune	Colored Man	Reicester Town Rd	Lot NE side on Keener's Land, $35, Imp his dwelling $10	Laborer		
Worthington, Abraham		Charles St		Gentleman	Maria 7, $20. Matilda 50, $30. Sophia 16, $80.	
Worthington, Charles		Charles St		Miller	Abraham 27, $125. Jenny 18, $80.	
Wright, Dr. Thomas		NW corner of Mulberry St		M.D.	Elisha 12, $40. Nancy 20, $80. Emma 18, $80.	
Wrightman, Rebecca	Colored Woman	Montgomery St	Lot on S corner of Ross St, $60 Imp dwelling $10			
Yeiser/Yeizer, John		Holliday St		Merchant	Henry 40, $125. Female, 30, $80. Female 16, $80. Female 10, $40.	

Free Blacks and Slave Owners in Baltimore City Tax Assessor's Ledger, 1818, Ward 10

NAME	RACE/ STATUS	RESIDENCE	REAL PROPERTY	OCCUPATION	ENSLAVED PROPERTY Name, Age, Value	COMMENTS
Young, Perry	Colored Man	Mulberry St	Lot N side W of North St $100, Imp his dwelling $200, Lot on any alley between North St & LaRue's Alley $30, Imp $10	Laborer		

Free Blacks and Slave Owners in Baltimore City Tax Assessor's Ledger, 1818, Ward 11

NAME	RACE/ STATUS	RESIDENCE	REAL PROPERTY	OCCUPATION	ENSLAVED PROPERTY Name, Age, Value	COMMENTS
Adrian, Geoge		Franklin St		Carpenter	Sarah 19, $80.	
Albright, John		Washington ST		Brickmaker	Raze 12, $40. Henson 5, $20. Rosetta 15, $80. Rachell 14, $80.	
Baer, Dr. Jacob		Market St			Bill 6, $20. Matilda 16, $80. Dina 7, $20.	
Bailey, Isaac	Colored Man	Bottle Alley	Lot N side E of Paca St $25, Imp unfinished $40	Wood Sawyer		
Ball, William		Pearl St		Painter St	Dennis 11, $40. Bett 36, $80.	
Barney, Joshua		Pearl St		Commodore	Fanny 50, $30. Milly 45, $30. Rachel 10, $40. Margarett 10, $40.	
Bauer, John J.		Hammond St		Butcher	George 16, $125.	
Bennett, Patrick		Paca St			Mary 5, $20. Roseanna 5, $20.	
Berry, Horatio		Market St		Carpenter	Eliza 22, $80. Kitty 11, $40.	
Berry, John W.		Mulberry St		Carpenter	Nancy 19, $80.	
Bill, Triolus	Colored Man	Asberry St	Lot W side S of Market St $20, Imp his dwelling $20	Drayman		
Bland, Theodorick		Paca St		Judge of the 6th Judicial District	Rachel 45, $30. Peggy 3, $10.	
Boyd, Mrs. James P.		Market St			Mary 15. $80. Nathan 28, $125. Augustus 6, $20. Henry 4, $10. Susan 35, $80.	James was an attorney & counselor at law
Brendle, Maria	Widow of Frederick	Green St			Betty 30, $80.	

Free Blacks and Slave Owners in Baltimore City Tax Assessor's Ledger, 1818, Ward 11

NAME	RACE/ STATUS	RESIDENCE	REAL PROPERTY	OCCUPATION	ENSLAVED PROPERTY Name, Age, Value	COMMENTS
Brightman, Rebecca	Colored Woman	Saratoga St	Lot NE of corner of Pearl St $75, Imp $250	Market Dealer		
Brown, John	Colored Man	Asberry St	Lot W side S of Market St $20, Imp unfinished $25	Drayman		
Brown, John (Kent of Brohn Agts)		Paca St			Isaac 10, $40. Solomon 8, $40. Henny 20, $80. Lucy 20, $80.	
Brown, Joshua	Colored Man	Pratt St	Lot N side E of Asberry St $30, Imp his dwelling $40	Carter		
Bruce, Upton		Franklin St		Gent.	Nell 14, $80. Walter 16, $125. Henson 9, $40. Nat 6, $20. Ann 22, $80. Sophia 14, $80.	
Bull, William		Pearl St		Grocer	Lewis 20, $125.	
Burk, Thomas	Colored Man	Pearl St	Lot E side S of Mulberry St $60, Imp his dwelling $20			
Caldwell, James		Eutaw St		Merchant	Jean 15, $80. Mary 18, $80. Robert 30, $125.	

Free Blacks and Slave Owners in Baltimore City Tax Assessor's Ledger, 1818, Ward 11

NAME	RACE/ STATUS	RESIDENCE	REAL PROPERTY	OCCUPATION	ENSLAVED PROPERTY Name, Age, Value	COMMENTS
Carroll, James		Washington St (Montclare Farm)	Land valued @ $31,500	Gentleman	Joseph 35, $125. Anthony 35, $125. Robert 30, $125. Peter 3, $125. Henry 30, $125. Isaac 30, $125. James 18, $125. Joshua 18, $125. Charles 14, $125. George 12, $40. Tom 8, $40. Sam 4, $20. Nelson 3, $10. Joe 3, $10. Abraham 30, $65. Debb 30, $80. Pegg 30, $80. Fanny 25, $80. Rachel 15, $80. Pollmary 15, $80. Mary 15, $80. Tamar 30 $40. Sal 18, $40. Harriot 4, $10.	Abraham is sickly. Sal is sickly.
Carroll, John	Colored Man	Market St	Lot N side W of Cove St $36, Imp his dwelling $125			
Cater, John		Jefferson St		Brickmaker	Phil 13, $40. Phillis 18, $80. Charlotte 12, $40.	
Chambers, Kitty	Colored Woman	Eutaw St	Lot W side S of Conway St $30, Imp $50			
Chase, Anna K.	Widow of Samuel	Eutaw St			Nick 15, $125. Scipio 48, $60. Susan 30, $80. Ruth 40, $40.	
Clapham, Jonas		Eutaw St		Gentleman	Daniel 27, $125. Polly 26, $80.	
Clark, Solomon	Colored Man	Bottle Alley	Lot N side E of Pratt St, $25, Imp unfinished $40	Laborer		
Clem, William		Clem's Lot			Hariotte 20, $80.	

Free Blacks and Slave Owners in Baltimore City Tax Assessor's Ledger, 1818, Ward 11

NAME	RACE/ STATUS	RESIDENCE	REAL PROPERTY	OCCUPATION	ENSLAVED PROPERTY Name, Age, Value	COMMENTS
Cook, George	George is son of William Cook	Clem's Lot			Charles 23, $125. Nancy 15, $80.	
Croskery, Bernard		Mulberry St		Nailer	Dick 21, $125. Matthew 7, $20. Linda $12, $40.	
Cugle, John		Market St		General Wayne Inn	Vincent 30, $125. Bill 22, $125. Sam 23, $125. Josh 8, $40. Betty 40, $80. Milly 30, $80. Lucy 20, $80. Harriot 9, $40.	
Cummings, Francis D.		Pearl St		Gentleman	Eve 12, $40.	
Cushing, Joseph		Pearl St		Bookstore on Howard St	Cara 35, $80.	
Dailey, Daniel		Franklin St		Plasterer	Charles 28, $125. Daniel 22, $125. Henry 5, $20. Peggy 32, $80. Mary 7, $20. Eliza 3, $10.	
Dashield, Rev. George		Fayette St		Rector of St. John's Church	Henrietta 15, $80.	
Davis, James	Colored Man	Asberry St	Lot W side S of Market St $20. Imp his dwelling $30, horse $10, dray $8	Drayman		
Deems, Jacob		Cove St		Tanner	Rachel 16, $80.	

Free Blacks and Slave Owners in Baltimore City Tax Assessor's Ledger, 1818, Ward 11

NAME	RACE/ STATUS	RESIDENCE	REAL PROPERTY	OCCUPATION	ENSLAVED PROPERTY Name, Age, Value	COMMENTS
Depestre, Mary	Widow resides in Low's house	Lexington St			Telime 40, $125. Jacques 40, $125. Louis 14, $125. Paul 7, $20. Joseph 3, $10. Fine 35, $80. Justine 40, $40. Fillette 35, $80. Nannette 18, $80. Roseanna 13, $40.	
Donnell, John		Frederick Town Rd		Merchant	Charles 25, $125. Jack 18, $125.	
Donovan, Richard		Pine St		Innkeeper	Peter 10, $40.	
Dorsey, Owen		Strawberry Alley		Accountant, conveyancer & justice of the peace	Susan 40, $40. Amelia 7, $20. Ned 4, $10.	
Dumest, Elizabeth	Widow	Green St			Jim 4, $10. Harriot 23, $80. Philis 21, $80.	
Dunn, Michael		Pearl St		Flour merchant	Polly 22, $80. Ruth 16, $80.	
Earls, David	Colored Man	Asberry St	Lot W side N of Pratt St $20, Imp his dwelling $30			
Edwards, William		Washington St		Carpenter	Susan 15, $80.	
Elder, Basil S.		Fayette St		Merchant	Anna 19, $80. Sarah 16, $80.	
Elliott, Howard		Cove St		Engs of Clifford Constable	Mary 40, $40.	
Elliott, Thomas		Paca St		Innkeeper	Jake 14, $125. Henry 3, $125.	

Free Blacks and Slave Owners in Baltimore City Tax Assessor's Ledger, 1818, Ward 11

NAME	RACE/ STATUS	RESIDENCE	REAL PROPERTY	OCCUPATION	ENSLAVED PROPERTY Name, Age, Value	COMMENTS
Emalong, Frederick		Paca St		Merchant	Harry 13, $40. Bob 4, $10. Sophia 30, $80. Fann 19, $80. Mary 8, $40. Nancy 12, $40.	
Evans, Lewis		Green St		Merchant	Lewis 7, $20.	
Finley, Ebenezer		Fayette St		Merchant	Leah 36, $80. Rachel 15, $80.	
Fitzgerald, John		Ferry Rd		Ropemaker	Thomas 11, $40. Bett 16, $80.	
Foltz, William		Pratt St		Formerly McClure & Foltz	Henry 8, $40. Ann 15, $80.	
Forman, Francis		Eutaw St		Merchant	Debby 28, $80. Aimey 15, $80.	
Forney, David		Green St		Grocer	Susan 17, $80.	
Fowler, Thomas	Colored Man	Third St	Lot E side S of Cross St $50, Imp his dwelling $50, Horse $10, 2 cows $10, cart $6	Laborer		
Freeman, Edward	Colored Man	Washington St	Lot S side W of Scott St $45, Imp his dwelling $35, old horse $10, Cart $6	Laborer		
Fulton, James		Paca St		Packer	Lyla 20, $80.	
Gadsby, John		Washington St			Mingo 32, $125.	
Gassaway, Henry		Pearl St		Dry Goods Merchant	Stephen 12, $40. Polly 20, $80.	
Gibson, John		Bloomsbury Rd @ Lorman's Land			Peter 38, $125.	

Free Blacks and Slave Owners in Baltimore City Tax Assessor's Ledger, 1818, Ward 11

NAME	RACE/ STATUS	RESIDENCE	REAL PROPERTY	OCCUPATION	ENSLAVED PROPERTY Name, Age, Value	COMMENTS
Goggin, Thomas		Saratoga St		Maypole Tavern	Joe 30, $125.	
Gould, Alexander		Ferry Rd		Butcher	Jacob 40, $125. William 6, $20. Darka 32, $80.	
Griffin, Charles		Green St			Charles 16, $125. Andrew 18, $125. Nancy 40, $40.	
Grove, Stephen		Green St		Merchant	Harriot 14, $80.	
Groverman, Anthony		Green St		China Merchant	George 8, $40. Mary 25, $80.	
Hall, Washington		Market St		Merchant	Chloe 18, $80.	
Hanson, Philip	Colored Man	Scott St	Lot W side S of Washington $16, Imp his dwelling $40	Brick Maker		
Harden, Henry	Colored Man	Pearl St	Lot W side S of Lexington St $100, Imp his dwelling $75	Preacher		
Hardy, Priscilla	Widow of John	Fayette St			Isaac 30, $125. Archibald 40, $125. George 25, $125. Bradley 20, $125. Anthony 16, $125. Albert 13, $40. Henson 7, $20. August 5, $20. Harriot 30, $80. Darcos 20, $80. Emma 13, $40. Kitty 10, $40. Maria 7, $20. Charlotte 4, $10.	
Harris, Col. David		Mulberry St		Merchant	Rosetta 22, $80.	

Free Blacks and Slave Owners in Baltimore City Tax Assessor's Ledger, 1818, Ward 11

NAME	RACE/ STATUS	RESIDENCE	REAL PROPERTY	OCCUPATION	ENSLAVED PROPERTY Name, Age, Value	COMMENTS
Harris, William	Colored Man	Asberry St	Lot W side S of Market St $20, Imp unfinished $30	Bootblack		
Haubert, Frederick (Estate of)		Lombard St			Gabriel 11, $40. Jane 28, $80.	
Hawkins, William (Estate of)		Market St			Perry 22, $125. Grace 10, $40.	
Heath, Gen. Richard K.		Lexington St			Bill 12, $40. James 5, $20. Betty 45, $30. Annette 5, $20.	
Hebrew, (No first name given)	Colored Man	Asberry St	Lot E side S of Market St $20, Imp $60	Dyer		
Henry, John		Market St		Harness maker	Henry 19, $125.	
Henry, Nancy	Colored Woman	Washington St	Lot W side S of Cross St $25, Imp her dwelling $15			
Hickley, Robert		Saratoga St		Merchant	Nancy 30, $80. John 6, $20.	
Higinbotham, Thomas		Fayette St		Merchant	Ben 32, $125. Dan 4, $10. Priss 30, $80. Esther 28, $80. Cora 10, $40. Elben 7, $20	
Hignutt, John		Scott St		Brick maker	Dency 12, $40. James 14, $125. Abraham 14, $125.	
Hines, James		Lombard St		Brick layer	George 12, $40. Lydia 12, $40.	
Hoffman, Daniel		Frederick Town Rd		Flour merchant	Limas 23, $125. Mintha 18, $80. Lott 10, $40.	

Free Blacks and Slave Owners in Baltimore City Tax Assessor's Ledger, 1818, Ward 11

NAME	RACE/ STATUS	RESIDENCE	REAL PROPERTY	OCCUPATION	ENSLAVED PROPERTY Name, Age, Value	COMMENTS
Honton/Honiton, Parish	Colored Man	Eutaw St	Lot W side S of Conway St, $30, Imp his dwelling $170			
Hook, Joseph Sr.		Green St		Lexington Market Master	Ann 11, $40.	
Hudson, Jonathon		So of ? Basin		Merchant	Ben 45, $60. Jacob 45, $60. Jim Cox 40, $125. Dick 35, $125. Joe 28, $125. Jake 20, $125. Robert 10, $40. Ned 40, $125. Jim Sheppard 35, $125. Susan 28, $80. Charles 40, $125.	
Hughes, Aquilla		Saratoga St		Grocer	Grace 12, $40.	
Israel, Beal		Green St		Cryer of the Court	Lydia 27, $80.	
Israel, Fielder		Green St		Justice of Peace	John 8, $40.	
Jackson, Bolton		Paca St			Jeffrey 40, $125.	
Jackson, Thaddeus		Fort McHenry		Innkeeper	Mary 40, $40.	
Jenkins, David	Colored Man	Asberry St	Lot W side S of Pratt St $20, Imp his dwelling $15			
Johnson, Benjamin	Colored Man	Pratt St	Lot S side E of Asberry St $30, Imp his dwelling $20	Laborer		

Free Blacks and Slave Owners in Baltimore City Tax Assessor's Ledger, 1818, Ward 11

NAME	RACE/ STATUS	RESIDENCE	REAL PROPERTY	OCCUPATION	ENSLAVED PROPERTY Name, Age, Value	COMMENTS
Jones, James	Colored Man	Asberry St	Lot W side E of Market $20, Imp his dwelling $30, horse $10, dray $8	Drayman		
Jones, William		Green St		Bricklayer	Mary 7, $20. Henny 3, $10.	
Kennedy, Dennis		Market St		Clerk	Jean 10, $40.	
Knabb, John		Ferry Rd		Carpenter	Elizabeth 12, $40.	
Konig, Frederick		Frederick Town Rd		Merchant	Bill 10, $80. Jacob 21, $125. Henny 22, $80.	
Krebbs, William		Washington St		Victualler	2 males between 14 and 45 years @ $125 each. 1 female between 20 and 36 $80. 1 female 10, $40.	
Krems, Joseph (Estate of)		Green St		Merchant	Saby 30, $80.	
Lakeintre, John L.		Lexington St		First teller U. S. Bank	Joseph 36, $125. Betsy 34, $80.	
Lawrence, Richard		George St		Crockery Store	Sarah 13, $80.	
Le Duc, Susan		Lexington St		Agt for Bonnefin	Charlotte 36, $80.	
Leclaire, Dr. Lewis S.		Mulberry St			Lewis 45, $60. Lelette 20, $80.	
Lieutaud, Bartholomew		Cowpen Alley		Gardener on McHenry's land	Victoire 28, $80. Catherine 6, $20.	
Lilly, Eli		Pratt St		Innkeeper Fun Tavern	Shaed 30, $125. Charles 12, $40. Nancy 35, $80. Juda 18, $80.	
Lloyd, Micha	Widow of Piola	Mulberry St			Sam 6, $20.	

Free Blacks and Slave Owners in Baltimore City Tax Assessor's Ledger, 1818, Ward 11

NAME	RACE/ STATUS	RESIDENCE	REAL PROPERTY	OCCUPATION	ENSLAVED PROPERTY Name, Age, Value	COMMENTS
Long, Elizabeth C.		Franklin St		Grocer	Lewis 10, $40. Charles 8, $40. Jean 33, $80. Phael 30, $80. Juliet 7, $20.	
Lynch, John		Franklin St		Watchmaker	Female 6, $20.	
Maslin, Michael M.		Lexington St		Hardware merchant	Dolly 35, $80.	
Mathews, John		Market St		Morroco Dresser	David 21, $125. Maria 18, $80.	
Mathews, Rachael	Colored Woman Widow	Saratoga St	Lot N side W of Green St $60, Imp $40, furn $5, 3 cows $15			
Maybury, Thomas		Mulberry St		Brick layer	Harriot 17, $80.	
Mayer, Christian		Eutaw St		Merchant	David 22, $125. Esther 38, $80.	
Maynard, Foster		Saratoga St		Carpenter	Poll 18, $80. Jenny 9, $40.	
McConckey, Capt. James		Saratoga St			Jim 23, $125. Maria 30, $80. Abraham 3, $10.	
Meads, Joshua	Colored Man	Back St	Lot W side S of Hammond St $34, Imp $40, 2 horses $25, an old cart $5	Carter		
Meredith, William (Estate of)		Franklin St			Henry 19, $125.	
Mollach, Candes	Colored Woman	Bottle Alley	Lot S side W of Eutaw St $25, Imp her dwelling $15	Seamstress		
Moore, Cyrus	Colored Man	Eutaw St	Lot E side S of Lexington St $30, Imp his dwelling $60			

Free Blacks and Slave Owners in Baltimore City Tax Assessor's Ledger, 1818, Ward 11

NAME	RACE/STATUS	RESIDENCE	REAL PROPERTY	OCCUPATION	ENSLAVED PROPERTY Name, Age, Value	COMMENTS
Nagel, Henry		Washington St		Brickmaker	Jim 32, $125. Ned 12, $40. Little Tom 32, $125. Nancy 23, $80.	
Neale, John G.		Pearl St		Stone cutter	Memory 14, $80. Delisla 35, $80.	
Nichols, Charlotte	Widow.	Resides at her county seat.			John 5, $20. Isaac 23, $125. Henry 6, $20. Richard 3, $10. Rachel 35, $80.	
Norris, Benjamin		Park Lane		Shoemaker	Patty 13, $40.	
Norris, James Jr.		Market St		Carpenter	Lucy 32, $80.	
Norton, John	Colored Man	Rock St	Lot W side S of Hammond St $25, Imp unfinished $40			
Norvell, Sarah	Widow of Dr.	Fayette St			Cato 35, $125. Aleck 30, $125. Beck 20, $80. Lydia 28, $80. Julianna 12, $40.	
O'Donnell, Columbus	In Skinner's house	Paca St		Gentleman	Otho 30, $125. Orson 7, $20. Bets 11, $40.	
O'Donnell, Sarah	Widow of John	Pearl St			Jean 25, $80. Mary Ann 31, $80. Sophia 20, $80. Tilda 13, $40.	
Owings, John		Franklin St		Merchant	Alley 20, $80. Betts 3, $10.	
Parker, William	Colored Man	Pearl St	Lot E side N of Saratoga St $75, Imp his dwelling $35	Laborer		
Pascault, Lewis		Saratoga St		Gent.	Arch 50, $60. Bunker 4, $10. Kate 35, $80. Julianne 7, $20.	

Free Blacks and Slave Owners in Baltimore City Tax Assessor's Ledger, 1818, Ward 11

NAME	RACE/ STATUS	RESIDENCE	REAL PROPERTY	OCCUPATION	ENSLAVED PROPERTY Name, Age, Value	COMMENTS
Patterson, Joseph	Son-in-law to Mrs. Nichols	Nichols Country Seat			Sam 22, $125 Fanny 19, $80	
Patterson, William P.		Washington St		Brickmaker	Peter 50, $60. Harry 50, $60. Jacob 50, $60. Phill 45, $60. Isaac 45, $60. Stephen 45, $60. Abe 22, $60. Dick 26, $60. Dick 23, $125. William 16, $125. Jacob 15, $125. Joe 15, $125. Charles 14, $125. Sam 12, $40. Moses 12, $40. Bill 10, $40. Jim 10, $40. Ben 15, $125. Belle 40, $40. Jean 14, $80. 2 males & 1 female between 3 and 5, $10 each.	Abe is crippled. Dick worth $60 due to King's Evil.
Phillips, Isaac Jr.		George St		Firm J.P. & Coy	Lucy 9, $40.	
Poor, Moses		Green St			Joe 11, $40. Anna 23, $80. Susan 4, $10.	
Powers, John		Green St		Flour merchant	Julia 17, $80.	
Ramsey, Charlotte	Widow of Col. Nathan	Lexington St			Jim 39, $125. Female 15, $80.	
Reip, Henry		Paca St		Tinner	Bob 9, $40. Nancy 22, $80. Patty 12, $40.	
Ridgeley, Mrs.		German St			Susan 40, $40. Ned 4, $10.	Rec'd slaves in transfer from Owen Dorsey.
Ringgold, Ann	Widow of James	Pearl St			Isaac 12, $40. Lavinia 8, $40.	

Free Blacks and Slave Owners in Baltimore City Tax Assessor's Ledger, 1818, Ward 11

NAME	RACE/ STATUS	RESIDENCE	REAL PROPERTY	OCCUPATION	ENSLAVED PROPERTY Name, Age, Value	COMMENTS
Robinson, Alexander		Market St		Gentleman	Jack 8, $40. Mingo 4, $10. Mingo 40, $125. Kitty 3, $10. Ellen 18, $80. Rose 26, $80. Cynna 38, $40.	
Rogers, John H.		Pine St		Brickmaker	Harry 30, $125. Stephen 30, $75. John 14, $75. Nancy 28, $80.	Stephen is sickly John is crippled.
Rollins, Benjamin		Ferry Rd		Rope maker	William 28, $125.	
Russell, Richard	Colored Man	Scott St	Lot E side S of Washington St $90			
Rutter, Thomas B.		Pearl St		Shipwright	William 4, $10.	
Schrener, John S.		Market St		Tanner	Stephen 22, $125. Harry 23, $125.	
Stansbury, Charles		Market St		Bricklayer	Lydia 30, $80.	
Stayler, Philip		Ferry Rd		Butcher	Nelson 12, $40.	
Stewart, William		Paca St		Merchant	John 3, $10. Jack 18, $125.	
Stinchcomb, John F.		Market St		Waggoner	Dick 30, $125.	
Stouffer, John		Eutaw St		Flour merchant	Fanny 14, $80.	
Sullivan, John		Eutaw St		Merchant	Peter 18, $125. Kitty 25, $80.	
Tanner, James		Fayette St		Clerk in bank	Nell 13, $40. Maria 22, $80.	
Taylor, William W.		Eutaw St		Merchant	Rhody 12, $40. Mina 5, $20. Eliza 23, $80.	
Tevis, Joshua		Eutaw St		Mechant	Lewis 10, $40. Minta 7, $20.	
Thomas, David	Colored Man	Asberry St	Lot W side S of Pratt St $20, Imp his dwelling $30	Brick maker		
Thomas, Philip	Colored Man	Near Cowpen Alley	Lot on Dr. Keerl's land fronting a lane $30, Imp $25			

Free Blacks and Slave Owners in Baltimore City Tax Assessor's Ledger, 1818, Ward 11

NAME	RACE/ STATUS	RESIDENCE	REAL PROPERTY	OCCUPATION	ENSLAVED PROPERTY Name, Age, Value	COMMENTS
Thompson, William	Colored Man	Scott St	Lot E side S of Washington St $30, Imp his dwelling $60			
Travis, Robert		Green St			Joseph 12, $40. Neisy 20, $80.	
Wallace, Joseph A.		Franklin St			Lewis 6, $20. Joshua 4, $20. Nancy 40, $40. Lydia 25, $80. Flora 30, $80.	
Walter, John	Walter is son of Peter	Pearl St		Stone cutter	Henny 20, $80.	
Warner, George		Washington St		Brickmaker	Adam 50, $60. Sampson 50, $60. Dick 35, $125. Moses 30, $125. Frank 29, $125. Bobb 28, $125. Isaiah 26, $125. Absalom 22, $125. Isaac 17, $125. Charles 13, $40. Aaron 13, $40. Dick 11, $40. David 5, $20. Nancy 26, $80. Fanny 15, $80. Louisa 12, $40.	
Warner, Michael		Eutaw St		Brickmaker	Joe 18, $125. Harry 47, $60. Perry 18, $125. Abraham 18, $125. Abraham 13, $40. Lewis 12, $40. Nan 14, $80. Mary 12, $40. Louisa 8, $40.	
Watkins, Thomas		Lombard St		Tailor	Abraham 20, $125. Dinah 32, $80. Lucy 16, $80.	

Free Blacks and Slave Owners in Baltimore City Tax Assessor's Ledger, 1818, Ward 11

NAME	RACE/ STATUS	RESIDENCE	REAL PROPERTY	OCCUPATION	ENSLAVED PROPERTY Name, Age, Value	COMMENTS
Watkins, William	Colored Man	Scott St	Lot E side S of Washngton St $30, Imp his dwelling $30			
Weaver, Casper		Paca St		Painter	Susan 14, $80.	
Welsh, Adam		Paca St		Merchant	Henry 7, $27.	
White, Resin		Market St		Carpenter	Benjamin 30, $125.	
Whiteford, David		Green St		Merchant	Jim 20, $125. Henny 24 $80.	
Williams, David		Market St			Joe 40, $125. Sam 17, $125. Perry 12, $40. Milly 20, $80.	
Williamson, Charles	Colored Man	Park Lane	Lot N side W of Pearl St $60, Imp $30	Brickmaker		
Wilson, Edward J.		Franklin St			Jacob 40, $125. Rachel 40, $40. Anna 16, $80. Pollie 17, $80. Patty 6, $20.	
Winters, Henry		Saratoga St		Blacksmith	Jack 20, $125.	
Yearly, Alexander		Green St		Accountant in the Bank of Baltimore	Belt 18, $80. Caroline 13, $40.	

GLOSSARY

Abated	Reduced; removed; lessened
Accountant	A person involved in auditing and maintaining accounts and financial matters
Apothecary	A person who prepares and sells drugs and medicines; a pharmacist or druggist
Biscuit Maker	A person who makes biscuits and cookies
Blacksmith	A person who works in iron with a forge and makes iron utensils, horseshoes, etc
Block and Pump Maker	A skilled woodcarver who makes two machines that ships need to sail: (a) the block and tackle that lifts heavy cargo or raises sails, and (b) the pumps that keep water from building up below deck
Bootblack	One who polishes boots and shoes
Bottler	One who bottles wines, beer, soda, water, etc.
Brass Founder	One who makes things from brass
Brewer	One who brews; one who prepares malt liquors and alcoholic beverages
Broker	One who mediates between a buyer and a seller
Butcher	One who prepares and sells meat for cooking
Carter	A man who drives a cart
Cashier	One who looks after the cash and often keeps the books for a business
Chemist	One who is qualified to dispense drugs on prescriptions from a doctor, pharmacist, apothecary, druggist
City Collector	A tax collector
City Gauger	A city official whose job it is to inspect and measure liquid goods entering the city
Clerk	One employed to keep records or accounts; a scribe; an accountant, or one employed as an assistant at a shop
Clothier	One who makes and sells cloth or clothes
Confectioner	A person whose occupation is making or selling candy and sweets
Constable	An officer of the peace who has power as a conservator of the public peace and is bound to execute the warrants of judicial officers

Consul	An official appointed by a government to live in a foreign city to protect and promote the government's citizens and interests; an ambassador
Cooper	One who makes and repairs barrels or other vessels made of staves and hoops, such as casks, tubs, etc.
Copper Refiner	One who removes impurities and other metals from copper
Cordial Distiller	One who extracts alcohol from fruits etc. in order to make a strong, sweetened aromatic liquor
Cordwainer	A shoemaker who makes new shoes from new leather
Counting House	An office or building in which the money and accounts of a person or company are kept
Crockery Store	A store where cups, plates, dishes and other similar items are sold
Currier	One who grooms the coat of a horse with a curry comb to loosen dirt and hair and to stimulate the skin to produce natural oils; one who dresses leather after it has been tanned for use by scraping, cleansing, beating, smoothing and coloring
Customs House Officer	A law enforcement person who enforces the legal fees on imported or exported items
Distiller	A person or company that manufactures alcoholic beverages
Drayman	One who drives a long strong 4-wheeled cart (a dray) without sides for carrying loads, usually beer kegs
Druggist	One who prepares drugs for sale
Dry Goods	Fabric, thread, cloth, clothing and related merchandise
Fancy and Ironmongery Store	A store that sells highly decorative items make of iron
Farrier	One who specializes in equine hoof care, including the trimming and balancing of horses' hooves and the applying of shoes on the hooves
Fig Blue	A commercial blue block stirred into the final rise water on wash day to disguise any hint of yellow and help linens to look whiter than white
Gauger	A worker or inspector who checks the dimensions or quality of machined work; a customs official, collector of excise taxes, or the like
Gent	Gentleman; a member of the gentry; a descendant from an aristocratic family whose income comes from the rental of his land

Goldsmith	A maker of gold articles
Grocer	Short for Greengrocer; someone who sells fruits and vegetables
Guilder	One who applies gold to pottery ware
Gun Smith	A person who makes, sells and repairs small firearms
Hackney	A coach man; a man who drives a carriage or coach for hire
Hatter	A man who makes and sells hats
Housewright	A person who builds and repairs houses, especially wooden houses
Innkeeper	A person who runs an inn or hotel
Inspector of Tobacco	A person authorized by law to examine tobacco for exportation and to approve or disapprove its quality
Iron and Commission Merchant	One who buys and sells iron for a percentage of the sale price
Iron Monger	A dealer of hardware made of iron
Jeweler	Someone who makes jewelry
Joiner	A skilled carpenter; one who constructs items by joining pieces of wood; a mechanic who does woodwork (stairs, doors, etc) necessary for finishing buildings
King's Evil	Tuberculosis; thought to be cured by the touch of royalty
Laborer	A person who does unskilled manual work for wages
Lime and Feed Store	A store where lime is sold to increase the ph level of acid in the soil, as well as feed sold for a variety of livestock and domestic animals
Lottery and Exchange Officer	A man who raises money through legal state lotteries for more than one state with quick pay outs
Market Dealer	A person who buys and sells goods
Market Master	An official, especially a municipal officer, who manages a town's market
Mariner	A sailor; a seaman
Mason	One who builds with stone or brick; one who prepares stone for building purposes
Meal Sealer	One who sells meal or flour

Measurer of Wood	A person who computes the size, weight or quantity of wood
Merchant	A person who buys and sells commodities for profit; a dealer or trader
Morocco Dresser	A person who tans or softens Morocco leather which is a type of goat skin leather that is lighter in weight than most leathers
Nailer	A person who makes nails; one who fastens with or drives nails
Notary	Someone authorized to draw up or witness contracts, wills, deeds, or similar documents
Notary Public	A person having the authority to act as an official witness when legal documents are signed
Painter Agent	Someone who helps a painter sell his work
Paver	One who lays paving stone or paved roads
Physician	A person qualified to practice medicine
Pile Driver	A construction crew member who uses a machine that hammers posts into the ground for the support of buildings or other structures
Pilot	A person who operates the controls of a ship
Plasterer/Plaisterer	A person whose job it is to apply plaster to walls, ceilings, or other surfaces
Porter Celler	One who ensures that a bar is fully stocked and kept clean
Postmaster	A person in charge of a post office
Potter	One who makes and sells ceramic items made of mud and clay
Register of Wills	An official charged with probate wills or with keeping the records of the probate court
Rigger	A person who worked with ropes for hoisting, lifting and hauling materials on a sailing ship
Ropewalk	A long building (nearly ¼ mile long) where skilled workers spun hemp fiber into yarn and then twine, cord and rope of various dimensions for the many sailing vessels
Saddler/Sadler	One who makes, repairs or sells saddles or other furnishings for horses
Scrivener	A person who could read and write and who made a living by reading and copying written material
Segar Maker	A maker of cigars

Ship Chandler	A retail dealer who specialized in supplies or equipment for ships
Ship Joiner	A person who constructs the woodwork on a ship
Silver Plater	One who applies a thin layer of silver as a coating on another metal
Silversmith	Someone who works with silver
Slater	A roofer who uses slate tiles
Stage Proprietor	The owner of a stage or entertainment venue
Stationer	A seller of paper and writing implements; a bookseller
Stone Cutter	A person who cuts stone from a quarry or who shapes and carves stone for use
Surveyor	A person whose occupation is to determine the size, shape, or boundaries of pieces of land
Tailor/Taylor	Someone who makes or repairs clothing
Tanner	One who tans (cures) animal hides into leather by soaking it in a liquid containing tannic acid
Tavern & Market Yard	A place where food and drinks are sold and consumed, also a place of whole sale fruits, vegetables and flowers
Tenant	A person who rents land or property from a landlord
Tinner	Someone who works in a tin mine; someone who works with tin
Tinsmith	Someone who works with tin
Tobacconist	A tobacco shop; a retailer of tobacco products in various forms and related accoutrements (pipes, lighters, matches, pipe cleaners, humidors, cigar cutter, etc)
Trustee	A person or party who acts on behalf of another person or persons, usually under the terms of a court order; a person who manages the affairs of a child or an incompetent adult
Turner	A person who is skilled in cutting, drilling, and sanding wood
Varnish Leather Manufactory	A factory where leather is produced already with a water resistant coating and a brilliant sheen which can extend the life of the leather
Veneering Sawmill	A saw mill where, using specialized tools, very thin layers of choice woods (rosewood, mahogany, satinwood, bird's eye maple, etc.) are sliced off and later heated and glued onto less quality woods to give the object a better appearance

Victualler	A seller of food and/or alcohol
Waiter	A customs officer or tide waiter; one who waits on the tide to collect duty on goods brought in. Also one who serves food in restaurants
Waiting Man	A servant; a valet
Waterman	Also a lighterman; someone who works with or on boats usually on rivers
Weigh Master	One whose job it is to weigh ore, hay, merchandise, etc.
Wheelwright	A maker or repairer of wheels for wagons, carts and carriages

Streets and Alleys where Blacks were Taxed for lots and Improvements, 1813/1818[1]

Aisquith St	Bridge St	Friend St
Ann St, E side	Bridge St	Friend St
Asberry St	Bridge St	Friendship St
Asberry St	Bridge St	Friendship St
Asberry St	Bridge St	Friendship St
Asberry St	Britton St	Friendship St
Asberry St	Britton St	Friendship St
Asberry St	Britton St	
Asberry St	Bussy Alley	Goodman St
Asberry St	Bussy Alley	Goodman St
Asberry St	Bussy Alley	Goodman St
		Goodman St
Back St	Calvert St	Goodman St
Bank St S. side	Calvert St	Gough St N. side
Biddle St	Camden St	Green St W Side
Bissey Alley	Camden St	Greenwich St
Bissey Alley	Camden St	Greenwich St
Bissey Alley	Caroline St E. side	Greenwich St
Bissey Alley	Caroline St E. side	
Bond St W. side	Caroline St W. side	Hammonds Alley
Bond St W. side	Caroline St W. side	Hammonds Alley
Bond St W. side	Caroline St W. side	Hammonds Alley
Bond St, N side	Caroline St W. side	Happy Alley, E side
Bond St, W side	Caroline St W. side	Happy Alley, E side
Bond St, W side	Caroline St, E side	Hill St
Bond St, W side	Caroline St, E side	Hill St
Bond St, W side	Caroline St, E side	Hill St
Bond St, W side	Caroline St, E side	Hill St
Bond St, W side	Caroline St, E side	Hill St
Bottle Alley	Chapel Alley	Hill St
Bottle Alley	Chapel Alley	Hill St
Bottle Alley	Coniwago	Hill St
Brandy Alley	Conway St	Hill St
Brandy Alley	Conway St	Hill St
Brandy Alley	Cowpen Alley, Near	Hill St
Brandy Alley		Hill St
Brandy Alley	Eden St E. side	Hill St
Brandy Alley	Eden St, E side	Holland St
Brandy Alley	Eutaw St	Honey Alley
Brandy Alley	Eutaw St	Honey Alley
Bridge St	Eutaw St	Honey Alley
Bridge St	Eutaw St	Honey Alley
		Honey Alley
	Falls St	Honey Alley
	Falls St	Honey Alley
	Falls Turnpike Rd	Honey Alley
	Falls Turnpike Rd	Honey Alley
	Fleet St, N side	Honey Alley
	Fleet St. S. side	Honey Alley
	Forest Lane	Honey Alley

[1] Each line represents one black taxpayer

Honey Alley	North St	Strawberry Alley, E
Honey Alley		Strawberry Alley, E
Honey Alley	Old Harford Rd	Strawberry Alley, E
Honey Alley		Strawberry Alley, E side
Howard St	Park Lane	Strawberry Alley, E side
Howard St	Pearl St	Strawberry Alley, W side
Howard St	Pearl St	Sugar Alley
Howard St	Pearl St	Sugar Alley
Howard St	Pet Alley W. side	
Howard St	Petticoat Alley, E side	Third St
Howard St	Petticoat Alley, E side	
	Petticoat Alley, W	Timber Neck Lane
In W. Biays House	Petticoat Alley, W	Timber Neck Lane
	Petticoat Alley, W	Timber Neck Lane
LeRue's Alley	Petticoat Alley, W	Timber Neck Lane
Liberty St	Pitt St	Timber Neck Lane
Liberty St	Pratt St	Tyson St
Liberty St	Pratt St	
Light St	Primrose Alley	Uhler Alley
Light St W. side	Primrose Alley	Union St
Lombardy St	Public Alley	Union St
Lombardy St	Public Alley	Union St
Low St	Public Alley	Union St
		Union St
Market St	Reicester Town Rd	Union St
McElderry St	Reicester Town Rd	Union St
Mechanical St	Reicester Town Rd	Union St
Montgomery St	Rock St	Union St
Montgomery St	Ross St	Union St
Montgomery St		Union St
Morris St	Salsbury St	Union St
Morris St	Salsbury St, S side of	
Morris St	Salsbury St, S side of	Wagon Alley
Mulberry St	Salsbury St, S side of	Washington St
	Saratoga St	Washington St
Neighbor St	Saratoga St	Woolf St W. side
New Harford Rd	Saratoga St	
New Harford Rd	Scott St	York Rd
New Harford Rd	Scott St	
New Harford Rd	Scott St	
New Harford Rd	Scott St	
New Harford Rd	Short St	
New Harford Rd	Smith St, S side	
New Lane	Smith St, S side	
New Lane	Smith St, S side	
North St	Strawberry Alley E. side	
North St	Strawberry Alley, E	
North St	Strawberry Alley, E	

SURNAMES THAT HAVE BECOME STREET NAMES

Aiken	Hillen	Schroeder
Aisquith	Hoffman	Sharp/Sharpe
Appleton	Hollins	Shipley
Armstead	Hopkins	Stansbury
Baker	Howard	Sterling
Bare	Hughes	Sterrett
Barnes	Hunter	Stevenson
Benson	Jackson	Stricker
Bond	Kennedy	Sumwalt
Buchanan	Keyser	Swann
Calhoun	Lemmon	Tessier
Campbell	Leonard	Tyson
Carey	McClellan	Vincent
Carroll	McComas	Walker
Caton	McCulloh	Waters
Chapel	McElderry	Watson
Chase	McHenry	West
Colvin	McKeen/McKean	Westwood
Conway	McMechen	Wheeler
Cook	Merryman	Wilkins
Cox	Millikin	Winchester
Cross	Montgomery	
Curtain	Mosher	
Davis	O'Donnell	
Decker	Oldham	
Durham	Oliver	
Edmondson	Osborn	
Egerton	Payson	
Ensor	Philpot	
Etting	Pinckney	
Evans	Pleasants	
Frailey	Pratt	
Fulton	Presbury	
Garrett	Presstman	
Gay	Raborg	
Gilmor	Ramsey	
Gittings	Ridgeley	
Gorsuch	Riggs	
Gough	Robb	
Green	Rogers	
Griffin		
Hamilton	Rusk	
	Russell	
Hargrove	Rutter	

FURTHER READING

Balkan, Evan. *Walking Baltimore: An Insider's Guide to 33 Historic Neighborhoods, Waterfront Districts and Hidden Treasures in Charm City.* Birmingham: Wilderness Press, 2013.

Baltimore City Censuses 1790-1860. Ancestry.com and Familysearch.org. Retrieved July 10-13, 2016.

Baltimore Gazette and Daily Advertiser, 1-3-1833, p.3.

Baltimore Sun. 11-18-1864, p.2.

Barnard, Ella K. "Mt. Royal and Its Owners." *Maryland Historical Magazine*, Vol. 26, No. 4, December 1931.

Birckhead, Solomon. http://www.findagrave.com/cgi-bin/fg.cgi. (Find A Grave #14721863) Retrieved 4-23-2017.

Birckhead, Solomon. Letter to James Madison. Baltimore, May 7, 1813. https://founders.archives.gov/documents/Madison/03-06-02-0277. Retrieved 4-22-2017.

Brown, C. Christopher. "Maryland's First Political Convention by and for Its Colored People." *Maryland Historical Magazine*, Vol. 88, No.3, Fall 1993.

Buyer, Stier and Related Families. https://buyerstierfamily.org. Retrieved 5-13-2017.

Curry, Leonard. *The Free Black in Urban America, 1800-1850: The Shadow of the Dream.* Chicago: University of Chicago Press, 1986.

Diemer, Andrew K. *The Politics of Black Citizenship: Free African Americans in the Mid-Atlantic Borderland, 1817-1863.* Athens: The University of Georgia Press, 2016.

"District Nominations." *Southern Aegis.* 10-24-1857.

Ellerbe, Kurt. "Baptiste v. de Volunbrun: The Events Surrounding an Early Nineteenth Century Freedom Petition Before the Maryland Court of Appeals." Legal History Publications 35. http://digitalcommons.law.umaryland.edu/mlh_pubs35. Retrieved 5-6-2017.

Fields, Barbara Jeanne. *Slavery and Freedom on the Middle Ground: Maryland During The Nineteenth Century.* Binghamton, New York: Vail-Ballou Press, 1983.

"Fifty Dollars Reward." *American and Commercial Daily Advertiser.* 9-28-1810.

"500 Dollars Reward." *American and Commercial Daily Advertiser.* 10-8-1818.

Fuke, Richard Paul. *Imperfect Equality: African Americans and the Confines of White Racial Attitudes in Post-Emancipation Maryland.* New York: Fordham University Press, 1999.

Gadsby, John. http://www.findagrave.com/cgi-bin/fg.cgi. (Find A Grave #81022536) Retrieved 8-30-2016.

Gadsby, John. Last Will and testament, March 11, 1844. Book 5, pp. 352-358, Box 16. http://bytesofhistory.org/Cemeteries/DC_Congressional/Obits/G/G_Gadsby_John.pdf. Retrieved 4-23-2017.

Gardner, Bettye. "Ante-bellum Black Education in Baltimore." *Maryland Historical Magazine*, Vol. 71, No. 3.: 360-366.

Garonzik, Joseph. "The Racial and Ethnic Make-up of Baltimore Neighborhoods, 1850-1870. *Maryland Historical Magazine*, Vol. 71, No. 3. Pp. 392-402.

Graham, Leroy. Baltimore, *The Nineteenth Century Black Capital*. Washington, D.C.: University Press of America, 1982.

Hayward, Mary Ellen. *Baltimore's Alley Houses*. Baltimore: The Johns Hopkins University Press. 2008.

Howard, George Washington. *The Monumental City: Its Past History and Present Resources*. Baltimore: J.D. Ehlers and Co., 1873.

Hughes, Christopher. http://www.findagrave.com/cgi-bin/fg.cgi. (Find A Grave #14743453) Retrieved 8-25- 2016.

"Indian Queen Hotel." http://www.battleofbaltimore.org. Retrieved 8-23-2016.

Jacob, Kathryn Allamong. "The Woman's Lot in Baltimore Town, 1729-1797." *Maryland Historical Magazine*, Vol. 71, No. 3.: 283-295.

Jarnagin, Laura. *A Confluence of Transatlantic Networks*. Tuscaloosa: University of Alabama Press, 2008.

Jones, Martha S. "The Case of Jean Baptiste, un Creole de Saint-Dominque." In *The American South and the Atlantic World*, Brian Ward, Martin Bone and William A. Link, Eds., 104-131. University Press of Florida, 2013.

"Lived To Be 105, Harriet Dickman a Colored Woman of Small Stature Who Was Born in 1793." Baltimore Sun. Vol. CXXII. Issue 89. Page 12.

Morrison, Brian. "African American Educational Efforts in Baltimore, Maryland During the Nineteenth Century." Ph.D. diss., Morgan State University, 2008.

Oppenheim, Samuel. "The Jewish Role in the Formation and Leadership of Scottish Rite Masonry." *American Jewish Historical Quarterly*, Vol. 19.

Phillips, Christopher. *Freedom's Port: The African American Community of Baltimore, 1790-1860*. Urbana and Chicago: University of Illinois Press, 1997.

Putney, Martha S. "The Baltimore Normal School for the Education of Colored Teachers: Its Founders and Its Founding," *Maryland Historical Magazine*, Vol. 72, No. 2, Summer 1977.

Rockman, Seth. *Scraping By: Wage Labor, Slavery and Survival in Early Baltimore*. Baltimore: The Johns Hopkins University Press, 2009.

"Solomon Etting, 1764-1847" MSA SC 3520-13490. Retrieved 9-12-2016.

"The Free Colored People's Convention." *The Baltimore Sun*, p.1. July 29, 1852. Washington, D.C.

"Town Meeting." *American and Commercial Daily Advertiser*. 9-29-1826.

Wade, Richard C. *Slavery in the Cities: The South 1820-1860*. London: Oxford University Press, 1980

"Washington Brewery." *American and Commercial Daily Advertiser*. 5-7-1818.

Whitman, T. Stephen. *The Price of Freedom*. The University Press of Kentucky, 1997.

Williams, Liz. "O Say Can You See." Stories From The National Museum of American History. http://americanhistory.si.edu/blog/2014/06/where-did-francis-scott-key-write-his-famous-lines.html. Retrieved 5-6-2017.

INDEX

Abraham, Capt. Wolbert, 74
Adams, Capt. Alexander, 74, 169
Adams, Eli, 206
Adams, John, 15
Adams, William, 99
Addison, Elizabeth, 74
Adkinson, William, 74
Adrian, Geoge, 222
Agnew, William, 193
Aiken, George, 39
Aisquith, John (Esq), 39
Aisquith, John, 123
Aitken, Robert, 39
Aitkins, Hannah, 169
Albers, Solomon G., 62
Albert, Jacob, 99
Albright, John, 222
Alcock, William, 206
Aldridge, Andrew, 55
Alexander, Ashton, 123
Alexander, Dr. Ashton, 39
Alexander, Isabella, 123
Alexander, Mrs. Isabella, 39
Allen, Elizabeth, 74
Allen, Hugh, 169
Allen, Nancy A., 193
Allen, Owen, 15
Allen, Richard, 55
Allen, Robert D., 169
Allender, Dr. Joseph, 91, 185
Allison, Ann, 26
Allison, Mrs. Ann, 110
Allison, Mrs. Mary, 133
Allison, Mrs., 49
Allnutt, James, 99
Almeda, Capt. Joseph, 74, 169
Alricks, Harmanus, 193
Amos, Benjamin, 193
Amos, John, 62, 151
Amos, William H., 62
Anderson, Capt. William J., 185
Annis, Benjamin, 26
Anthony, Daniel, 74
Appleby, Mr., 110
Appleton, William G., 206
Arcambal, Madame, 74
Armat, Christopher, 39
Armitage, Benjamin, 99
Armour, Mrs. Mary, 74
Armstead, Mrs., 110
Armstrong, James C., 151
Armstrong, James, 62, 151, 206
Armstrong, John, 123
Arnest, Dr. John, 55
Arthur, Damarls, 206
Ashbaw, Francis, 151

Athey, Walter F., 206
Atkinson, Angelo, 39
Atkinson, Isaac, 91, 185
Atkinson, Joshua, 74
Auld, Capt. William, 185
Austin, Capt. Purnel, 169
Avise, Charles, 99
Avisse, Charles, 15
Ayres, Jacob, 133
Baartsheer, William, 74, 185
Baconais, Louis, 39
Baer, Dr. Jacob, 222
Bailey, Elijah, 15
Bailey, Elisha, 206
Bailey, George Jr., 206
Bailey, George, 15
Bailey, Isaac, 222
Bailey, James, 99
Bailey, Margaret, 99
Bailey, Rachel R., 74
Bailey, Thomas, 193
Baker, Dr. Samuel, 123
Baker, George S., 39, 99
Baker, James, 62
Baker, Providence & Betsey Baker, 151
Baker, Thomas B., 39
Baker, Thomas, 39
Ball, Elizabeth, 151
Ball, William, 49, 151, 222
Baltzell, Lewis, 15
Baltzell, Thomas, 26
Bandel, George, 74, 169
Bandell, Michael, 193
Bangs, John, 141
Baque, Margaret, 55, 141
Bare, John, 15
Bareman, Joshua, 99
Barker, William, 74, 169
Barklie, Thomas, 206
Barnes, Capt. James, 91, 185
Barnes, Levin P., 133
Barnes, William P., 185
Barnes, William T., 91
Barney, John H., 39, 152
Barney, John, 99
Barney, Joshua, 222
Barns, Whitly, 75
Barol, James, 206
Barrickman, Hannah, 62, 152
Barry, Dinah, 193
Barry, Elizabeth, 193
Barry, Lavallin, 62, 152
Barry, Richard, 15
Barry, Robert, 55
Barton, Thomas, 169
Basset, Ann, 62
Bassett, Mrs., 99

Bateman, Benjamin, 152
Bateman, Catherine, 169
Batturs, Richard, 15, 110
Bauer, John J., 222
Bausman, John, 99
Baxley, George, 15
Bayreau, Monsier, 39
Beacham, James, 185
Beal, Evan, 152
Beal, John W., 133
Bear, William, 123
Becker, Simon, 26
Beckley, Henry, 15
Beckly, Mrs., 99
Beho, Moses, 99
Belt, James Jr., 185
Belt, James, 91
Belups, Robert, 26
Benedict, 26
Beneland/ Benillant, Stephen, 75
Benelant, Stephant, 169
Bennett, Fielding/Fielder, 91
Bennett, Patrick, 222
Bennett, Peter, 193
Benson, Joseph, 39
Benson, Peter, 99
Benson, Robert, 123
Benson, Samuel, 133
Berry, Benjamin, 26
Berry, Horatio, 222
Berry, John and Tho. L., 100
Berry, John W., 222
Berry, John, 26, 100
Berry, Mrs., 100
Berry, Robert, 123
Berry, Thomas L., 100
Berteau, Peter, 62
Betts, Enoch, 169
Betts, Solomon, 40, 123, 206
Biays, Col. Joseph, 91, 185
Biays, James Col., 92
Bier, Jacob, 75
Biev, Jacob, 169
Bill, Triolus, 222
Billard, Martha, 15
Billington, William, 55
Bingham, Gordon, 141
Birckhead, Solomon, 40, 123
Birkhead, Hugh, 110
Biscoe, James, 40
Bishop, Charles, 49
Bivins, Baker, 152
Bixler, David, 15
Black, Arthur, 100
Black, James, 62, 152
Black, Vison, 26
Blair, James, 15

INDEX

Blair, Michael M., 206
Blair, Mrs., 100
Blake, Ruth, 152
Bland, Theodorick, 222
Blondell, William, 55
Boggs, Harmanus, 55, 133
Bohme, Charles G., 123
Bohn, Charles, 15
Bolgino, Francis, 141
Bolte, John, 152
Bond, Eleanor, 15
Bond, Ellenor, 100
Bond, Margaret, 92
Bond, Mary, 194
Bond, Mrs. Margaret, 185
Bond, Peter, 62, 153
Bond, Thomas W., 62
Bond, Thomas, 100
Bonefono, John, 141
Bonfiel, John (Heirs of), 185
Bonnefin, Nicholas, 40
Bonner, Hugh, 49
Bonner, John, 141
Bonnett, Joseph, 63, 153
Bornard, Jambia, 15
Bosley, Daniel & James, 141
Bosley, Daniel, 55, 169
Bosley, James B., 141
Bosley, James, 49, 75
Bosley, William, 49, 169
Boss, Hays, 75
Boughan, Augustin, 26
Boughan, Augustine, 110
Bounds, Capt. Joseph, 185
Bouthier, Peter Francis, 92
Bowen, Catherine, 153
Bowen, Pitt, 206
Bowen, Richard, 75, 170
Bowen, Ruth, 206
Bowen, Susan, 207
Bowser, Rebecca, 75, 170
Boyce, Prettyman, 75
Boyce, Theodore R.C., 100
Boyce, Theodore R.S., 15
Boyd, Alexander H., 123
Boyd, Ann Mrs., 49
Boyd, Ann, 133
Boyd, Elizabeth & Mary, 123
Boyd, James P., 40
Boyd, Miss Elizabeth and Mary, 40
Boyd, Mrs. James P., 222
Boyd, Peter, 55, 170
Boyer, Jacob, 170
Bradenbauch, John, 49
Bradenbaugh/Breidenbach, John, 133
Brandt, Jacob, 49
Brannon/Brannan, John Francis, 75

Branson, William, 40, 123
Bray, Joseph (Estate of), 63
Brendle, Maria, 222
Breston, Jacob, 110
Brewer, Nicholas, 185
Brice, Henry, 15, 100
Brice, John, 123
Brice, Nicholas, 40, 123
Brightman, Rebecca, 223
Briscoe, Alexander, 49, 153
Briscoe, James Alexander, 153
Briscoe, James, 110
Briscoe, Samuel, 63, 153
Brister, Moses, 75
Bromwell, William Jr., 153
Bromwell, William, 153
Brown, Alexander, 40, 124, 194
Brown, Amos, 16, 100
Brown, Charles, 110
Brown, Dixon, 186
Brown, Dr. George, 49, 133
Brown, Jehu, 63, 153
Brown, John (Kent of Brohn Agts), 223
Brown, John, 49, 223
Brown, Joshua, 223
Brown, Mary, 154
Brown, Samuel, 41, 124
Brown, Stewart, 49, 207
Brown, Valentine, 75
Brown, William, 194
Browning Mrs., 110
Browning, Peregrine G., 16
Bruce, Upton, 223
Bruff, Mrs., 100
Brundige, William, 110
Brune, Frederick, 26
Brunelot, Francis B., 49
Brunett, John F., 55
Bruscup, John, 154
Bryden, Capt. William, 194
Bryson, Nathan G., 154
Bryson, Nathaniel G., 63
Buchanan, Misses Sidney & Margaret, 133
Buchanan, Elizabeth, 154
Buchanan, James A., 41, 124
Buchanan, Lloyd, 16
Buchanan, Miss, 49
Buchanan, Mrs., 133
Buchanan, Thomas (Esq), 41
Buchanan, William, 26
Buck, Benjamin, 75, 170
Buck, Christopher (Heirs of), 170
Buck, Jacob, 55, 141
Buck, William, 207
Bucklin, John C., 207
Bull, Elisha, 133
Bull, Jarrett, 16

Bull, William, 223
Bunbury, Capt. M. S., 75
Burges, Rachel, 110
Burgoyne, Cheston, 170
Burk, Thomas, 223
Burke, David Esq., 186
Burke, David, 92
Burke, Henry, 170
Burke, Thomas, 186
Burneston, Isaac, 26
Burrell, Charles, 100
Burt, Andrew, 26, 207
Busch, Henry, 154
Bush, William, 186
Butler, James, 63
Butler, Sarah, 207
Byrnes, Samuel, 16
Caduc, John, 170
Caduc, Raymond, 92
Caldwell, James, 223
Caldwell, Thomas, 154
Calhoun, James, 41
Calhoun, Lydia, 124
Calhoun, Mrs. Lydia, 41
Callender, John, 141
Camp, William, 55, 141
Campbell, James, 41, 124
Campbell, John R., 16
Campbell, William, 49, 133
Campsall, Michael, 100
Canby, Hannah, 170
Cane, Anthony, 75
Cannon, Mary M., 124
Canon, Mary, 133
Cappeau, Ann, 63, 194
Carey, Richard, 101
Carnigham, James, 55, 141
Carr, John, 92
Carr, Joseph, 55
Carr, Thomas, 141
Carrere, John, 49, 133
Carrol, John, 26
Carroll, Acquilla, 75, 170
Carroll, Charles Jr., 26
Carroll, James, 224
Carroll, John, 224
Carroll, Richard, 207
Carson, Andrew (Estate of), 154
Carson, Andrew, 63
Carson, Nehemiah, 101
Carter, John S., 194
Carter, Peter, 26, 110
Carter, William B., 194
Carthouse, Charles W., 154
Casey, Mary, 154
Casey, Robert, 27, 110
Cater, John, 224

INDEX

Cathel, Capt. Clement, 75, 170
Caton, Richard, 76, 171
Cator, John, 55
Caughan, David M., 186
Caughey, Patrick, 207
Chalk, Mordecai, 194
Challie, Susanna, 92
Chalmers, Capt. Timothy, 92
Chalmers, James, 16, 194
Chalmers, William, 194
Chambers, Daniel, 154
Chambers, Kitty, 224
Chamillon, Joseph, 124
Chanehe, Mr., 27
Chapel, John, 27
Chapman, Christopher, 76, 171
Chappell, John G., 186
Chase, Anna K., 224
Chase, Capt. John, 186
Chase, Capt. Thorndick, 186
Chase, Samuel, 207
Chase, Thorndick, 92
Chatard, Dr. Peter, 16
Chater, Capt. James, 76
Chavilier, John R, 41
Chayter, Capt. James, 171
Chears, William, 27
Cheers, William, 110
Chenoweth, Richard B., 155
Chenoweth, Richard, 63
Cheston, James, 27, 110
Chevolleaux, Alice, 171
Chew, Philemon, 41
Child, Richard, 101
Churchman, Enoch, 194
Clagett, Hezekiah, 101
Claggett, Eli & Co., 171
Claggett, Eli, 101
Clampsel/Campsall, Michael, 27
Clapham, Jonas, 224
Clare, Thomas, 171
Clark, James, 171
Clark, John L., 76
Clark, John, 110
Clark, Solomon, 224
Clark, Stephen, 134
Clayton, Philip, 207
Clem, William, 224
Clendennin, Dr. William H., 92, 186
Clery, Madame, 76
Cloney, James, 92, 186
Clopper, Andrew, 207
Clopper, Edward N., 16, 207
Coake, James, 27
Coale, Edward J., 124
Coale, William H., 141
Coates, William, 76, 171

Coats, Jeremiah, 194
Cobb, Lyman H., 155
Cochran, William G. (Estate of), 124
Cochran, William G., 49
Cochran, William, 41
Cock, Matthew T., 92
Cockey, Thomas, 155
Cockrill, Thomas (Heirs of), 186
Cockrill, Thomas, 92
Coe, William, 124
Coffield, Martha, 27
Cohen, Jab. J., 101
Cohen, Jacob J. Jr, 41
Cole, Dr. Skipwith H., 171
Cole, Edward J., 16
Cole, John, 41, 110
Cole, Matthew, 63
Cole, William, 55, 141
Coleman, John, 64
Colhoun, Benjamin, 16
Collins, Benjamin, 76
Collins, George C., 64
Collins, James W., 110
Colter, Alexander, 124
Colvin, Ann, 155
Colvin, Miss Rachel, 76, 171
Comegys, Cornelius, 27
Comegys, Jesse, 76
Conn, Daniel, 195
Conn, William, 155
Connell, Patricia M., 171
Conner, Hanibal, 110
Connoway, Darcus, 76
Constable, Charles, 64, 111
Constable, John, 155
Conway, Robert, 76
Conway, William, 64, 155
Cook, Capt. Robert, 171
Cook, George, 41, 225
Cook, John L, 64.
Cook, Robert, 76
Cook, William (Estate of), 101
Cook, William Sr., 16
Cooke, George, 124
Cooke, William, 142
Cooms, Capt. Solomon, 171
Cooper, Robert, 186
Cooper, Samuel B, 111
Cooper, Sarah J., 111
Cooper, Wells, 101
Cordery, James, 92, 186
Cork, Matthew T., 187
Corner, James, 77, 172
Corrages, James, 27
Corwine, Jehu, 207
Coulson, George, 172
Coulter, Alexander, 41

Coulter, Dr. John, 77, 172
Count, Mr., 111
Count, Stephen, 27
Courage, Anthony, 16
Courtenay, William, 172
Coward, Capt. Thomas, Jr., 77
Cowchois, John, 92
Cox, David, 195
Cox, James, 41, 124
Cox, Joseph, 41, 125
Cox, Peter, 142
Craig, Capt. James, 77
Craig, Henry, 77, 172
Craig, John, 187
Crawford, John, 27
Craycroft, Sarah, 207
Creamer, Joshua, 195
Creery, John, 101
Creery, Jonathan, 134
Crig, Thomas, 27
Crock, Charles, 156
Crocket, Mrs. Jane, 41
Cromwell, Dr. John, 42
Cromwell, John, 125
Crook, Walter, 64, 156
Crosdale, George, 27
Croskery, Bernard, 225
Cross, Andrew & John, 64
Cross, Andrew (Heirs of), 172
Cross, Andrew, 64
Cross, William S, 64
Cross, William, 156
Croutch, William, 111
Crow, Ann, 64
Crow, Sarah, 92
Crowl, Henry, 134
Croxall, John, 16
Cry, Frederick, 195
Cugle, John, 225
Cummings, Francis D., 225
Cummings, John, 27, 111
Cunningham, Capt. John, 92
Cunyngham, Capt. John, 187
Curlett, John, 156
Curran, John, 64
Currie, John, 172
Curtain, Mrs. Mary, 92
Curtain, Thomas, 195
Curtis, Capt. James, 92, 187
Curton, Mrs. M., 111
Cushing, Joseph, 225
D'Arcey, John N., 195
Dagan, Mary, 111
Dailey, Daniel, 225
Daley, Daniel, 16
Dall, Eleanor Mrs., 111
Dalrymple, James, 156

INDEX

Dalrymple, John (Heirs of), 172
Dalrymple, John, 77
Dalrymple, William P., 172
Dalrymple, William, 77
Dangirord, Mary, 156
Darden, Henry, 142
Dare, Elizabeth, 208
Dare, Nathaniel C., 111
Dare, Nathaniel E., 27
Dashield, Rev. George, 225
Dashiell, Capt. Henry, 93, 187
Davey, Capt. Hugh, 93
Davidge, Dr. John B., 42
Davidge, John B., 125
Davidson, Capt. William, 93
Davidson, Margaret, 64, 156
Davidson, Sarah, 17
Davis, Capt. Peter, 172
Davis, Henry, 77
Davis, James, 225
Davis, Joseph, 93, 187
Davis, Peter, 77
Davis, Samuel, 172
Davy, Capt. Hugh, 187
Dawes, James, 50
Dawes, Mary, 156
Dawson, Capt. Henry, 64
De Butts, Dr. Elisha, 17
Deagan, Mrs. Mary, 42
Deal, Hannah, 93
Deale, Capt. James, 195
Deale, Mrs. Hannah, 187
Dean, Capt. Henry, 172
DeBontz/DeBonis, Peter M., 28
Decker, George, 17, 101
Deems, Jacob, 225
Deffenderffer, John D., 65
Delacour, David, 208
Delinat, Charles, 101
Delinotte, Charles, 17
Delozier, Mrs., 111
Delsher, George, 195
Delsher/Delcher, Jemima, 195
Delsher/Delcher, John, 195
Delvecchio, Peter, 42
Demangin, Charles, 17
Denees/Dewees, Andrew, 172
Denmead, Adam, 195
Denson, John, 172
Denys, Benjamin, 17
Depestre, Mary, 226
Derkheim, Capt. Meyer, 65
Desan, Nicholas, 101
Deshon, Christopher, 77, 172
Despeaux, Joseph, 93, 187
Dew, Ann, 65, 142
Dew, James C., 195

Dewees, Andrew, 77
Deweese, Andrew, 101
Dickehut, George, 42
Dickinson, Mrs. Catherine, 93
Dickinson, William, 134
Didier, Henry Jr., 28, 125
Didier, Henry Sr., 208
Diffendall, John, 142
Diffenderfer, John, 156
Diffenderffer, Charles, 156
Diffenderffer, Michael (Estate of), 65
Diffenderffer, Peter, 55, 142
Dilahunt, John, 208
Dinsmore, Henry W., 17
Distance, William, 208
Dobbin, Catherine Mrs., 172
Dobbin, George (Estate of), 65
Dobson, Priscilla, 142
Doda, Julian, 77
Doda/Dode, Julian, 172
Doddral, James, 65
Donaldson, Dr. William, 111
Donaldson, James L., 28
Donaldson, James W., 56
Donaldson, Jane, 156
Donaldson, John, 28, 208
Donaldson, Joseph, 17
Donaldson, Marriot V., 101
Donaldson, Richard, 101
Donaldson, Samuel J., 28, 125
Donnell, John, 50, 134, 226
Donovan, Richard, 226
Donsee, Leopold, 101
Donsee, Leypold, 17
Dooley, Capt. James, 173
Dorry, Dr. Henry, 77, 187
Dorsey, Allen, 102
Dorsey, Allen, 28
Dorsey, Bachel (Estate of), 102
Dorsey, Edward Hill, 208
Dorsey, John E., 28
Dorsey, Julia, 111
Dorsey, Lucinda, 196
Dorsey, Owen, 226
Dorsey, Vachel, 17
Dorsey, Walter (Esq.), 125
Dorsey, Walter, 42
Dosh, John M., 42
Dougherty, Theophilus F., 28
Douglas, George, 102, 125, 196
Douglass, George, 42
Dounan, Lewis M., 28
Dowell, George M., 50
Doxey, Joseph, 93, 187
Dublin, Thomas, 42
Ducatel, Dr. Edme, 56
Ducatel, Edme, 142

Ducatel, Germain, 56
Dugan, Cumberland, 56, 142
Dugas, Lewis J., 112
Duke, Basil, 102
Dukehart, Elizabeth, 56
Dumest, Elizabeth, 226
Dunbar, George T., 17, 102
Duncan, Rev. James M., 112
Dunham, Jacob, 173
Dunington, William, 102
Dunkel, George A., 17, 102
Dunkin, Peregrine, 77
Dunn, Michael, 226
Dunwoody, Robert, 50, 134
Duon, Honore, 56
Duppin, James, 196
Durham, John, 112
Durkee, Pearl Capt., 173
Dushane, John, 102
Dyer, William B., 77
Earls, David, 226
Earnest, George, 17
Eaton, William, 28
Edmondson, T & J, 112
Edmondson, Thomas & Isaac, 28
Edwards, Jonathan, 56
Edwards, William, 226
Egerton, Charles C., 65
Egerton, Charles, 125
Eichelberger, George, 17, 102
Eichelberger, Martin, 28, 112
Elbert, Dr. Laudman, 173
Elder, Basil S., 226
Elderkin, William G., 156
Ellery, Eppes, 156
Elliott, Hartman, 102
Elliott, Hartmann, 17
Elliott, Howard, 226
Elliott, John, 65, 157
Elliott, Robert, 17, 102
Elliott, Thomas, 226
Emalong, Frederick
Emery, Thomas L. Jr., 125
Ennis, Benjamin, 112
Ennis, Joshua, 77, 173
Ensor, Luke & William, 78, 173
Ensor, William, 196
Ernest, George, 102
Esmanard, John B., 65
Essender, John, 29, 112
Etting, Solomon, 17, 102
Eunick, Thomas, 142
Evans, Griffith, 65, 157
Evans, Hugh W., 208
Evans, Joseph, 65
Evans, Lewis, 227
Evans, Mrs. Elizabeth, 112

253

INDEX

Evatt, Edward, 125
Everett, Rebecca, 112
Everett, Thomas, 29
Fadon, John M., 173
Fahnestock, Dederick, 102
Fahnestock, Derick, 17
Fahnestock, Peter, 17, 102
Fairbairn, Thomas H., 134
Falkonar, Perry, 17
Farnandis, Samuel, 42
Farnandis, Walter, 126
Farquharson, Charles, 134
Farrell, James, 187
Faulks, John, 103
Faure, Blanc, 56
Faure, Blanche, 143
Feigare, Mrs. Louisa, 173
Femister, Alexander, 143
Fenby, Peter, 187
Fennell, Caleb, 78
Ferguson, David, 208
Ferguson, John Capt, 29
Findlay, John, 208
Finlay, Hugh, 143
Finley, Ebenezer, 227
Finley, John & Hugh, 56
Finley, Thomas, 208
Fisher, Henry M., 134
Fisher, John, 18, 112
Fisher, Robert, 208
Fissour, John M., 42
Fitch, Capt. Daniel, 173
Fitch, Gideon, 196
Fitch, William of H., 78
Fitch, William, 196
Fitgzhugh, George, 157
Fitze, John, 187
Fitzgerald, John, 227
Fitzhugh, John, 65
Fitzhugh, Mrs. Elizabeth, 134
Flanagan, William, 65, 173
Floyd, Thomas, 196
Folkes, Henry, 173
Foltz, William, 227
Fonderay, William, 103
Fonerden, Adam, 50
Ford, Joseph T., 78, 173
Ford, Samuel, 196
Ford, Stephen H., 18, 208
Foreman, Elijah (Estate of), 143
Foreman, Elijah, 56
Forman, Francis, 227
Forney, David, 227
Forney, Peter, 103
Forrister, Ralph E., 157
Forsyth, Alexander Jr., 208
Forsyth, Alexander Sr., 209

Fosbenner, Daniel, 112
Foster, John, 209
Fowler, Benjamin, 126
Fowler, Col. Benjamin, 78
Fowler, Thomas, 227
Fowler, William, 143
Fox, Mrs. Elizabeth, 18
Fox, Mrs., 103
Frailey, Leonard, 18, 103
France, Joseph, 29, 112
Franciscus, John, 78, 143
Franciscus, William, 65
Francois, Magdaline, 209
Frazier Capt. James, 78, 173
Frazier, Joseph, 196
Frazier, Richard, 157
Freeberger, John, 29
Freeman, Edward, 227
Freise, John F., 209
Freise, Phillip R. J., 29
Frelet, Augustus, 134
Frelet, Claude Joseph, 50
French, Ebenezer, 143
French, William, 42
Frick, Peter, 56, 143
Frick, William, 126
Frieze, Philip R.J., 112
Fry, Elizabeth, 78
Fry, James, 188
Fry, Samuel, 18
Fulford, William, 50, 126
Fuller, Ann, 112
Fulton, David, 18
Fulton, James, 227
Furguson, Capt. John, 112
Fusselbaugh, John, 66
Gadsbey, John, 29
Gadsby, John, 113, 227
Gale, Joseph, 197
Galland, John B., 56, 143
Gallaway, Ezekiel, 188
Gallaway, James, 197
Gallon, Absalom, 103
Galloway, James, 78
Galloway, William H., 209
Galloway, William K., 30
Galt, Peter (Esq.), 93, 188
Gambrall, John, 18
Gants, Adam, 56
Gantt, Capt. Christian, 197
Garetson, Mary, 56
Garnett, Henry, 30
Garretson, Benjamin, 197
Garrett, Henry, 113
Garts, Charles (Deceased Estate), 30
Gassaway, Henry, 227
Gatchell, Increase, 135

Gates, Mrs., 126
Gauline, John B., 157
Gavot/Gavet, Capt. John, 78
Gay, Deborah, 173
Gemmell, Capt. David (Heirs of), 78
George, Archibald, 18
Gertz, Mrs. Catherine, 113
Gettings, Mrs. Mary, 173
Geuiran, Isadore, 66
Ghequeire, Charles, 30
Gibson, Capt. James, 78, 174
Gibson, Dr. William, 209
Gibson, John, 18, 209, 227
Gibson, William, 209
Gilbert, Harry, 157
Giles, Jacob W., 157
Giles, James, 78, 174
Giles, Rebecca, 66
Gill, John, 56, 143, 157
Gillard, Jacob, 157
Gilliard, Jacob Sr., 197
Gilmor, Robert Jr., 50, 135
Gilmor, Robert Sr., 50
Gilmor, Robert, 135
Gilmor, William, 18
Gilmore, William, 143
Ginnar, Francis, 143
Giraud, Dr. John J., 50, 135
Gist, Job, 78
Gitchell, Increase, 42
Gittings, Mary, 209
Gladden, Samuel, 197
Glassgow, Dr. John & Hannah, 56
Glaveney/Glavarry, Francis A, 30
Glendy, Rev. John, 79
Glenn, Elias, 30, 209
Glenn, James, 79
Glenn, John W., 66, 209
Goames, Nathan, 113
Godfraid/Godfroid, William, 56
Godfroid, William (Estate of), 143
Godfroy, Maxmillian, 113
Goetz, Mrs., 103
Goggin, Thomas, 228
Golder, Robert, 126
Goldsmith, Sarah, 66
Goldthwait, Mary, 157
Goldthwait, Mrs., 79
Gooding, John, 56, 144
Goodwin, Caleb D., 30
Goodwin, Elizabeth, 126
Goodwin, Melcah, 113
Goodwin, Milcha, 30
Goodwin, Thomas, 103
Gorsuch, Joshua, 66, 157
Gorsuch, Nicholas, 66, 157
Gott, Ruth, 197

INDEX

Goudon, Ferdinand, 113
Gough, Prudence, 158
Gouing, James, 197
Gouiran, Isadore, 158
Gould, Alexander, 228
Gould, Capt. Peter, 42, 126
Gould, Paul, 30
Gouldsmith, Sarah, 158
Govens, Daniel, 197
Gover, Ephraim G., 158
Govins, Daniel, 66
Gowan, John, 18, 103
Gowan, Lloyd, 126
Grace, Redmond, 209
Gracy, Redmond, 66
Graff, Frederick C., 103
Grafton, Nathan, 113
Graham, Dr. William T., 79
Graham, Dr. William. L., 158
Graham, Hamilton, 79, 174
Graham, Robert, 66, 113
Grahame, William, 31
Grant, Daniel, 31
Grant, Elizabeth, 113
Grasham, Margaret, 158
Graves, Robert, 79, 174
Gray, Henry W., 197
Gray, Joseph, 174
Gray, Lynch, 79
Gray, Sarah, 113
Grayham, Charles, 197
Green, Armisted, 144
Green, Benjamin, 158
Green, Charles R., 158
Gregg, John, 79, 135
Griffin, Charles, 228
Griffin, Luke, 198
Griffith, Catherine, 42
Griffith, Charles, 18
Griffith, Henry B., 135
Griffith, John, 210
Griffith, Susanna, 57, 126
Griffith, Thomas W., 126
Griggs, James, 79, 174
Grimes, Nero, 103
Grock, John A., 31
Grosh, Capt. John, 93
Grove, Stephen, 228
Groverman, Anthony, 228
Grundy, George, 210
Grundy, Thomas Byrum, 210
Gudgeon, Jesse, 198
Gudgeon, Providence, 198
Guestier, P. A., 174
Guestier, Peter A., 79
Guiese, Lewis, 113
Guildener, Charles, 158

Gunby, Stephen, 93
Gunn, James, 210
Guthrow, Elizabeth, 31
Gwinn, Caleb D., 113
Gwinn, Charles, 135
Gwynn, Mrs. 18, 103
Gwynn, William (Esq.), 43
Gwynn, William of John, 126
Hackeman, Herman Henry, 31
Hackett, Henry W., 114
Hackett, Margaret, 198
Hadkis, Samuel H., 198
Hagthrope, Edward, 93, 188
Haley, Mrs. Mary, 79, 174
Hall, Benjamin W., 126
Hall, Capt. John, 79, 174
Hall, Don Carlos, 174, 198
Hall, Dr. Richard W., 43
Hall, George, 79, 174
Hall, H. W., 103
Hall, Isabella, 19, 210
Hall, Richard M., 126
Hall, Richard W., 114
Hall, Richard, 158
Hall, Sophia, 174
Hall, Stephen, 31
Hall, Teresa, 174
Hall, Thomas, 174
Hall, Washington, 228
Hamilton, Dr. Thomas, 135
Hamilton, Jacob, 198
Hamilton, James, 210
Hamilton, Pliny, 57
Hamilton, Robert, 158
Hammon, William L., 159
Hammond, Harriot, 31
Hammond, Miss Harriot, 126
Hammonds, John L., 144
Hanan, John, 79
Hancock, Capt. Robert, 175
Hand, Moses, 210
Hane, James, 103
Hanna, Alexander B., 79, 175
Hanna, Ann, 67
Hanna, John, 188
Hanson, Charles W., 57
Hanson, Philip, 228
Hanson, William H., 175
Hanson, William, 159
Harden, Henry, 228
Harden, Samuel, 31
Harden, William, 31, 103
Hardester, Benjamin, 80
Hardy, Priscilla, 228
Hargrove, John, 175
Hargrove, Rev. John, 80
Harker, John, 198

Harmange, Anthony (Estate of), 114
Harmange, Anthony, 31
Harper, Robert G., 57, 144
Harris, Col. David, 228
Harris, Dr. Edward, 19, 103
Harris, John F., 43, 126
Harris, Robert, 198
Harris, Samuel, 80
Harris, William, 229
Harrison, Hall, 31, 175
Harrison, Jonathan, 188
Harrison, Thomas (Heirs of), 93, 188
Hart, Capt. Robert, 80, 175
Hart, Joseph, 80, 175
Hartshorne, William, 31
Harvey, Polly, 198
Harvey, Samuel, 43
Haskins, Govert, 57, 144
Haslam, John, 159
Haslet, William, 50
Hassard, John & Ralph, 19
Haubert, Frederick (Estate of), 229
Hawkins, James L., 19, 135
Hawkins, William (Estate of), 229
Hay, Martha, 159
Hayes, Reverdy, 43
Hays, John, 67
Hays, Martha, 80
Hays, Walter C., 80
Hays, William, 67, 159
Hayward, Harriot, 31
Heath, Gen. Richard K., 229
Hebrew, (No first name given), 229
Heddinger, Michael, 159
Heddricks, Thomas, 175
Heddricks/Hedrick, Thomas, 80
Heide, George, 43, 127
Heidelbaugh, John, 31
Heighe, James, 210
Henck, Frederick W., 43
Henderson, Robert, 94
Hennecke, George, 19
Hennely, John H., 210
Hennick, George, 103
Henry, John, 229
Henry, Nancy, 229
Henshaw, James, 159
Herring, Henry, 175
Herring, Ludwig (Heirs of), 175
Herring, Ludwig, 80
Herter, Ignatius, 198
Heslip, John, 144
Hessilius, Mary, 19
Hewitt, Eli, 114
Hewitt, Elie, 31
Hewitt, William, 175
Hickley, Robert, 19, 229

INDEX

Hickley, Sebastian, 159
Hicks, John, 67, 159
Higginbotham, Ralph, 210
Higinbotham, Thomas, 229
Hignutt, John, 229
Higson, George Esq., 175
Hildon, Abraham, 114
Hill, George, 43, 175
Hill, George, Jr., 80
Hillen, John, 67, 159
Hindman, James, 57, 210
Hines, James, 229
Hines, John, 104
Hobson, George, 159
Hodges, Benjamin M., 43, 127
Hodgkin, Mrs. Susanna, 80, 175
Hoffman, Daniel, 19, 229
Hoffman, Frederick G., 67
Hoffman, George, 32, 114
Hoffman, John, 43, 127
Hoffman, Peter Jr. 43
Hoffman, Peter, 127
Hogg, John, 104
Holbrook, Capt. Joseph, 80, 175
Holland, Littleton, 104
Hollingsworth, Zebulon, 210
Hollingsworth, Mrs. Ann, 135
Hollingsworth, Racheal L., 43
Hollingsworth, Samuel, 32, 114
Hollingsworth, Thomas, 50
Hollins, John S., 57, 144
Hollins, John, 43, 127
Holmes, Capt. John H., 188
Holmes, James, 210
Holmes, Thomas, 175
Honeycomb, John, 67
Honton/Honiton, Parish, 230
Hook, Joseph Sr., 230
Hooks, Joseph Jr., 104
Hooper, James, 104, 188
Hooper, William, 81, 176, 199
Hope, Daniel, 114
Hopkins, Sarah, 159
Hoppe, Daniel, 32
Hoppe, Justice, 211
Horlon, James, 159
Horne, Thomas, 159
Horsey, Mrs. Sarah, 176
Horton, William L., 144
Houlton, William, 176
House, Samuel, 114
Howard, Col. John E., 211
Howard, Diana, 199
Howard, Dinah, 211
Howard, Dr. Henry, 44
Howard, Henry, 50, 127
Howard, John, 159

Howard, Rebecca, 114
Howe, Capt. Thos. C., 188
Howe, Mrs. Margaret, 94
Howell, William Sr., 32
Howell, William, 176
Hoy, (No first name given), 176
Hubball, Ebenezer, 50
Hubbell, Josiah, 114
Hubble, Josiah, 44
Huberts, Dr., 81
Hudson, Jonathan, 104
Hudson, Jonathon, 230
Hughe, Mrs. Jane, 114
Hughes, Aquilla, 230
Hughes, Christopher Jr., 32
Hughes, Christopher Sr., 32, 115
Hughes, George M., 176
Hughes, Jonas, 81
Humphreys, Kerr, 188
Hunt, Barbara, 160
Hunter, Rebecca, 115
Hurst, Shadrach, 67, 160
Hurxthal, Frederick, 104
Hurxthal, Lewis, 104
Hurxthall, Ferdinand, 19
Hussey, Nathan, 19
Hutchings, Daniel, 67
Hutchings, Elizabeth, 144
Hutchins, John, 57
Hutton, James, 57, 144
Hyde, Samuel G., 160
Hynson, Joseph, 199
Hynson, Nathaniel, 176
Ingles, Silas, 81
Inglis, Rev. James, 44
Inloes, Joshua (Heirs of), 94
Inloes, William, 176
Ireland, Edward, 57
Ireland, Edward (Estate of), 145, 211
Irvine, Alexander, 19, 104
Isaac, Mrs. Elizabeth, 176
Isaacke, Elizabeth, 81
Isett, John, 104
Isfett, John, 19
Israel, Beal, 230
Israel, Fielder, 230
Ives, James, 57
Jackson, Ann, 199
Jackson, Anthony, 104
Jackson, Bolton, 104, 230
Jackson, Henry, 19
Jackson, J.E., 104
Jackson, Stephen, 199
Jackson, Thaddeus, 230
Jackson, William, 94, 188, 211
Jacobs, Capt. Wm., 81
Jacobs, Mrs. Jane, 94

Jacobs, Samuel, 160
Jacquin, Paul, 160
Jakes, Frederick, 211
Jamart, Michael, 160
James, Daniel, 188
James, Edward, 211
James, James W., 81
James, James, 211
James, Tudor, 104
James, William, 94, 188
Jamison, Caecilius, 81
Jamison, Joseph, 57, 145, 160
Jarrett, John, 44
Jarvis, Leonard, 211
Jarvis, Ormand, 115
Jefferson, Hanson, 211
Jefferson, William, 212
Jenkins, David, 230
Jenkins, Edward, 50, 135
Jenkins, Henry, 199
Jenkins, Michael, 44, 127
Jenkins, Mrs. Sarah, 81
Jenkins, Sarah, 212
Jenkins, Thomas C., 44, 127
Jenkins, Walter, 19
Jenkins, William, 50, 136
Jenney, Rebecca, 94
Jennings, Dr. Samuel K., 104
Jennings, Thomas, (Esq.), 104
Jessop, Dominic, 19
Jessop, William, 19, 104
Johns, Hosea, 145
Johnson, Abraham, 212
Johnson, Benjamin, 230
Johnson, Christopher, 104
Johnson, David, 81, 176
Johnson, Edward (Esq.), 82, 176
Johnson, George, 115
Johnson, James, 189
Johnson, Jane, 199
Johnson, Samuel, 115
Johnson, Thomas, 199
Johnston, Christopher, 19
Johnston, Samuel, 32
Johnston, Thomas, 32
Joice, Charity, 199
Jones, Aubray (Estate of), 145
Jones, Awbreay, 57
Jones, Capt. Levin, 94
Jones, James, 231
Jones, Joshua, 50
Jones, Richard H., 32
Jones, Talbot, 105
Jones, Talbott, 19
Jones, Thomas S., 127
Jones, William, 231
Joshua Brown, 44

INDEX

Kaminskey, John C., 127
Kaminsky, Christopher, 44
Kane, John M., 32
Karrick, Joseph, 105
Karthause, Peter A., 67
Kaylor, George, 57, 145
Keenen, Charles, 105
Keener, David, 127
Keener, John, 51, 136
Keener, Susan, 212
Keerl, Dr. Henry, 19, 105
Kell, Thomas, 51, 160
Kelly, Thomas, 127
Kelso, Thomas, 199
Kelty, Catherine, 115
Kemp, James (D.D.), 212
Kemp, Thomas, 82
Kempton, Samuel A., 67
Kempton, Samuel, 176
Kennedy, Dennis, 231
Kennedy, John F., 32
Kennedy, John, 212
Kerns, Capt. John, 177
Kerr, Capt. Archibald, 94, 189
Key, Abner, 51, 136
Keys, John, 57, 145
Keyser, Derick, 20
Keyser, Diderick, 105
Keyser, George, 20
Keyser, Samuel, 105
Kierstead, Luke, 94
Kiersted, Luke, 189
Kilbourne, Capt. Russell, 177
Killburn, Capt. Russell, 82
Kimmel, Anthony Sr., 20
Kimmel, Michael, 105
Kincaid, James, 160
King, Henry, 20
King, James, 82
King, Samuel, 160
Kinnard, Nicholas, 177
Kinnard, Samuel, 189
Kipp, John, 20, 105
Kittinger, Michael (Say Heddinger), 67
Kitts, Barnet, 199
Klinefelter, Michael, 161
Knabb, John, 231
Knight, Isaac, 115
Konig, Frederick, 20, 231
Konkey, William M., 177
Kraber, Martin, 212
Kramer, Frederick, 20, 105
Krebbs, William, 231
Krebs, John, 20
Krems, Joseph (Estate of), 231
Krous, George (Estate of), 105
Kurtz, Rev. Daniel, 136

Kyle, Adam B., 115
Lacy, Hannah, 57
LaFaranier, Mrs., 177
Laferty, William, 199
Lakeintre, John L., 231
Lamb, Joshua, 161
Landsdale, Richard, 105
Lanney, Peter, 161
Lanney/Lannay, Lewis J., 32
Lansdale, William M., 44, 127
Larantry, Michael P., 20
Larsh, Abraham Jr., 57
Larsh, Margaret, 32, 145
Latimer, James P., 127
Latimer, Mrs., 128
Lattee, Joseph, 189
Laudeman, Mrs., 189
Lauden, Michael, 58
Laurenson, Philip, 20
Laurenson, Phillip, 105
Lavaly, Mary, 145
Lawder, Benjamin, 67
Lawrence, Richard, 94, 189, 231
Lawson, Elizabeth Mrs., 20
Le Duc, Susan, 231
Lebon, Charles, 20
LeBon, Eliza, 212
Leclaire, Dr. Lewis S., 231
LeClaire, Peter Cazeaux V., 212
LeClere, Francis, 212
Lee, Mrs., 20, 105
Leeke, Nicholas, 82, 177
Legrand, Samuel D., 58, 145
Leigh, John, 21
LeLoup, Monsier Louis F., 82
Lemmon, Mrs., 21, 115
Lemonier, Alexander L., 105
Leonard, Joseph Capt., 33
Leonard, Joseph, 116
Leone, Jasper/Gasper, 82
Letta, Thomas, 67
Letter, Thomas, 161
Lettig, Philip, 128
Letto, Barbara, 213
Levering, Enoch, 21
Levering, Jesse, 21, 105
Levering, Nathan, 33, 116
Levering, Peter, 33, 116
Levy, Hetty, 21
Lewis, Abraham J., 136
Lewis, Mrs., 94, 189
Leypold, Frederick, 51, 136
Librou, Anthony, 44, 128
Lieutaud, Bartholomew, 231
Liggett, George, 51
Lilley, Elie, 21
Lilly, Eli, 231

Lindenberger, George, 33, 213
Lindenberger, Jacob, 44, 116
Ling, Robert, 189
Linville, James M., 128
Lister, John, 33
Littig, Philip, 44
Littlejohn, M. (Estate of), 116
Littlejohn, Miles, 44
Littlejohn, Thomas, 200
Lloyd, Micha, 231
Lock, Nathaniel, 44
Logan, James, 213
Lomax, David, 177
Loney, Phoebe, 82, 177
Long, Elizabeth C., 232
Long, Henry, 67, 161
Long, Kennedy, 213
Long, Reuben, 21
Long, Reubin, 116
Long, Thomas, 177
Lorman, William, 128
Louderman, Frederick (Heirs of), 94
Louerwine, Peter, 21
Lourens, Robert, 95
Love, Dr. John, 58
Love, Elizabeth, 44
Lovell & Sultzer, 189
Lovell, William Jr., 82, 189
Lovell, William, 21, 136
Lovering, Francis, 58
Low, Cornelius, 33, 116
Lowrey, John, 177
Lowry, Samuel, 161
Lupeerre, Clelie, 68
Lusby, Henry, 161
Lyeth, John, 21
Lyles, David, 116
Lynch, John, 232
Lyons, Nace, 200
Lytle, Mr., 82
Macatee, Francis, 51
Mackall, Richard, 51
Mackenzie, Colin, 145
Mactier, Alexander, 45, 128
Maerst, James M., 58
Magauran, James, 68
Maggs, Jane, 51, 136
Magruder, Ellen, 34
Magruder, William B., 34
Maher, Martin F., 161
Maidwell, John, 68
Mainard, Foster, 21
Makeff, Richard, 105
Malden, Mrs., 116
Mallory, Capt. John, 200
Mann, Dr. Anthony, 45, 200
Manning, Capt. Thomas, 82

INDEX

Manro, Jonathan, 105
Manroe, Jonathan, 21
Marche, John, 58, 145
Maris, George, 128
Marks, William, 136
Maroste, D., 136
Marshal, Francis, 116
Marshall, Thomas, 82
Martiacq, John, 34
Martin, Capt. James M., 189
Martin, Dr. Samuel B., 177
Martin, James, 51, 136
Martin, John, 21, 213
Martin, Luther (Esq.), 45
Martin, Luther, 128
Martin, William, 34, 116
Maslin, Michael M., 232
Mason, Peter, 105
Mathews, John, 232
Mathews, Rachael, 232
Matthews, William, 136
Maxwell, Elizabeth, 83
Maxwell, John, 200
Maybury, Thomas, 232
Mayer, Christian, 232
Mayer, Lewis, 116
Maynard, Foster, 232
Mays, George. 177
McAllister, Robert, 68
McAllister, John, 161
McCausland, Marcus, 213
McCauslen, James, 161
McCleary, William, 51
McClellan, Samuel, 136
McComas, Elizabeth, 162
McCombs, Solomon, 83
McConckey, Capt. James, 232
McConkey, William, 83
McConky, James, 51
McConnell, Miss Elizabeth, 145
McConnell, Thomas, 83
McCreery, Mrs., 116
McCubbin, Moses, 21, 105
McCulloh, James H., 213
McCulloh, James W., 128
McDonald, Col. William, 83, 177
McDonald, John, 106
McDowell, Dr. Maxwell, 106
McDowell, George, 136
McDowell, Maxwell, 21
McElderry, Elizabeth, 200
McElderry, John, 200
McFadon, John, 83
McFerran, John, 51
McFerrin, John, 137
McGaughan, David, 95
McGill, George, 213

McGill, Mary Miss, 34
McGill, Mary, 117
McGill, William, 83
McGinnes, John, 162
McGinnis, John, 68
McGwinn, William, 83
McHenry, James, 128
McIlvaine, Alexander, 45
McKean, John, 117
McKeen, John, 34
McKenzie, George, 51, 137
McKim, John Jr., 45, 137
McKim, Samuel, 58, 145
McKim, William D., 213
McKinze, John, 58
McKinzie, Dr. Colin, 83
McLaughlin, Matthew, 117
McLaughlin, Peggy, 68
McManus, Owen, 34
McMechen, William, 45, 145
McNeal, Capt. Daniel, 95
McNulty, John, 213
Meads, Joshua, 232
Meagher, Timothy D., 200
Meeteer, Samuel & William, 68, 162
Meredith, William (Estate of), 232
Merfeld, John, 34
Meridith, Thomas, 106
Merkle, Jacob, 213
Merrica, James, 21
Merriott, Mary D., 83, 177
Merryman, Elizabeth, 128
Merryman, Job, 21
Merryman, John, 45, 128
Merryman, Micajah Sr., 162
Merryman, Sarah R., 128
Messersmith, Mrs., 128
Messick, Baptist, 95
Messick/Mezick, Capt. Joshua, 83
Metzger, William, 214
Meyer, Andrew, 68
Mezick & Johnson, 178
Mezick, Capt. Baptist, 189
Mezick, Capt. Joshua, 178
Middleton, Richard, 58, 117
Miery, Augustus, 22
Miles, Jane Mrs., 178
Miles, John, 68, 178
Milhau, Michael, 58
Millard, Joseph Lee, 95, 189
Miller, Catherine, 146
Miller, George W., 68, 162
Miller, George, 68
Miller, Jacob, 68, 162
Miller, John Jr., 58
Miller, John, 69
Miller, Lewis, 200

Miller, Robert, 34
Miller, Sarah, 162
Mills, Levin, 51
Mills, William P., 146
Mills, Capt. George, 178
Mills, Ezekiel, 146
Mills, Robert, 214
Miltenberger, Anthony, 22
Mince, Joseph, 83, 178
Mingo, John, 106
Mingo, Kitty, 106
Mitchell, Alexander, 58, 146
Mitchell, Col. George, 214
Mitchell, Francis J., 106
Mitchell, Mrs. Margaret, 45
Mitchell, Richard B., 214
Mitchell, Richard, 83, 178
Mo??in, James, 162
Moale, Ellen, 34, 117
Moale, Samuel, 51, 137
Mohler, Henry, 58
Mohler, Peter, 162
Molding, John, 34
Mollach, Candes, 232
Mondell, William, Esq., 178
Monker, William, 178
Monsarrat, Capt. David, 189
Montalibor, Martha, 214
Montgomery, Amos, 178
Montgomery, John Esq., 200
Montgomery, John, 34
Montgomery, Martin, 179
Moody, Isaac, 200
Moore, Abbey, 201
Moore, Anthony, 214
Moore, Cyrus, 232
Moore, George W., 22
Moore, Molly, 106
Moore, Philip (Esq.), 83, 179
Moore, Samuel, 117
Moore, Stephen H., 128
Moore, William S., 137
Moore, William, 201, 214
Morehead, Turner, 117
Morgan, Edward, 69, 162
Morin, Francis, 69
Morin, Francois, 162
Morrin, James, 69
Morris, Thomas, 95
Morsell, Hetty, 214
Morton, Capt. Robert, 95
Morton, John A., 214
Morton, John, 179
Moscrop, Henry, 34
Mosher, James, 128
Mousinier, Madame, 84
Mousnier, Lacouste/Laurent, 163

258

INDEX

Mullanphy, John, 34
Muller, Caspar Otto, 45
Muller, John C., 84
Mulliken, Rignald, 106
Mullikin, Basil, 128
Mullikin, Benjamin H., 34
Mullikin, Mary, 214
Mullikin, Richard D., 45
Mummey, Thomas, 22
Mummy, Thomas, 106
Munroe, Isaac, 146
Murphy, Thomas, 163
Murphy, William, 214
Murray, Alexander, 179
Mushet, Walter, 34
Mushett, Walter, 214
Muskett, John, 84
Mycroft, John, 201
Myer, Jacob, 35
Myers, Andrew, 163
Myers, Elizabeth, 69, 163
Myers, Godfrey, 137
Myers, Henry, 215
Myers, Jacob, 51, 137, 215
Myers, Jane, 69
Myers, John, 137
Myers, William, 69, 201
Nagel, Henry, 233
Nance, William, 35
Neal, Abner & Bosley, Daniel, 45
Neal, Abner, 128
Neal, Hannah, 117
Neale, John G., 233
Neel, Hannah, 35
Negro Ben, 22
Neild, Richard, 163
Neilson, James C., 22
Neilson, James, 163
Neilson, Robert H., 215
Nelson, Rachel, 22
Nelson, Richard C., 117
Nelson, Richard, 215
Nesbit, Alexander, 163
Nettis/Neutes, Jack, 117
Newburn, Mary, 58
Newton, Anthony, 146
Nichol, Samuel, 106
Nicholas, Bathesard, 58
Nichols, Charlotte, 35, 233
Nicholson, John, 69, 137
Nicholson, Joseph H., 22
Ninde, James, 146
Noland, Mrs., 106
Norman, Capt. T. W., 117
Norman, Thomas, 35
Norris, Benjamin, 233
Norris, Harriet, 58

Norris, James Jr., 233
Norris, John, 58
Norris, Richard, 215
Norris, William Jr., 52, 117
Norris, William, 51, 117
Norton, Frank, 118
Norton, John, 233
Norvell, Sarah, 233
Norwood, Mrs., 118
Nowland, Dennis, 22
O'Connor, Dr. John, 179
O'Connor, Hannibal, 35
O'Donnell, Columbus, 233
O'Donnell, Sarah, 233
O'Rourke, Devizeau Mrs., 22
Ockerman, George, 84
Ogden, Nathan, 163
Okely, John, 69
Oldham, John, 52, 137
Oliver, Robert, 58, 201
Olliver, Robert, 146
Onion, Elizabeth, 69
Orme, Archibald E., 215
Orrick, Capt. John W., 118
Osborn, Christopher, 118
Osborn, William, 35
Osburn, William, 118
Osgood, Robert H., 118
Owen, Dr. John, 45
Owen, Kennedy (Estate of), 215
Owens, Joseph, 52, 138
Owens, William, 58, 146
Owings, John, 233
Owings, Mary, 215
Pacolet, Valentine, 215
Paduzi/Peduzi, Peter, 95
Page, Daniel, 69, 163
Page, Fanny, 84
Page, James, 179
Palmer, Edward, 35, 118
Pamphillion, Thomas, 95, 190
Pannell, Edward, 52, 138
Parker, Elizabeth, 52
Parker, Joseph, 201
Parker, Samuel, 163
Parker, Thomas, 215
Parker, William S., 179
Parker, William, 233
Parks, Abraham, 179
Parks, Maybury, 69
Parks, William, 84, 179
Partridge, James, 45
Partridge, Rosanna, 69
Pascault, Francis, 201
Pascault, Lewis, 233
Patridge, James, 129
Patten/Potter, Dr. Nathaniel, 118

Patterson, Edward (of William), 146
Patterson, John, 138
Patterson, Joseph, 118, 234
Patterson, Robert, 45
Patterson, Susan, 215
Patterson, William and Robert, 84
Patterson, William P., 234
Patterson, William, 52, 138
Pawley, James, 215
Payson, Henry, 35, 118
Pechin, William, 85
Peck, Francis, 85
Peck, Frank, 179
Peck, Henry, 22, 118
Peduzi, Peter, 190
Peirce, John, 95, 190
Pendleton, Daniel, 179
Pennington, Joshua, 138
Penrice, Capt. Thomas, 179
Penrise/Penrice, Capt. Thomas, 85
Pentz, Joseph, 163
Periel, Alexander, 179
Perine, William, 215
Perkins, John, 58, 146
Perry, Jeremiah, 129
Perry, Rogius, 35
Person, Jesse, 69
Peterbottom, John, 85
Peterkin, Capt. William, 85
Petherbridge, John, 163
Pew, Peggy, 46
Pew, Rebecca, 46
Phenix, Elizabeth, 70
Philippe, Joseph, 146
Philips, Perry, 85
Philips, William, 106
Phillips, Capt. James, 85, 179
Phillips, Isaac Jr., 234
Phillips, Isaac, 215
Phillips, William, 22
Phips, Ann, 215
Phoenix, Thomas, 164
Pierce, Israel, 164
Pierce, Levy, 216
Pilch, James, 190
Pilkington, Thomas, 190
Pinkney, William (Esq.), 52
Piper, James, 201
Pitt, Capt. Richard, 190
Pitt, William, 85, 164
Pitts, Spencer, 106
Pleasants, John P., 216
Pogue, Elizabeth, 106
Poleny, Mary, 118
Poncet, Lewis, 59, 146
Ponter, Leonard, 216
Pontier, Anthony, 52

INDEX

Pontier, M., 129
Pool, Rezin, 138
Poor, Dudley, 216
Poor, Moses M., 46
Poor, Moses, 234
Porter, Michael, 106
Porter, William, 52, 164
Poughe, Mrs., 23
Poumairat, John, 118
Powers, John, 234
Pratt, John H., 46
Prendiville, Ann, 95
Presbury, George G. 1st, 59
Presbury, George G. III, 70, 146, 201
Presbury, Priscilla, 201
Pressman, Mrs., 118
Presstman, William, 35
Price, Hezekiah, 216
Price, John, 95, 190
Price, William, 96, 191, 201, 216
Priestly, Edward, 70, 164
Priffith, Samuel G., 118
Printz/Prints, Casper, 96
Proebstino, Theodore C., 107
Prout, James, 85
Prout, Richard, 202
Prout, Robert, 107
Puder, Leonard, 23
Pue, Peggy, 129
Pue, Rebecca, 129
Pulett, William, 23
Pullett, Nehemiah, 179
Purnal, Isaac, 23
Purviance, James, 23
Purviance, Robert, 23, 118
Purviance, William, 216
Quail, Robert, 46, 129
Queen, Henry, 129
Queen, Stephen, 114, 118, 129
Quin, Stephen, 35
Quinn, William M., 180
Raborg, Christopher (Estate of), 138
Raborg, Christopher Jr., 52
Raborg, Christopher Sr., 52
Raborg, Samuel, 52
Raborg, William, 23
Ramsey, Charlotte, 234
Ramsey, James, 96, 191
Ramsey, Joseph, 85, 191
Randall, Elisha, 164
Randall, John, 35
Raney, William, 164
Raphael, Aquila, 216
Raven, Thomas, 86
Rawlings, Benjamin, 52
Readel, John, 53, 138
Redding, John, 129

Reddy, Samuel, 86
Reese, Elizabeth, 180
Reese, John, 107
Regnier, Charles L., 216
Reigart, Philip, 138
Reinecker, George, 23, 107
Reinecker, Mrs. Maria, 107
Reip, Henry, 234
Renshaw, James, 70
Repold, George (Estate of), 46, 129
Repold, Mrs. Metta, 119
Rescaniere, Monsier, 46
Rescaniere, Peter, 129
Rhees, John, 23
Ricaud, Mrs., 119
Ricaud, Thomas P., 129
Rice, Shields, 180
Rice, Thomas K., 164
Richards, John C., 35
Richards, Rev. Lewis, 70
Richardson, Daniel, 164
Richardson, James, 202
Richardson, Mary, 165
Richardson, Robert R, 107
Ridgeley, Mrs., 234
Ridgely, Greenbury, 70, 165
Ridgely, Greenbury, Jr., 146
Ridgely, Miss, 107
Ridgely, Nicholas, 23
Ridgely, Noah, 70, 119
Ridgley, Lot, 59
Rigden, John E., 35
Riggs, George W, 53
Riley, William, 119
Ring, Capt. Thomas, 96
Ringgold, Ann, 23, 234
Ringgold, Dr. Jacob, 86
Ringold, Benjamin, 119
Ringold, Catherine, 59
Riston, George, 119
Robb, John, 165
Roberts, George, 180
Robertson, George, 107
Robinson, Alexander, 235
Robinson, Charles, 86, 180
Robinson, Eve, 23, 107
Robinson, Joseph, 46, 86, 129, 180
Robinson, Mrs. Deborah, 86
Robinson, William, 86
Rodgers, Caesar, 107
Rodrigues, Lewis, 87
Rogers, Edward, 180
Rogers, Jacob, 53, 138
Rogers, John H., 235
Rogers, Philip, 202
Rogers, Richard Jr., 70
Rogers, Thomas, 71, 180

Rogers, William C., 165
Rollins, Benjamin, 235
Rollins, James Capt, 35
Roney, William, 59, 165
Ross, Reuben, 53, 138
Ross, William, 165
Rowe, John K., 36
Rowles, Rezin, 87, 180
Roy, John, 139
Ruckle, John, 36, 119
Rusk, Robert, 202
Rusk, William, 165
Ruso, Peter, 71
Russell, James, 119
Russell, Richard, 235
Rutter, Thomas B., 235
Rutter, Thomas (Estate of), 217
Ryan, Thomas (for the Heirs of Andrew H
Sadiler, Philip B., 46
Sale, King, 202
Salmon, Charles, 146
Salnave, James, 202
Sampson, 119
Sands, Benjamin N., 107
Sands, Benjamin, 23
Sauervine, Peter, 107
Schaeffer, Frederick G., 139
Schaeffer, William A., 147
Scharf, William, 165
Schmidt, William L, 71.
Schnauber, George, 36
Schrener, John S., 235
Schroeder, Henry Jr., 46
Schroeder, Henry, 46, 217
Schultz, John E. C., 36
Schultz, Conrad, 23
Schultze, Lucy C., 107
Schwartz, Frederick, 36
Schwartze, A. J., 119
Scott, John, 23, 46, 107, 129
Scott, Joseph, 23, 107
Scott, Thomas, 23
Seankins, Clem, 119
Sears, William, 202
Seller, Abraham, 130
Sellers, Abraham, 46
Sellman, Jonathan, 71
Selman, Johnsee, 217
Servary, Peter, 217
Seth, James G., 217
Sewel, Elizabeth, 165
Sewell, James H., 71, 180
Sewell, Richard, 165
Sewell, Thomas, 217
Sewell, William H., 53
Sexton, Charles, 87, 180
Shaffer, Frederick Esq., 180

INDEX

Shane, Joseph, 108
Shanley, James, 36, 119
Sharp, James, 87, 180
Sharp, Mrs. Ann, 191
Shaw, John, 87, 181
Shears, Joseph, 87
Shedden, John, 59
Sheppard, Major Thomas, 191
Sheppard, Thomas, 96
Sherlock, John, 53
Sherrer, George, 119
Shipley, Richard A., 108
Short, John, 130
Shorter, Ann, 120
Shortt, John, 47
Shutt, Bartholemew, 71
Simeon, (No first name given), 36
Simington, James, 47
Simmons, Matthew W., 24, 120
Simonson, James, 120
Simpson, John, 24, 71, 108
Sinclair, William, 181
Singleton, Mrs. Elizabeth, 139
Singleton, Mrs., 53
Sinners, Elijah R., 139, 191
Skinner, John S., 130
Slade, Elizabeth, 165
Slater, Hannah, 139
Slater, William, 53
Slingluff, Jesse, 24
Sloan, James, 47, 130
Small, Jacob, 36, 120
Small, John, 53, 130, 181
Smith, Job, 59
Smith, Arnold (Estate of), 147
Smith, Arnold, 181
Smith, Capt. Joseph, 71
Smith, Capt. Robert, 71
Smith, Dennis A., 47
Smith, Dr. James, 47
Smith, Elizabeth, 147, 166
Smith, Gen. Sam, 139
Smith, Gen. Samuel, 53
Smith, George C., 36, 59, 87, 147
Smith, Jacob G., 217
Smith, James, 71, 166
Smith, Job Jr., 166
Smith, Job, 147
Smith, John, 87, 96, 191, 202
Smith, Mrs. Mary, 87
Smith, Pamela, 181
Smith, Ralph, 47, 130
Smith, Richard W., 181
Smith, Richard, 87
Smith, Robert (Honorable), 120
Smith, Robert, 36
Smith, Sally, 36

Smith, Samuel R., 36, 217
Smith, William, 47, 87, 147
Smyth, Samuel, 217
Smythe, Dr. James, 217
Smythe, James, 147
Snow, Hezekiah or Zedekiah, 24
Snuggrass, William, 217
Snyder, Capt. John, 96
Snyder, Peter, 217
Sollars, Joseph, 108
Sollers, Basil, 59, 147
Sorenson, Catherine, 87
Spalding, Richard B.
Sparks, Acquila W., 202
Spear, Barbara, 147
Spear, Capt. William, 87
Speck, Capt. Cornelius, 181
Speck, William A., 191
Spencer, Jonathan, 203
Spencer, Robert, 166
Spiars, Capt. Thomas, 203
Spicknell, John, 120
Spies, John P., 108
Spiknell, John, 47
Spottwood, David, 203
Sprague, Charles, 71
Sprigg, Thomas, 59, 147
Sprole, William, 59, 147
Spurrier, William, 147
Stafford, Capt. Patrick, 96
Stall, Edward H, 71.
Stallings, Benjamin, 59
Stansbury, Charles, 87, 235
Stansbury, Daniel, 108
Stansbury, Darius, 166
Stansbury, Dr. James, 192
Stansbury, Nicholas, 96, 192
Stansbury, Solomon, 181
Stansbury, Thomas, 203
Stansbury, William (of Abraham), 71, 166
Stansbury, William (of Elijah), 71, 72
Stapleton, Joseph K., 130
Starke, George, 24
Starr, Hezekiah, 53
Starr, William, 139
Stayler, Philip, 235
Steel, Capt. John, (Heirs of), 97, 192
Steinbeck, Christian, 108
Stenson, William, 139
Stephens/Stevens, Capt. Richard, 87
Stephenson, Sater, 217
Sterett, Col. Joseph, 59
Sterett, Joseph, 139
Sterett, Samuel, 59
Sterling, Achsah, 87
Sterling, James, 203
Sterrett, James, 59, 148

Sterrett, Samuel, 217
Sterritt, Benjamin, 108
Steuart, Col. William, 181
Steuart, Dr. James, 53, 181
Steuart, Major William, 88
Steuart, Robert (Esq.), 88, 181
Steuart, Robert St. John, 181
Stevens, Capt. J. H., 181
Stevens, Capt. Richard, 166
Stevens, Mary, 36
Stevens, Mrs. Ann, 181
Stevenson, Capt. William (Heirs of), 88
Stevenson, Dr. Cosmo, 72, 203
Stevenson, George P., 218
Stevenson, Joshua, 203
Stevenson, Josiah, 166
Stevenson, Josias, 72
Steward, Mrs. Ann, 97
Stewart, David (Estate of), 148
Stewart, David C., 130
Stewart, David, 59
Stewart, John, 72
Stewart, Mrs. Ann, 192
Stewart, Richardson, 36, 120
Stewart, William, 235
Stickney, Henry, 72
Stien, George, 24
Stiles, Capt. George, 88
Stiles, Edward, 53
Stiles, Hon. George, 181
Stiles, Mrs., 130
Stinchcomb, John F., 235
Stockett, Barbara, 97
Stockett, William Capt., 181
Stockton, Richard, 218
Stokes, William, 108
Stonebraker, George, 108
Stouffer, Henry, 24, 108
Stouffer, John, 24, 235
Stricker, John, 130
Strike, Nicholas, 36
Stump, Samuel, 36, 120
Sullivan, John, 235
Sultzer, Sebastian, 182
Summercamp, Mr., 130
Summerwelt, Elizabeth, 120
Sumwalt, Frederick, 218
Sumwalt, George, 36, 120
Sumwalt, Philip, 88, 182
Sunderland, Elizabeth, 97, 182
Sutherland, John, 120
Sutliff, Thomas, 148
Swaes, Basil, 120
Swan, Gen. John, 130
Swan, General John, 47
Swan, John, 108
Swann, William, 218

INDEX

Swear, Joseph, 166
Sweeton/Sweeting, Thomas, 37
Sweetser, Seth, 53
Sykes, John, 72, 167
Tanner, James, 235
Tanner, P. & L., 72
Tapiau, Vital, 60
Tate, Alexander, 218
Taylor, Joseph, 108, 167
Taylor, Lemuel G., 182
Taylor, Lemuel, 47, 130
Taylor, Robert, 88, 203
Taylor, Samuel, 108
Taylor, Thomas, 53
Taylor, Vincent, 182
Taylor, William W, 235
Taylor, William, 47
Tenant, Thomas, 97, 148
Tensfield, Zachariah, 47
Tessier, The Rev. John , 218
Tevis, Joshua, 235
Tharp, George, 139
Thomas, Allen MD, 120
Thomas, Barton, 88, 182
Thomas, Daniel L., 167
Thomas, David, 235
Thomas, Ebenezer S., 130
Thomas, John, 47, 131
Thomas, Julius, 218
Thomas, Philip, 120, 235
Thomas, Rachal L., 24
Thomas, Richard, 88
Thompson, Ann, 37, 121
Thompson, Capt. Alexander, 97, 192
Thompson, Capt. John, 182
Thompson, Capt. Nathaniel, 97
Thompson, Edward, 88
Thompson, Hugh, 60
Thompson, John R., 167
Thompson, John, 72
Thompson, Stephen J., 131
Thompson, William, 108, 236
Thornbury, George, 37
Tiernan, Luke, 47, 121
Tiernan, Patrick, 218
Tilden, Marmaduke, 53
Tilghman, Mary Lloyd, 131
Tinges, Charles, 88
Tittle, Jeremiah, 203
Todhunter, Joseph, 37
Tolbert, John, 60
Tonson, Thomas, 218
Tool, John, 167
Torrance, Charles, 60, 148
Towson, Madame Amie, 88
Towson, Philemon, 148
Towson, Rebecca, 131

Travers, Julia, 37
Travis, Robert, 236
Travis, Susan, 72
Trippe, Edward, 37
Troop, Elizabeth, 218
Tryall, Joshua, 48
Tupper, Mary, 167
Tupper, Nathan, 72
Turrell, John, 218
Tyler, Mrs., 192
Tyson, Nathan, 37, 121
Uhler, Barbara, 121
Uhler, Erasmus, 37, 121
Uhler, Philip, 121
Uhler, Phillip, 37
Urie, James, 53
Urie, Jeremiah, 54
Usher, Mary, 131
Vail, Mr., 121
Vallette, Charles, 54, 139
Van Wyck, William (Estate of), 148
Vance, William, 131
Vanwyck, William, 60
Vaughen, Charles, 203
Vickers, Capt. Joel, 88, 182
Vincent, Samuel, 48, 167
Vintkler, John, 148
Volunbrun, Jean M., 60, 149
Wagner, George, 97, 192
Walker, Archibald, 37
Walker, Isaiah, 140
Walker, Samuel P., 48, 131
Walker, Thomas, 24
Wall, George, 24
Wall, John E, 72, 149
Wallace, Joseph A, 236
Wallace, Joseph., 218
Wallace, Major, 204
Wallace, Ruth, 24
Wallace, William M., 218
Wallis, John Jr., 121
Wallis, Philip, 218
Walraven, John, 48
Walsh, Jacob Jr., 88
Walsh, Robert, 48, 131
Walter, John, 37, 236
Waltham, Mary, 182
Waltham, Thomas, 89
Ward, Elizabeth, 48, 131
Ward, William, 89, 108
Ware, John, 167
Warfield, Charles, 37, 121
Warfield, George F., 24
Warfield, George T., 108
Warner, George, 236
Warner, Henry, 24
Warner, Michael, 236

Warner, William, 149
Warrell, Thomas, 89
Waters, Catherine, 204
Waters, Darcus, 89
Waters, Hezekiah Esq., 192
Waters, Hezekiah, 97
Waters, Joseph G., 108
Waters, Joshua, 182
Waters, Peter, 182
Waters, Richard, 60, 182
Waters, Sarah, 89
Watkins, Thomas, 236
Watkins, Tobias, 121
Watkins, William, 108, 236
Watson, Robert, 131
Watson, Thomas, 167
Watts, Dickson B., 182
Watts, Jeremiah, 204
Watts, Richard K., 37
Weary, Peter, 97
Weaver, Casper, 237
Weavy/Weary, Peter, 192
Webster, William, 121
Weeks, Capt. Benjamin, 89
Weeks, Samuel, 109
Weems, Capt. Charles, 89, 182
Weems, Capt. George, 192
Weems, Dr. William, 89
Weems, George, 97
Weise and Boehm, 48
Weise, Felix, 61, 149
Weise, S.L., 140
Welch, Jacob Jr., 182
Welch, John, 219
Welch, Peter, 183
Welford, Robert, 131
Welks, Benjamin Capt. 183
Wellmore, William, 24
Wells, Benjamin (Estate of), 109
Wells, Benjamin, 24
Wells, Joshua, 24
Wells, Nelson, 121
Wells, Rev. Joshua, 131
Welmore, Margaret, 149
Welsh, Adam, 237
Wesley, Thomas, 149
West, Capt. William, 89
West, John, 61, 149
West, Maria, 149
West, William, 89, 183
Westwood, John, 167
Wetherall, William, 24, 121
Wheeler, John, 219
Wheeler, Leonard, 25, 109
Whelan, Thomas, 37, 121
Whipper, Isaac, 219
Whitaker, Thomas, 72, 167

INDEX

White, Abraham, Jr., 204
White, Capt. Thomas, 89
White, Dr. John C., 140
White, George (Estate of), 109
White, George, 25
White, Henry, 25
White, Jacob, 219
White, Jane, 131
White, John J., 183
White, John, 54, 140, 219
White, Resin, 237
White, William, 89, 204
Whiteford, David, 237
Whitney, Elizabeth, 204
Wickham, Capt. Peter, 90
Wilhelm, John, 167
Wilkins, ???? (No first name given), 37
Wilkins, 121
Wilkins, Dr. Henry, 131
Wilkins, Henry, 48
Wilkins, John, 38
Wilkins, Joseph, 38, 121
Wilkinson, Capt. Shubael/Shubal, 97
Wilks, Letty, 219
Willhelm, John, 72
Williams, Amos A, 219
Williams, Amos A. & George, 219
Williams, Benjamin, 38
Williams, Caesar, 219
Williams, Capt. William N., 140
Williams, Catherine Mrs., 54
Williams, David, 237
Williams, Ezekiel, 90, 183
Williams, George, 219
Williams, Jacob, 204
Williams, James, 131
Williams, John S., 97
Williams, Martha, 90
Williams, Matthew, 204
Williams, Mrs. Catherine, 183
Williams, Nathaniel F., 219
Williams, Nathaniel, 48
Williams, Richard, 204
Williams, Samuel, 204
Williams, Spinler/Spinter, 205
Williams, Thomas, 122
Williams, William N., 73
Williamson, Basil, 131, 168

Williamson, Charles, 237
Williamson, David, 48
Williamson, James, 140
Willis, Joshua, 90, 183
Wills, Francis M., 38
Wills, Joseph, 122
Wilmer, John W., 38, 122
Wilmer, Simon, 38
Wilson, Benjamin, 192
Wilson, Charlotte, 205
Wilson, Edward J., 237
Wilson, Gerard, 61
Wilson, James (Estate of), 168
Wilson, James C., 122
Wilson, James of William, 54
Wilson, James, 73, 140
Wilson, John, 25, 73, 168, 219
Wilson, Joseph, 149
Wilson, Lydia, 220
Wilson, Nixon, 38, 122
Wilson, Robert, 140
Wilson, Robert, 54
Wilson, Samuel, 205
Wilson, Thomas, 132
Wilson, William Jr., 38
Wilson, William Sr., 132
Wilson, William, 48, 122
Winand, Jacob, 25
Winchell, James F., 54
Winchester, Charles, 122
Winchester, David, 54
Winchester, George, 38, 132
Winchester, Jacob, 90, 183
Winchester, Sarah, 38
Winchester, William, 109
Winder, Gen. W. H., 132
Winder, Rider H., 73
Winder, William, 73
Wingate, Capt. Peter, 98
Winkler, John, 61
Winstanley, William H., 73, 183
Winters, Henry, 237
Wintkle, Elizabeth, 54, 140
Wirgman, Charles, 61, 220
Wirgman, Peter, 132
Witmor, Mrs., 122
Wolf, Dr. George, 109
Wood, Thomas, 48

Woodland, William, 122
Woods, Corfel, 73
Woods, Wesley, 220
Woods, William H., 132
Woods, William Jr., 205
Woods, William, 38, 122
Woodward, Abraham, 109
Woodward, Capt. Abraham, 183
Woodward, William W., 122
Woodyard, Neptune, 220
Woodyear, Edward G., 73
Woodyear, Edward, 168
Worley, Joseph, 25, 109
Worrall, Margaret, 140
Worrell, Elizabeth, 38
Worrell, Mrs., 109
Worrell, Thomas, 183
Worthington, Abraham, 220
Worthington, Charles, 220
Worthington, Henry, 73, 168
Worthington, Nicholas, 25
Worthington, Thomas, 205
Wright, Dr. Thomas, 220
Wright, James I, 61.
Wright, John, 168
Wrightman, Rebecca, 220
Wyant, Peter (Estate of), 122
Wyant, Peter, 38
Wyvill, Marmaduke, 150
Yates, John, 73
Yates, Major Thomas, 90
Yearly, Alexander, 237
Yearly, Henry Capt., 184
Yeiser/Yeizer, John, 220
Yellott, George (Estate of), 122
Young, Ann T., 168
Young, Capt. William, 90
Young, Hugh, 122
Young, John S., 184
Young, John, 73, 168
Young, Miss Ann, 48
Young, Mrs., 122
Young, Perry, 221
Young, William L., 109
Zane, Joseph, 98
Zane, Peter, 90, 168
Zollers, Dr. Charles, 61
Zollers, Dr. Charles, (Estate of), 150

www.ingramcontent.com/pod-product-compliance
Lightning Source LLC
Chambersburg PA
CBHW080409300426
44113CB00015B/2450

9 780806 358581